PRAISE FOR *REVISE THE PSALM*

"This anthology is an homage of monumental proportions. It is a literary offering from a partial list of poets and writers who honor the major twentieth century American figure, Miss Gwendolyn Brooks, Chicago poet, champion for Black expression in American letters, advocate for the underdog in our society and all children everywhere. It is a must for every library."

—Ana Castillo, author of *So Far From God*

"Gwendolyn Brooks provided us with sun to flower. In *Revise the Psalm*, the brilliant writers she influenced and inspired measure up to and magnify Brooks' challenging, inclusive, disciplined art."

—Joanne V. Gabbin, Furious Flower Poetry Center

"*Revise the Psalm* revisits and revitalizes the power of Gwendolyn Brooks' legacy of 'literary citizenship.' Tributes from multi-ethnic writers, mostly poets, attest to her transformative poetic practice, her sharp attention to audience, her compassion for younger writers. This anthology, edited by Quraysh Ali Lansana and Sandra Jackson-Opoku, is a necessary intervention into forgetting, as we approach the 100th anniversary of one of the most brilliant poets of the twentieth century and, I daresay, the twenty-first."

—Cheryl Clarke, author of *After Mecca: Women Poets and the Black Arts Movement*

"The works of Gwendolyn Brooks are our heritage. We receive her remarkable artistic testament, the fruit of her imagination and artistry and commitment. For other poets and writers, this heritage is endlessly generative [. . .] In all her writing, one recognizes her enormous capacity to respond with wisdom and sympathy to human frailty and failure, to encourage and to set an example, and to sustain her fierce loyalty to everyday life. Her poems encompass men and women working, singing, suffering, loving, and grieving; joyous, sad, and angry; dejected, despairing, and foolish; hopeful, helpful, and heroic [. . .] From the very beginning of her artistic career, she was deeply engaged with her art, championing with her poetic range and brilliance the humanity of those whom she portrayed. As another poet once said to me long ago, Brooks' virtuosity was the proof of her commitment to black life. To life. She stood with the great cause of civil rights and also wrote of the great travails of being human in an uncivil time and place. She wrote with special warmth, honesty, and realism about children. Her work and her person have directly and indirectly inspired, counseled, advised, and challenged all who write poetry and fiction, and all who read. Nothing could be more fitting or more welcome in the centennial year of Brooks' birth than this moving collection of tributes to her."

—Reginald Gibbons, author of *Sweet Bitter*

REVISE
THE PSALM

WORK CELEBRATING
THE WRITING OF
GWENDOLYN
BROOKS

EDITED BY
QURAYSH ALI LANSANA &
SANDRA JACKSON-OPOKU

CURBSIDE SPLENDOR PUBLISHING

Published by Curbside Splendor Publishing, Inc., Chicago, Illinois in 2017.

First Edition
Copyright © 2017 by Quraysh Ali Lansana and Sandra Jackson-Opoku
Library of Congress Control Number: 2016958546

ISBN 978-1-940430-86-7
Cover art by Dirk Hagner
Woodcut on washi, 2001; 38 x 22.5 inches (97 x 57 cm)

Quraysh Ali Lansana photo by Alan Tarin
Sandra Jackson-Opoku photo courtesy of Swatch Art Peace Hotel, Shanghai
Book design by Alban Fischer

Manufactured in the United States of America.

WWW.CURBSIDESPLENDOR.COM

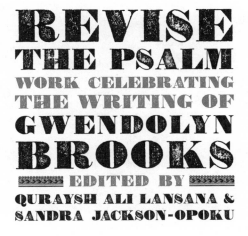

REVISE
THE PSALM
WORK CELEBRATING
THE WRITING OF
GWENDOLYN
BROOKS
EDITED BY

QURAYSH ALI LANSANA &
SANDRA JACKSON-OPOKU

Quraysh Ali Lansana. Quraysh Ali Lansana's wife, Emily, and sons, Nile and Onam, with Miss Brooks at her home in Hyde Park, August 2000. Taken just four months before her death, this was one of the last known photographs of Miss Brooks.

To Emily, Nile, Onam, Ari, and Brooks
To Kimathi and Adjoa
(in faith and in family)

To Nora and Henry III
(for sharing their mother with the world)

And always and forever,
the inimitable Miss Brooks!

CONTENTS

Part 6

Artwork Gallery

INTRODUCTION:
OF MEMORY AND REVISION

> Behind the scurryings of your neat motif
> I shall wait, if you wish: revise the psalm
> If that should frighten you: sew up belief
> If that should tear: turn, singularly calm
> At forehead and at fingers rather wise,
> Holding the bandage ready for your eyes.
> —*Gwendolyn Brooks, "The Children of the Poor"*

How does one engage the glory of a well-turned phrase? Capture the magic of the contoured word? How do you celebrate such a thing? We sing *Gwendolyn*. A moan of wind as it blesses the earth. *Brooks*. The music of water kissing stones, reshaping them into something different.

"Voice" is an artist's style, theme, manner, and mode of expression. Among other sources, voice is shaped from what the artist has witnessed and internalized—memory and childhood and trauma, history and myth and dream. Whether deliberately or unconsciously, we "cover" and interpret, retell and riff upon songs we've heard, films we've seen, artwork we've encountered, and literature we've read.

Miss Brooks, as she preferred to be addressed, once said, "I've always thought of myself as a reporter." From that vantage point she bore witness to over eight decades of pain, progress, setbacks, and struggle in American life and the world beyond. She became a pivot in literary history, straddling multiple experiences, generations, and communities.

Gwendolyn Brooks came into literary prominence during a time between the New Negro Renaissance of 1918-1935 and the Black Arts Movement of the early 1960s through the mid-1970s. Literary critic Lawrence Jackson identifies the period from 1934-1960 as "the indignant generation." Although the Civil Rights and Black Power Movements are largely credited with bringing about a radical shift in political consciousness, they were actually preceded by a thirty-year period of active resistance to the forces of political, racial, and economic injustice.

Sweeping events like World War II, Jim Crow segregation, the Great Depression, the Great Migration, the growth of American Communism, and international decolonization movements helped color the consciousness of a generation of black writers and critics. In *Black Metropolis: A Study of Negro Life in a Northern City*, his groundbreaking study with St. Clair Drake, sociologist Horace Cayton identifies this as a powerfully political and deeply emotional moment that altered "the sentiments sanctioning the processes."

Miss Brooks bridged this period into the next generation, bringing a sense of craft into the exciting stridency but sometimes loose discipline of the Black Arts Movement. As she moved toward a racially conscious art, some of the more conservative literary forces, both black and white, began distancing themselves from the overt political content of her message. Yet she remained an inclusive figure among progressive communities. Although she never identified as a feminist, Miss Brooks was tenderly embraced by the women's movement, as well as old and new guard black literati, and most notably, a vast general readership of those old and young, urban and rural, gay and straight, black and white.

"What I'm fighting for now in my work," Miss Brooks insisted, ". . . is for an expression relevant to all manner of blacks, poems I could take into a tavern, into the street, into the halls of a housing project."

The epigraph at the beginning of this introduction, excerpted from a poem in Gwendolyn Brooks' Pulitzer Prize-winning volume *Annie Allen*, demonstrates her proficiency with language, her complexity of form, and the socio-political underpinnings that inform her work. "The Children of the Poor" ponders what fate will befall the most vulnerable among us, those "adjudged the least-wise of the land."

This quintet of sonnets forms a message from a mother to her children in a time of war. What does she tell her children who are poor? Religion offers no easy answers, prayer no panacea. The simple directive, "revise the psalm," presents a series of challenges. Look beyond doctrine to find a source of solace within oneself. Create your own narrative of survival or suffer the outcome of blind belief.

This volume is a diverse chorus of survival narratives, a gathering of works that challenge conventional dogma. Gwendolyn Brooks said, "I am interested in telling my particular truth as I have seen it." In that spirit, these artists present their own personal truths with the honesty, bravery, and candor that is at the heart of Miss Brooks' art.

I shall wait, if you wish: revise the psalm

We wanted to investigate what is embodied in the act of revision, though not in the literal sense of correcting errors in a written work. That is editorial revision. What you will witness within these pages is a project of literary and artistic revision, the process of "talking back" to works that inspire, teach, challenge, and engage.

How do these artists speak to the children of the poor? To the "kitchenette folks"? What do they say to love, to a lynching? To DeWitt Williams in the back of a hearse, "nothing but a plain black boy"? To the unborn children a mother felt unable to give breath? While some celebrate in the poetry for which Miss Brooks was best known, the prose writers, photographers, and painters are also present and accounted for.

Some have revisited themes, passages, ideas, and images presented in her works. Poet and essayist Patricia Smith responds to Miss Brooks' poem, "A Bronzeville Mother Loiters In Mississippi. Meanwhile, A Mississippi Mother Burns Bacon" with a memoir piece that contemplates her coming of age on the west side of Chicago: "Meanwhile, a Lawndale Girl Burns Cornbread" (p. 205).

Some have penned and painted portraits in tribute. Others have chosen the parody, a work designed in the style of the original. Tony Medina (p. 172), Roger Bonair-Agard (p. 165), and Kevin Coval (p. 154) take on Miss Brooks' exceedingly popular poem about a group of young men whiling away their time and their lives in a neighborhood pool hall: "The Pool Players. Seven at the Golden Shovel," a work most known as "We Real Cool."

In homage to that very work, poet Terrance Hayes invented "the golden shovel." Lines are taken from an inspiration poem, and each word in that line becomes an end word in the new poem. Joan Wiese Johannes' "Child-free" is a case in point (p. 3).

Revise the Psalm: Works Celebrating the Writing of Gwendolyn Brooks is organized as follows:

Part 1 presents the experience of motherhood, from the abortions that "will not let you forget" in works like Georgia A. Popoff's "I, Too, Am the mother" (p. 5). We see too the familiar archetype of the nurturing mother; we witness its challenges and joys from the perspective of those who do mother, and those who are mothered. Also explored are the experiences of women who have not mothered, as in Angela Jackson's "The UnMother" (p. 10).

Part 2 extends this theme to examine other aspects of womanhood: the struggle towards love and self-acceptance, the recognition of worth in oneself and others of like lineage and gender. The mysteries of womanhood are explored in pieces like Kimberly A. Collins' "A burning lesson" (p. 33), a reminiscence of the straightening comb ritual that black women (and some men) of a certain age know all too well. Both Kalisha Buckhanon (p. 34) and jessica Care moore (p. 40) recall the special role Gwendolyn Brooks played in their coming of age as women and writers.

So many of Miss Brooks' works explore the act and art of loving. "To Be in Love" is both "to touch with a lighter hand" yet also "to be free/with a ghastly freedom." The works of heartbreak and healing in **Part 3** reflect upon what builds, destroys, affirms, and frustrates that "golden hurt" experienced between lovers, parents and children, "would-be wives," and in one whimsical piece, a radio.

Part 4 moves onto the perils and pleasure of brotherhood, from teenagers lurching toward an uncertain manhood, to ladies' men and boys with weapons. From Tony Medina's "brown angels" and "preacher's brothers" to father figures, mothers' sons, and heroes lifted from history, ancestry, and everyday life (p. 99). Desire and sexual orientation, overburdened family providers, infirmities, and incivilities are all explored in this section.

Part 5 encompasses pieces of an overt political nature: works that examine genocide, apartheid, wars, rumors of war, and the various "violences" we visit upon one another.

The works in **Part 6** evoke place, the backdrops against which we conduct the business of our lives in urban, suburban, rural, and international settings. In response to Gwendolyn Brooks' Bronzeville, Reggie Young invokes his own Bluesville (p. 123, 201). Miss Brooks' definitive yard (back yards, front yards) as the open space of the urban dweller is revisited within this volume. There are also pit mines and housing projects, cityscapes and cemeteries, natural and constructed worlds set in this life and the hereafter.

Having honed her natural gifts since early childhood, Gwendolyn Brooks was a master of craft. She perfected classic forms like sonnets and ballads, and also crafted epic poems and open verse using subtle rhyme, alliteration, anaphora, oxymoron, and more. Adrienne Christian and others reflect on topics like Miss Brooks' innovations in nontraditional lineation, i.e. "the Magic of the Line" (p. 292). *Part 7* speaks to those elements of craft that have inspired the works of other artists.

Part 8 consists of memories and impressions from those who may have known Miss Brooks intimately, and those who know her only by her works and reputation.

As writers and editors, we were pleased to discover "Gwendolynian" influences in the visual arts. Arlene Turner-Crawford's images chronicle the Black Arts Movement when Gwendolyn Brooks marked her passage into "the kindergarten of consciousness" (color insert). Roy Lewis' iconic 1969 photo shows Miss Brooks sporting the fairly new Afro she would wear for the rest of her life. It is said to have been her favorite portrait (color insert). Joyce Owens, Rose Blouin, Malaika Favorite, Felicia Grant-Preston, and Satoki Nagata also contribute their artistic visions in painting, photography, and mixed media.

Revise the Psalm is a testament to what Gwendolyn Brooks best represented—an art that is disciplined in craft and culturally conscious, yet one that is widely inclusive, from our youngest contributor at eighteen years old to an elder of Miss Brooks' own generation. We of many races, cultures, nations, genders, and sexual and religious persuasions have come here by way of Miss Brooks, and here we replenish for the journey ahead.

Come inside and be quenched.

—Quraysh Ali Lansana and Sandra Jackson-Opoku

FOREWORD

Gwendolyn Brooks' spirit and body of work was broad shouldered and audacious, like the city she made famous. Everything she wrote was a sacred, loving homage to the people whose rugged, eloquent stories flowed through her veins, her blood, and the beating heart of every word she wrote. Her mission was to channel those stories into the wider world. Miss Brooks' legacy as a woman, wife, mother, activist, poet, teacher, writer across genres, and world treasure continues to evolve and nourish new generations of writers and readers.

Revise the Psalm is a praise-song, a blessed event showcasing the power of one writer who wedded herself to all humanity, to inspire an abundance of creative magic in anyone touched by her mentorship, or her words. In these pages, veteran voices mingle with the sound of new, emerging writers edging into the spotlight. That is how I am sure Gwendolyn Brooks would have wanted any celebration of her work and impact to be structured—democratic, egalitarian, and totally surprising.

Read this book carefully. Savor the striking tenderness, precision, and mystery of the language, and the courage of these meditations, whether, prose, poetry, narrative, or visual art. These pages are a canvas in vibrant tones that echo the history of a blues people, a canvas that bears witness to their often unheralded beauty. The artists and writers in *Revise the Psalm* are "Miss Brooks' children" and they learned their lessons well. They have brought forth a new world, one sculpted from the love Gwendolyn Brooks inspired. They have given us new ways to honor and remember a woman who was our griot, our "chief," our Queen.

> —**Marita Golden,** author of over a dozen works of fiction and nonfiction, including the memoirs *Migrations of the Heart* and *Saving Our Sons*

Part 1

And you create and train your flowers still.

—Gwendolyn Brooks, "For Black Women"

JOAN WIESE JOHANNES

Child-free

(A Golden Shovel from Gwendolyn Brooks' "The Mother")

Now beyond a decade since the change, I
still possess a fertile mind and heart, have
no regrets for choosing heartbeats heard
and sleepy head against a lover's chest in
easy love. Fulfilled, I freely sacrificed the
fertile eggs while other women's voices
cooed to children, crooned sweet songs of
Bye o' Baby Bunting ilk, and welcomed the
sexless love of motherhood, still as wind
that does not gust and fails to spawn the
hurricane of carnal joy. No lustless voices
hailed me, and all was well when blood of
monthly flow ran thick and clotted down my
thigh. Intent that prospects should not dim,
my Dalkon shield protected as it killed
the eggs that could have been my children.

JODI JOANCLAIR

Barbed Wire

Spiked spine where a womb
should be. No clouds. No rain.
Just scorched earth, brown-orange
from neglect. No shade of green. No
shade from leaves. Just naked branches
reaching upward asking for just a little.
Because too much of one thing will always
poison. Because equilibrium is harder to
maintain than to attain. The precarious teeter
tot telling us we are open flowers with no
guarantee of pollination. That we will wilt, have
been wilting, since the moment we full-bloomed.
And petals, like arms, can't hold up forever. That
wombs have expiry dates and mine only grows
barbed wire to keep out new life. My womb will
never know. I have chosen myself instead. My
eyes, my nose, my mouth, my ears to sustain
my sense of me. Will never know of tiny
hands and feet. I will use my fingers
and toes to count life's milestones.

GEORGIA A. POPOFF

I, *Too, Am* the mother

Abortions will not let you forget.
You remember the children you got that you did not get,
　　—Gwendolyn Brooks

Mother's Day is one of my least favorite days of the year. Not just because I have been without my mother since shortly after my fourteenth birthday, but also because I am not a mother. There is the universal expectation that a woman of my age, now sixty-two, would have had children. I am among a growing number of women who have not married, have not raised children, and who are aging without meeting many societal expectations, what I generally refer to as the "Cinderella Myth" that imbues nearly every level of our upbringing.

In June 1971, I showed up at my high school graduation, only to discover the school administration was not expecting me. I had completed my minimum requirements for a NYS Regents diploma in December and I began full-time work, six days a week waiting tables in our neighborhood diner. I had started the job the summer I turned sixteen to help my father, widowed just two years before, to help my family, and to give myself options: clothes, entertainment, future tuition. It did not dawn on me that the school would not know I was intending to be among the graduates. I walked the stage that day in a wrinkled gown, cap tilted uncomfortably on my head. A few weeks later, I had my first pelvic examination at Planned Parenthood, which confirmed I was pregnant.

After my boyfriend and I informed my father, wheels were set in motion. We were decidedly too young to start a family. Too much was at stake. We did not tell his parents. I had an appointment for an abortion a couple of weeks later. This is significant in that New York had legalized abortion months before the Supreme Court's historic decision of *Roe v. Wade*. Were this not the case, my child would now be forty-four years old.

The morning I was to have the abortion, my father dropped me off at the hospital clinic, planning to come back for me later. Waiting in the examining room, I was alone.

As the doctor, still in his residency, examined me in preparation for the procedure, he developed a sudden look of terror. He informed me that he would not continue. I was confused. He explained that the previous doctor who had examined me had misjudged my circumstance, that I was too far along. I got dressed and asked to use a phone to call my father.

My uncle was a doctor. He pulled strings. My boyfriend and I took the funds from our tuition savings, and I was admitted to the hospital for a late-term abortion. I had no concept of what was ahead of me. I had little understanding of anything beyond how and why I got a period. That much I learned from sixth grade film strips. My mother died before she could help me know more about womanhood.

I was in the hospital, alone, for two nights. I had a full, arduous labor and a most unfortunate delivery. When I asked how big the fetus was, the nurse, who disdained cleaning me up, said, "Big enough to live." Three days later, my breasts began to lactate. Three weeks later, I left for college, stunned, numb, alone.

I was haunted by the voice of that almost baby. I cried. I felt horrid guilt. Eventually my boyfriend fell in love with another. That left me alone with all the what ifs. Years later, I wrote about it.

As I continued through what I believed was my fate, I found myself pregnant several more times. In each circumstance, I truly believed myself unable, perhaps even unfit, to bring the child into the world. And the voices continued to echo of each that I *did not get*. When younger, I believed that I had plenty of time, that there would be a man who would fall in love with me and want to parent, with me, and we would be a family, the family I fantasized about throughout high school and college. But these pregnancies were none of that. I chose termination and still trust that each was the correct choice.

One time, I walked through picket lines at a clinic 150 miles from where I lived, the only one that had an appointment available to safely end my pregnancy within the healthy, legal timeframe. Alone with the pain in a motel in a strange city. Ridiculed by pro-life activists before and after. Solitary with my fear, guilt, and grief.

The voices echoed each year and sometimes when I did not expect. Eventually, as I entered my forties, I started the process of accepting that I was not going to be a mother. Another grief. Another empty reconciliation. Eventually, I found the courage and relief of putting it into language, into a poem, "Hog-Nose Adder," that would later appear in my second book, *The Doom Weaver*. Two stanzas are particularly poignant each time I return to the poem to remember:

Deep within I carried you
captive in a fragile shell.

Had I chosen another way
we would sit together
and speak of your lunge
into the world,
your tender tear anthem.

With no real model for what to expect as I aged and approached menopause, I took my last pregnancy test at fifty-two, not trusting it was the gradual decline of my fertility. Thankfully, I was peri-menopausal. But there was also something very painful in releasing that fear of becoming a single mother one last time. Soon thereafter, I discovered that Gwendolyn Brooks had looked into the heart of each of us who has faced and accepted the choice of not bringing a child into the world, that she knew what we all bear, branded with emotion and doubt. That she spoke on behalf of me, of all of us. There was also a bond I felt between Miss Brooks and myself, a recognition of the veracity of my own articulation that became the last stanza of my lone abortion poem:

Still I rue never naming you
or answering the brittle laugh
of your rattle.

There was something familiar, parallel in my words that could only be borne of a common knowledge, and I felt united with this magnificent poet as both artist and woman. *the mother* is not only an affirmation of my own poem of years ago, but it also confirms there is a sisterhood among us, we the mothers of the *never made*. There is not a woman I know who has opted for abortion who did so cavalierly. I do not know one who did not regret some element of making that choice. But we all have believed that it was for the highest good for all involved. I also had to acknowledge that there was a re-markable boldness in *the mother*, considering the time in which it was written and, subsequently, published. Imagine coming forth with this poem more than twenty-five years before women earned the legal right to choose. Con-sider the risk of revealing compassion for women who had secured, endured illegal abortions in the 1940s, much less the risk of doing so as a Black woman in that time. Frankly, it is astounding that the poem made it to print at all. But I am ever grateful it did.

In finding *the mother*, I found a deeper language for all I had still not said. I found the language that united me further with all women who have had life sucked out of them. And I found the language of those women who did not have the legal authority over their own bodies, so they took the law into their own hands. I also discovered the words crafted to speak for all those who could not articulate the deep loss for themselves, the empty solitude of an *un-finished reach*.

Several weeks after my first abortion, I spent an evening with my grandmother, during which she gently shared that she knew I had made the choice to not mother. Startled and a bit humiliated, I did not know how to respond. She took the lead in the conversation and, looking down at the floor, her hands in her lap, she told me she had terminated a pregnancy. It would have been her fourth child. It was during the Depression. Her mar-riage was turbulent. Her husband would soon be sent to jail, though I don't know if she knew that at the time. She did know that she did not feel she could support another child. She said my grandfather beat her badly when he found out. I have often wondered about the network of women that led my grandmother to the person who would help her. I considered her help-lessness in making the decision and in enduring the brutal blows of her hus-

8

band's hands. I also considered that she had carried this secret alone, deep within her, for decades.

There is nothing new about unwanted pregnancy. I know of women who have attempted self-abortion. I know of herbs that will halt gestation that have been relied upon for millennia. We have had a relatively short period of time in which western women have been granted safe, legal options to secure their own futures, their highest good. Most women do not have this privilege and it is currently threatened for American women.

I drive by Planned Parenthood frequently and notice that, most often, the majority of those protesting in front are men, often elder men, grayed and hunched a bit, usually of European descent. I am curious about their motivation. They could not know the depth of the fear a woman faced with aborting her child experiences. I cannot presume to know if Miss Brooks took her inspiration from personal experience or from listening to the voices of women in quiet, sacred circles. It is enough that she captured the fear some of us have of beating our children, of neglecting them, of poisoning them, of loving them too much. Throughout *the mother*, there is a bell tolling a deliberate rhyme scheme that is not too deliberate, of a rhythm that is the song of the rocking chair against floorboards. It is the sobbing late at night and waking each morning with a resolve to keep moving forward, to live among the echoes.

The last time I was privileged to be in the company of Lucille Clifton, she read *the mother* to a rapt audience in an all-star tribute to Miss Brooks at the 2012 AWP conference in Chicago. Knowing that Ms. Clifton not only cherished her dear friend and missed her dearly, and that she had her own profound knowledge of these words that weighted her voice, the poem wound through the air, and settled into my body. The dirge, the light beyond it, the truth of *Believe me, I loved you all* were both penance and restitution, yet did not absolve me of tears. I rushed from the room. I needed just a moment to catch my breath, alone. To relish and then let *the voices of my dim killed children* drift off once again. To recognize that I among legions and generations of sisters who chose a similar fate, possibly to save their own lives. To forgive myself still another time.

ANGELA JACKSON

The UnMother

(homage to Gwendolyn Brooks' "The Mother")

Barrenness will not let you forget.
You remember the children you wanted you did not get.
The small, quick bodies who ran like scattered seeds.
The singers and musicians who never played their reeds.
You will never scold or whip
them, or shush a trembling lip.
You will never coat a thumb with hot sauce
or tell monsters under the bed you're the boss.
You will never go out the door, longing for them
already, returning to hold them with arms sure and steady.

I have loved them the children of mothers,
fed them food of comfort and sugary sweets,
let them suck from bottles I warmed,
and burped them after they were replete.
But then I knew they were not mine
and never would they ever be.
Though they lay in my arms and slept
and ran to me when they came to sit on my knees.

If I deprived them of birth and names,
Their hollerings and their hand-games.
Their romances, and raps, and squabbles
and scowls, marriages, illness and
deaths.
If I stole their only attempts at breath,
Believe that the crime was not solely mine.

He never came to father you, cure me kind
                              and tenderly.
And so you could not be.

Barrenness will bring regret.
I gave myself to other gifts.
But believe me
And this truest that I can recall.
I wanted you. I wanted you all.

JEANNE TOWNS

Dialogue Between Two Women at the Clinic

It got easier after three, said Elsa. I mean, I divorced myself from the act and left my body there while I tended to the business of living. I hoisted my feet up in those steel stirrups, pushed my body down and placed my bare ass on that slab of death. And when he put the cold anesthesia in me, and whispered that it will all be over in a few minutes, I began my travels. I left behind the menacing whirl of the vacuum, the face of my unborn that might have borne freckles, or might not. I left behind all the simple joys that are given with new life.

I traveled to exotic places, and sometimes I stayed and made wild love to my man, held him inside of me to ease the ache of a memory wrought with despair. I went anywhere, as long as I could place distance between myself and reality—myself and the bastardly act. You'll see, she said patting her head with a hesitant smile.

And slowly the second girl found her voice. And with misty eyes burrowing into Elsa's she said, I don't think it ever gets easy. And though I will staunchly defend your rights (and mine) to choose, I cannot, dare not imagine it easy.

The act of stealing a life while it lay becoming of breast, becoming round and tender in anticipation of cold unfamiliar hands probing all my secrets of laying ass naked on a cold, lifeless table fighting screams and regrets, wrestling with I shoulda and I coulda, of taking laughter and tumults of missing the blossoming of the me that I gave so much of myself to, is something that never gets easier. It gets bearable, yes. But, never, never easy.

Motherhood

It is what I have become in every breath and in the space between in stillness and in motion it expands as I contract and sometimes it is more than I am.

For nine months we dutifully prepared. I read every book I could get my hands on. I read about birthing methods and about nutrition. I read about how to have a smarter baby and about raising conscious children. We gathered Onesies, A&D ointment, diapers, board books, black and white toys, a super powered breast pump, and collection of lullabies; and on that morning when he began to press his path into this world, I thought I was ready.

The journey was long for all of us and we welcomed the caress of skin, the rooting, the tasting, the searching, and knowing. We wrapped you carefully in blues and greens and dutifully kept you hidden from as much as possible for as long as possible. As spring unfolded we lifted the covers ever so slightly and suddenly complete strangers were drawn to us.

Too often, they exclaimed, "Oh my! What a beautiful baby. He is gorgeous."

He was, but we saw this precious tiny gift with such different eyes.

We had slipped into uncharted territory and I was terrified. I realized that no one had written, "What to expect when you are expecting a beautiful black boy in an America that is terrified of young black men."

I looked into stranger's eyes and wondered. "Yes, he is swaddled and innocent but as he grows his limbs will lengthen, his body will find its center, he will discover his voice and I believe that it will frighten you." Especially the strangers who are so enamored with him now. He will no longer be blameless and beautiful and I suspect that these unsuspecting strangers will become suspicious observers holding their purses more tightly when they see him approaching, crossing the street "just to be safe."

Part of the problem in this moment is that I don't know when it will happen and I don't know how to arm him for it. Will there suddenly be a moment when he is nine or ten, eleven or twelve when his innocence gives way to adolescence and as he learns how to walk into manhood the world around him prepares a case against him?

I worry and wonder about how I should guide him. Are there tools he will need? How do I teach him to stand tall, to walk with determination, to speak with conviction but not to frighten unsuspecting strangers who are already afraid of a mysterious black male teenage myth?

When will the moment come and how do I plan? I wonder about how long I can enjoy this moment of swaddling and cradling, of nursing and rocking and about the moments that will follow. On this pilgrimage I learn that each of these moments will pass before I have time to mourn them and that perhaps this is the balm and the gift. With no warning, suddenly there will be a moment when he no longer wants to be swaddled or rocked or nursed. There will be a moment when he no longer wants bottles or baby food or *Blue's Clues*. There will be a moment when his onesies no longer fit and he needs overalls, when his feet need shoes and not footsies so that he can stand and walk and run. When he needs a bed and not a crib so that he can rise and face the world in his own time. When he no longer needs me to hold his hand as he crosses the street but as he mourns a friend. And the problem with each of these moments is that they will come and go without warning and if I am too busy reminiscing I will miss the moment at hand.

And that is how I have traveled with my firstborn from sky blue blanket to hoodie. He ventures out of my sight and I pray that the world will remember how beautiful he still is.

First Journey

"... *you did not know you were going.*"
—Gwendolyn Brooks, "To the Diaspora"

In my mother's old photograph album
is she and I.
She a young woman
and I three months old.
She holds me on a small tricycle.

I have a questioning look on my face.
I am not sure what she is doing, but she is.
Maybe it was a gift
and my father or her sister took the photo
to send to the giver.

In spite of the uncertainty, I was *home*.
It would be wheels that took me on journeys
to places across the land
and wheels that took me
to the final departure of she and I.

But there in the photo
the pedals I could not yet reach.
The road I did not know was there.

RITA DOVE

Daystar

She wanted a little room for thinking:
but she saw diapers steaming on the line,
a doll slumped behind the door.
So she lugged a chair behind the garage
to sit out the children's naps.

Sometimes there were things to watch:
the pinched armor of a vanished cricket,
a floating maple leaf. Other days
she stared until she was assured
when she closed her eyes
she'd see only her vivid own blood.

She had an hour, at best, before Liza appeared
pouting from the top of the stairs.
And just *what* was mother doing
out back with the field mice? Why,
building a palace. Later
that night when Thomas rolled over and
lurched into her, she would open her eyes
and think of the place that was hers
for an hour—where
she was nothing,
pure nothing, in the middle of the day.

CHIRSKIRA CAILLOUET

My Mother's Clothes

Momma holds the universe on her hips
Spans 'cross galaxies and dips

'round like the Earth

Birthing planets into the Milky Way

Orbiting around the *Young and the Restless*, her thesis, Daddy and
me

Colliding like the moon with the tides
Feeling the pull of gravity on her

She sleeps like Pluto
making
Herself
a mountain in the bed

Her strength eclipsed by blankets

She fades like her threadbare green skirt

KIMBERLY A. COLLINS

Washer Woman

Wrinkled fingers wring excess water.
Clothes pinned lips, she hangs the bright

with the faded. The same weight—
time makes them blend.

Seeing his dreams flapping, drip dried
in Chicago's soot sprinkled wind,

Daddy removes his load.

My mother's weather worn hands
pass me pins. I hang mixed colors

we wear in prayer for a forgiving wind
to not

blow away labor we have learned to trust.

Tax Deadline

I disagreed when you told me
that I worked best under pressure

Yes, I would strive to meet the occasion
rise to answer the mandatory

as I saw you do day after day after day
Returning with grace and a joke

from the place that took your smile
made you bite your lips, narrow your eyes

You brought us stories of those you helped
who kept unopened bills in shopping bags

saving intricate fiscal complexities for your unknotting,
how they relied on your gentle understanding,

lay priesthood, advice they annually ignored.
I learned how to purposefully procrastinate

to file for an extension reflexively
gain time to sift and sort what's due

recalibrate, recalculate, shift weight
how I wish I could have done this for you.

Fixing Face

I have fixed my face mommy,
time and again straightening up
before confronting ever hostile audiences
minding my ps and qs
trying to be a credit to you
your well pressed appropriately dressed
cool esthetic and love combinations
I always wear clean underwear,
chew with my mouth closed
thinking before I speak,
hiding my sword, using it only as necessary
less provoked, less provocateur
Though yes I still do whatever
the hell I feel like doing
though not as often as I feel like doing it
avoiding that trip to hell in a handbasket
because so much of this is hell why go further?
'specially since I can no longer hear what you told me,
my hard head hurting my behind soft
I can no longer squeeze your boo-doos
You're not here for me to roll my eyes at,
hug or speak to in that tone of voice
watching my mouth make more trouble
maybe maybe magic
I still sit up straight, holding my head up high
and I'm still not sure where it is I think I'm going
yes, yes for all you gave me
something to cry about until you take me
out the world you brought me into

They say "... When you can see your future children in his eyes."

The sting sliced at the crack
of my eye—the top knuckle
on his longest finger reached
that far. His palm's cave carried burn
to my jaw, hairlines scattered
down my twisted neck. Had he been standing,
it would have caught my ear
instead. But I was, and forgot
his quick reflexes—had no chance
to rub my future children calm

Round and swaddled,
skin of overripe plums, dark
and bound to split
at the first sharp edge
they howled rage
only innocents can muster,
having never stood in the backdraft
of thoughtless acts.

milk bath

i.

momma always said that i'm the cream—
the good stuff—'cuz cream always rises
to the top—i always told momma her
analogies don't make sense—but it's a
nice thought how milk coats the palate
of your tongue but doesn't cleanse it—

ii.

are ya proud of how fast my name
travels 'round these parts? momma
always said my name would stick to
tongues—i wonder how she'd feel 'bout
the context—momma always said better
my soul than my name spread like fire

iii.

if i hear my name again i swear i'm gon
get ya
if i hear my name again i swear she gon
get me

if i hear my name again swear i'm gon
get ya if she don't get me first
if i hear my name again

i swear i do bite n i swear we gon get ya
together then but that's how they know
me now, ain't it?

iv.

i cried over the first gallon of spilt milk
but i found my guts in the second n i
haven't spilt any since—

& i swear i'll never cry again—

if i hear my name again—

momma always said—

v.

momma always said god would take care
or control—i can't remember which—but
this truck doesn't have power steering
and i think i'm an atheist now because of
it

vi.

how much milk am i wasting tryna cover
up the taste of my name

Part 2

Sisters,
where there is cold silence—
no hallelujahs, no hurrahs at all, no handshakes,
no neon red or blue, no smiling faces—
prevail.

—Gwendolyn Brooks, "For Black Women"

Horse and Carriage on the Plaza

You pretend you are free
but you like being blinded too,
forced to only look straight
ahead and just be pretty,
teeth clicking over bit and trot
to keep time, to never stray.

We are both big and beautiful,
prized for our teeth;
you understand me.
Strong and graceful we
shudder at the slightest touch,
run when we are afraid.
Tremble in thunderstorms
and rush hour horns.

The secrets we share with our eyes;
it's much easier to carry
and pull countless others
in the name of service
rather than ourselves in the wild.

CRYSTAL SIMONE SMITH

A Slip into History

A self-portrait the quest—
sit mirror-side like van Gogh,
track back & forth, the ghosts
of a bright white page, the faint
silhouette charcoaled in,
the silver flash of a reflection.
Measure & place your features
Meticulously—locks tied up & spilling out,
mind thirsty, young eyes, sable & smiling.
To be, at last, hung among the others
in class. Only then you spot
what's grossly wrong—
the bandana overdrawn, a flaw
that resembles a head rag
worn centuries ago by a woman
someone would own.

My Face

My mothers wild
bug
eyes
dance
Syracuse hymns
in my face I carry
her rhythm

Aunt Emma's
black ball kisses fit
perfectly to each space on
my left and right
cheekbones
like warrior marks
of a people who refuse
to go away

my father's cold
cracked/jaw
holds my
tongue
sharpened in armor
the curvature of my jowl
always spells out
h-i-n-e-s

I was a sweet baby
smelled like sugarcane
people kissed my face

so often
my lips
got swollen
stayed that way

my favorite aunt
Debra brought her full sculpted cheeks
taught me how to laugh when I felt
like crying chiseled each side of my face to look like
half of a heart

cousin Ameena filled
my pupils with chocolate glaze and hazelnut

great grandma Minnie sewed my eyelashes
from peacock feathers
dipped in ink

my sister poured some of her sunshine
in my mouth she made my smile warm
like fresh loaves of bread

can't stop rolling
my eyes thinking about all the years
I spent trying not to see you

blk(s)

> "People who have no children can be hard:
> Attain a mail of ice and insolence:"
>   —Gwendolyn Brooks, "The Children of the Poor"

weena crispy
blk bruda(s) call her
ooon fufu

weena roun(d)
blk eczema polka
dot her leg(s)

brudda(s) walk up
to her puff
dey cheek(s) go
boogah

boogahboogah
wuggahboo boo
boogah laf

point at weena

hair lock(d) sista(s)
whisper *dem thing(s)*
smell like pee

weena hear'em
cross lunchroom

locker|room
sista(s) whisper
her hot pocket
got tuna in it
her hear'em

in hallway
femi ax her
if her receive him
30 cent(s) today

say him been
sponsorin african(s)
since 1987

den laf & point
like all other brudda(s)
& sistah(s) do

femi got nerve
him las(t) name bankole

weena las(t)
name jones
all her friend(s) **WHITE**
girl(s) who speak erything
wif question mark(s)

keep brudda(s) & sista(s) talkin
weena a wanna be

& weena wonderin
y blk(s) stupid
y blk(s) laf at africa

y blk(s) dunno her
hear'm whisper

weena daydream
her gonna perish one day
soon underneef a **WHITE**
husban(d) who will tickle
her beautiful into beleef

weena draw(s) herself
jumpin double-dutch wif kima
raquel davina ashlee
& brandon

weena daydream
femi lip(s) on her neck
him arm(s) roun(d) her
as her eat(s) at lunch-
table wif blk(s)

who call her *sista*

The Night After You Have Been Fired From Your Job

Do not be afraid
of the wide eyed, past midnight silence.
Break it like a wish bone with a prayer,
open your sleepless mouth and breathe.
Chant silently as not to break the children's sleep,
There is but one life, that life is God's life . . .
Do not be afraid
of the cold towel pressed to your face
as you throw up ideas and fears
in the bathroom sink at 3:00 a.m., those
possible curses placed upon you as demise.
Do not be afraid
of the fall back into peace only to be rattled
by your alarm to get ready for nothing
and to go nowhere, at least not today.
Do not be afraid.

KIMBERLY A. COLLINS

A *burning lesson*

A keloid kiss graces the tip of her ear lobe.
It is Sign and Signifier of discarded pink ribbons
wound tight around plaited braids.

Some girlfriend said it was time.
Mary Janes and white ankle socks
be handed down along with cotton hair bows.

Cupping her ear, Bessie sat almost still—eyes watching
the iron combs spilling heat, promising straight
edges gaining momentum to correct her beauty.

A slight movement in the wrong direction.
The first scorch of being grown.

KALISHA BUCKHANON

She Was My First

We were girls of all colors, shapes, sizes, backgrounds, hair textures, fashion styles, and future aspirations back in the winter of 1997 on that chilly University of Chicago campus, where the abysmal 2-3 percent student of color ratio meant what was going on in an upper room of the main student center was a miracle.

Some young women on campus had gotten tired: tired of the questions about our hair, tired of the strain to prove our "talking points" for grades, tired of the need for silence over battles in public, tired of helping visitors who thought we worked there, tired of being blamed for mishaps or imaginary offenses in the dorms, tired of requests to rap on the spot, and tired of having to wait hours, if not days, to see a friendly cinnamon, lemon, chocolate, or nutmeg-hued face say: "How you doin', sista?" As tired and pressed as we were, we had been exceptional enough to make it through the doors of the institution which would make us fight hard for the future it promised. This exceptionality dictated that when girls like us got tired, we did not rest. We got up and fought harder.

A Haitian upperclassmen (amidst grueling pre-medical school studies), two African-American friends earning law and business degrees, and a future African-White British journalist were all looking for more friends in an unfriendly place. Sistafriends was born, an organization with the lone stipulation that only Black women of color could cross the thresholds of any room we gathered in. I was a freshman on campus at this time, and I attended the first meeting of Sistafriends with eagerness to talk to the women I wanted to count in my fold, hold in my arms, and see in my life. When the leaders spoke, it sounded like a prayer.

Within a few years those young women would graduate and I would succeed them as leader. At that time the group's primary need was a faculty sponsor to warrant its authority. We needed their help to book free space on campus and request money to carry out the mission statement. Recently, we had welcomed a long-legged and vocal Dean of Students who looked like she could be our older sister. Her name was Michelle Obama, and with her Princeton undergraduate experience and Harvard law degree she was in high demand in a place where *Dear White People* could have easily been filmed. We were hungry for minds who were not shocked we existed, who did not marvel at the notion that we could perform as well as the top heap of students, and other hearts unbroken by the idiocies preventing us from fitting in on our own terms. With excited surprise at the request, Mrs. Obama sponsored Sistafriends, thus was born an organization that is still in necessary existence today.

I was a young woman who moved from the fringes to the center of the organization. We popped in quietly and sporadically for fortifying boosts when we had a trip and discussion on *Love Jones*, held soul food potlucks, and brainstormed panels to create for the scarce black female professors. With some credibility and slight presence, it came time to make a bigger statement to the university community: we would organize a visit for a celebrated black woman to appear on our behalf, as a symbol for all Sistafriends could be. In the upper room of a gray student center, we held the early planning meeting of our biggest event yet. Then, my small-town hillbilly face showed itself. The name "Gwendolyn Brooks" rolled onto the table as a local possibility we could afford; she was not too far from us, therefore the lack of travel and lodging gave us an approvable budget to pay her. I am not sure we could have made a bigger statement.

Gwendolyn Elizabeth Brooks was born in Topeka, Kansas, in 1917. A little over two years after she spoke to our school, she would pass on at age eighty-three in Chicago. For me, the lone member of Sistafriends and one of few on campus who thought about the job of "writer" as one I could have, she was a god walking the Earth. In those days before Internet ubiquity and You-Tube, my only sense of her was in black and white, as her photo most often appeared in the schoolbooks of my youth.

In my small town public schools, so far from more progressive urban education programs and community activist groups, Miss Brooks joined a carousel of standards my English textbooks and Black History Month programming showed how I could be one day; Langston Hughes, Maya Angelou,

Nikki Giovanni, and Sonia Sanchez were among the other safe bets to teach the half-black and half-rural school district. They spoke most often of home and joys, not the world and hatred. Textbook editors chose their works with soft veiled political commentary in witty anecdote and innocuous jazzy style. These selections kept our classes snapping fingers, reciting rhymes, coloring pictures, and delivering reports on them. I may have heard her voice at that point, in gray footage for a PBS-like special on black women perhaps. But no matter what my sense of her was, she was a *writer*. A real one. She was an early haunt of my soul and an impress to my mind on what any woman who looked like me can do.

For this reason, and my newness to the elite university setting which breeds entitlement into its young as a rule, I did not think someone like her would ever answer to us, much less come to us. However, she or her handlers did answer to us, quite quickly as a matter of fact. But she had taught long ago at University of Chicago, a fact uncovered quickly. Suddenly, most of us felt less deranged about putting ourselves in such an all-white and foreign environment; it mattered to us that she had done so willingly as well. Her response was such validation we probably grew hair and fingernails on it. Within weeks I was calling home to tell people the poet Gwendolyn Brooks ("Yes, 'We Real Cool' Gwendolyn Brooks!") would be the first guest speaker for my ad-hoc colored girls sorority, Sistafriends.

She was my first.

Prior to Miss Brooks, I had never met a human being whose words I read and knew and loved, so I had fabulized about writers' existences. Like Olympic gold medalists and Oscar winners, writers were shadowy people I was meant to watch and talk about with flesh-and-blood people as we flipped through the magazines or channels that talked about them. But me becoming one? Certainly not.

Miss Brooks arrived from further south in Chicago after an agreeable chauffeur in an upperclassman's Honda or Toyota or something like that, with the small request for an escort to help her to and from her wheelchair. I dressed as I would for church because I had no protocol on how to meet a real writer. What I would learn only later, when I started to meet more larger-than-life figures on campus as well as make the rounds of my own books, is that writers become so embedded in their readers' psyches as if they are giants, but they almost always appear very small in person. I am unsure what I was expecting of a soft-spoken, mannered, precise poet like her. A Chicago Bull? The Sphinx? A female Goliath? I stood star-struck among my sistas and the faculty who supported us with just one thought in mind for minutes, as she sat ahead of but near me: "Oh, wow, she is so small."

Because I had branded myself as a "writer," I was among a few students who opened for her with our own attempts at this process that Miss Brooks was an anointed master of. My adopted Chicago uncle was Clarence Waldron, then the Features Editor of *Jet* Magazine who kept in touch with me after he conducted my remote Columbia University admissions interview. He wandered into the large hall normally reserved for student snacks and study just in time for Miss Brooks' ascension to the podium. Once he arrived, I felt grounded and consoled back to my place as just a young person doing things good people were proud of. I relaxed, steadied, and slipped into the moment for real when Miss Brooks was in the same room with me, and I with her.

Her largesse, that trick of the mind the greatest writers have entranced their publics with, reignited in how she approached the stage set for her. She corrected any of us naïve onlookers who were worried she was frail or could fall. The same stage we tried out our burgeoning identities on in student events appeared to have been waiting for her all along. It was hers. She knew it, well. She could have walked it in her sleep. Her feet could have tracked it like fingertips on Braille. In her eighth decade of life, the place she was made for at birth was just set up on a South Side of Chicago campus where people who looked like us scarcely walked but to work. Scarcely to sit in classrooms. Scarcely to head classrooms. Almost never to speak at large.

And Gwendolyn Brooks showed me how writers work, for real. At one mid-point to a complicated sonnet I had never been taught, I tapped a sista and said: "She isn't reading it. She just knows it." The words fell from her entire body, not just her tongue. She looked us in our eyes and challenged us with her stares. Yet still she cradled us affectionately and warmly like students she may have greeted in the community workshops and teaching artistry that were her trademarks, thinking we knew a little something when we had so much more to know. Only later, when I returned to the University of Chicago in my late twenties for a PhD English, would I study and take in the whole of her that she showed us that night. How silly I was . . .

What was so remarkable about that evening was that she belonged to all of us. Her enthralled audience was a mixed bag of South Siders, Black students, and administrators, and more non-Black students, faculty, and community members than we had expected. Thankfully, we ordered enough food for the reception afterwards. The cascade of admirers approaching Miss Brooks afterward never trickled down, and her enthusiasm to talk back to them never did either. It stayed steady until she was tired, well past a time when others of her seniority would have nodded off in front of the television or retired to their bedrooms.

So, "tireless" is just not a good enough word for Miss Brooks, a poet so careful about her words I dare not attempt to describe her in too many. "Genius" is not adequate either, because it undercuts the work behind her brilliance and talent. "Star" is too small. So are "writer" and "poet."

The best I can come up with is "Gift."

Word spread quickly among us when Miss Brooks died in the winter of the first year of a new millennium. We talked about how we had just met her in person, and had handwritten thank you letters to her not too long ago, and awaited complaints that never came from her team when our inexperienced young organization cut her honorarium check late. We cried.

And only then, after she was gone, did the miracle of what she helped us accomplish settle in for what it was. Because of her, Sistafriends transformed and evolved from just another assumed gripe group into one of the most respected and active student entities the school had ever seen. En route to becoming doctors, lawyers, professors, corporate bigwigs, community leaders, and yes, writers, we gained emboldened self-respect from Miss Brooks and later those we brought to follow her, including iconic poets Sonia Sanchez and Derek Walcott. We volunteered in the city and snatched up colored girls behind us before reverse minority psychologies did. I am not sure it would have gone that way had Miss Brooks not come there for us at the very beginning.

Gwendolyn Brooks is as big a black female goddess as they come. But, no matter her age or state, she was never too big to come down and make us all feel bigger.

A Poem for Gwendolyn Brooks on her Centennial Birthday

a crescendo of little girls
affording themselves an imagination
line up for the front line, polka dot
dresses, striped ankle socks & black
shoes.

they watch the world from this place
they've been told is the battlefield
they only know what their stomachs
have told them.
their hearts connected by a thread of
courage men have yet to own.

she is hungry for a language
she won't want to turn into waste quickly
a freedom that only a Gwendolyn Brooks
can offer.

these girls, classic black oil
standing in their own mythology
armed with poems, pressed into
sunday curls & pink nail polish

blues, have not found their way to them
sorrow is for the old.

they have found poetry so fierce
it can't be contained inside their bodies
no casket can bury its capacity to live

so they laugh and giggle and smile
and sometimes they are quiet and mysterious
as a half moon.

a constellation of poems lives in their wombs
waiting to be born again. a ballad of wounded
birds flying between their bones.
assembled by a whistle, manufactured by a wish.
foremothers, who gave their lives to craft
who insisted voice included their throats, their
aborted womanhood.

a silk dark flower, growing despite being unrooted
from its original, rich diaspora soil.
Brooks gave us all permission to blossom in
the belly of unforgiving acts against our humanity,
our brown girlhood.

she told us the light eyed and the dark skinned
are the stars of our dna.
our hearts, a gold dug too deep &
mixed gently with fire and blood.

Brooks taught us flowers are not to be worn
to simply mourn a death. they are an extension of
the living. their branches form from our mouths,
the seeds of our thoughts,
our actions.

so, live on Gwendolyn Brooks
queen of 100 races around the sun.
purple hyacinth buried inside your afroed coif.
we are grateful your typewriter located our perfume
walking past,

your second floor apartment
in chicago.

your poems attached arms and legs
& complexity to the rhythmic souls of our walk,
our pool game. our death traps, our cool, personified.

live on, peculiar cactus
in this dense desert of cement.
write on, among the angels, Miss Brooks.

we understand.
our pigtails & lace dresses,
hide stories/bombs, waiting to be discovered,
or explode, depending on the weather channel
predictions
or if granny cooked the greens,

just

right.

Gwendolyn Brooks.

gave us all permission
to be human. to live. to love, to fight
to return
from the uncertainty of the frontline,
quickly push off our shiny black shoes,
feet searching for the familiar grooves of a slanted
oakwood shotgun house floor.

rush to find a table, a piano top, a dinner napkin
take a moment to laugh at it all

& remember

to

just write.

Part 3

You are the beautiful half
Of a golden hurt.

—Gwendolyn Brooks, "To Be in Love"

Sister Flossie's Jam

I.

She took that jam
Split it straight down the middle
Shipped both jars north through
A post office assembled
At North State Line, a road that divides
Southern cities. It's funny
The moments baked into
Memory, how I cannot
recall my great-grandmother's face
but remember a single
morning in December
I sat on the kitchen floor, fingered
the box's label, envied
Its journey and split
Its flaps open to begin
the search through fruit cakes,
Tea cakes, and sweet potato pies, past
Desserts with no names. Deeper
South into the box, I searched
As if its bottom could
carry me back to her and found
A single jar of red berry jam
Sent just for me. I pulled crackers
From my pocket and dug in, my nail beds
Gleaming, tiny seeds tucked
Between.

II.
At birth, I was given two middle names
One of which came from her
So here in this decade where I am always
looking back I've planted
my first garden of berries
and mason jars, wait for harvest.

L.D. BARNES

Recipe

It's a raw lamb's foot
Not easy to chew
It's a bloody pig's heart
Main ingredients for my brew.

It's a dirty look
From the butcher behind the case
It's a pinched nose scowl
Thrown right back in his face.

It's a cluster of black feathers
Plucked from my rooster's tail
Keeping them birds in my yard
Could easy land me in jail.

It's a handmade fancy knotted
Mud covered length of rope
It's studded with the shattered glass
Left from the night you acted like a dope.

It's a swatch of cloth
From your favorite shirt
It's the one you wore
Every night you snuck off to flirt.

It's a low pitched buzz
An over the shoulder flutter
It's an invisible black winged avenger
With a baritone mutter.

It's a white paper parcel
Left on your door step
It's a gift fit for a funeral
Where not one tear will be wept.

It's a mystery gift for you
Open it if you dare
Its magic will work
No matter what you care.

Radio

The cat swallowed the radio
Every-now-and-then she tries
To turn it on by twisting her gut

She tunes in to a station
And purrs but switches
When it is not the purring channel

A lullaby is what she wants
She settles for easy listening
Curls up in the soft blanket of her dreams

Wakes hours later
Stretching her arched body
After a soft soprano whine

The radio is blasting
The advertisement for cat food
Guides her to the waiting bowl

For the lover who eats my poems . . . and all the loving in-between bites

I write for these sounds of bruised whispers. Lovely indigo painted hands. Sea-washed coral brocade covers shuddering loveliness. I gasp for mercy. Scarred rainbows leave a trail of ladies-in-waiting. Trails of spent ripeness. Trails of skin so close I can hear it breathe bleed fruit into lush. It is an evening of breaking branches that we will bandage at sunrise. Your tongue is a beckoning forest. Star-lit. Liquid whole face conjuring a delectable pilgrimage. My hair is the only map you need. Coarse uncharted navigation deep into this tangled web of throttle rhythm infinite symphonies horizons of songs. We are tangled in binding breath to prayer. Our history of sound becomes a snare drum. A decoration of ancestral thrust. A declaration of the summer when we were full of tongues kinky mornings. You prefer a feast of hair but I offer neck shoulders a delicacy of sleepless wrists singing ribs and dangerous unhinged ankles and feet. A smile holding seven seas and unmentionable continents. We wade through a millennium of oceans tropical spasms fierce star bursts. We have stolen this land this cocoon of earth for harvest deliverance birthing of new face new love new skin. It is not a shackled dance. It is not a voodoo hoodo dance. It is not a midnight flower we bring screaming head first into this world. It is all the voices you sewed inside my heart. It is all the nights of mothers waiting. It is all the Decembers of a son's lynching. It is all the mornings swept clean of hungry ghosts. It is all the love we can carry beneath our tongues. A tenderness so wanton it lashes petals wind the inside outside of our house. Here is the place to sow. Here is the space to scalp mercy siphon full moon mirror. We are this tangled confession. Blazing bare shadows. A treason of midriffs. Honey-laced thighs. Uncouth sighs. Neon heartbeats . . . and in this *while* it is enough to slide my fingers down into a stammering heartbeat and wait for you to become my primal scream. We breathe a soundless tsunami. We become the oak covering our windows. Our roots collapsing with thunder rising beneath masked skins and a rain that claims us.

To Be In Love

(after Gwendolyn Brooks)

Call it bondage   blue lake girding
            my wrists and viscera
swell under plum   trench of skin

Call it *vernissage*   harness spotlight
            gather   I feel
what you make   in your imagination

bleakness blackness   every animal nosing air
            What do you desire?
My hanging here   My serums' burgeoning

gape Beautiful   half golden hurt ·
            salted in sweat
My love I want   to be rigged

To Be

"You are the beautiful half
Of a golden hurt."
—Gwendolyn Brooks, "To Be In Love"

the cynics who cannot imagine themselves
as birds and say that there is nothing

left to say that hasn't already been
said: that is a flapping

too. i am lying
on the couch trying my best not to

die, and be golden. to be metallic as a tooth
in the yaw of the night, missing

you and careless that a fallen tower to heaven
had been built from the bricks

of indecision—the words
are not new but this weight in my hands

and that window, over there. this being of a bird
with a certain relationship to glass.

Knife in the Wall

Add to the clenched fist, the tattooed veteran
with his shirt off strumming an acoustic guitar.
Add to the three brothers and their dreams

of chrome rims, rusted car parts and roses
tattooed to the bottoms of their feet. Add to the
house music rising from traffic and children tied

es

est's tears,

noved

the doorway

im. Add

from

tible.

KEITH WILSON

Chalk

> I keep my keys away that she
> May never have to find
> The enameled winter of your heart,
> The Pastels of your mind.
> —Gwendolyn Brooks, "Priscilla Assails the Sepulcher of Love"

and why bother to name a thing except to hold it
close like a coal

that might subside inwardly? that we might refer to it as that
one, who thumbs my tears

into the folds of me, keeps a collapse
from happening, at bay—whatever the religious say instead

of Keystone, the anvil of sky. hold me
together. this is no hurricane,

for a storm has one constant eye. let's wrap like two trees
into a third, the light like ivy, everything

with roads of little green and then a yellow-gold as when the sky
becomes a moment you see

finally. your eyes betray you
when you sleep. innocence is the egg that breaks

to make love. when were you last a child? when it was easy
to say anything and be a root

that no foundation could crumble. that's what i was praying,
every time, i didn't speak.

when your silence will not save you

in the aftermath you remember the fist
upside her head. did you see. saying no
almost instinctively, you say no. again

you remember no audio with the beating
to follow in the alley. you remember
clearly not thinking. the woman got beat

from the other side of the street. imagine
you witnessed her "walker of the night,"
illusion to fantasy built up. in your head

the after-scream. in the alley she could be
dead. you thought no one would remember
the freeze-frame each night whispering

in your ear: you could have saved me . . .

CRYSTAL SIMONE SMITH

Fine Art School

I wrote of the panels at San Vitale
4th century Byzantine art,
my mother dusted portraits
in the alcoves of public buildings.
I keenly describe the basilica's
gold mosaics depicting
the emperor and empress
as if Rome were my own heritage,
and perhaps in some way
this forte was in my blood.
My father, the ever out-of-work vet,
could illustrate and paint
with the ease of an expert.
Self taught and better than the taught,
he was a master—his angle
always perfect as if traced,
even when he struck my mother's face.

Combatives

that night she told me
about the man she killed

how he forced her to the ground
pressed himself against her

how he took her
how she wrenched a blade

from her boot slid it sideways
into his navel—pulled it

like a zipper to his chin
how he leaked black bile

and she burned her clothes
before the chopper carried her

from the FOB in the morning
confusion she shakes in my arms

afraid to close her eyes but
I don't fight it when her fingers

tighten around my throat
as we make love

JERICHO BROWN

Stay

(after a line from "The Coora Flower")

All day, I kept still just to think of it—

Your body above mine, what was
A lack of air between us—hot but restful

As I sat center on my bed of learning,

Mouth open, memory touching nothing
That misses you when I stay quiet and un-necessary.

abracadabra

long before you knew
something changed inside

you became stone cold still
as if what lay before us

you knew the road to nowhere
winding through our hearts

the lump in your throat
before you left, yes you knew

each lie we would tell
when you said i'm gone

& i split, too, even before
we made love disappear

Psalm 23 at 15

Molly is my daughter; she will not speak
—not to me, at least.
Nightly I would carry her to the green
pastures of imaginary Ireland, make
Keltic ocean noises in my mouth and
throat, soft waves on pebbles
until she slept. I resettled her soul.

    Then came divorce and the shadow
of the valley. Now she sets a table
for anyone but me, rod and staff
bolt the door of her heart. I fear.
It has been fifteen years.

    Surely my dadness has followed her?
    Surely she remembers my name?
I stood that day in the back of the
church as she changed it. Per agreement,
I snuck out through the cellar, unreceived.
All the days.

visitation one

after divorce, my mother takes me
out of town every other weekend
to a roadside Dairy Queen
considered neutral ground

highway traffic through restaurant
window is one lane overlooking
another as my mother wears nervous
patience like her own mistakes

with a child's anger i believe
his absence teaches me more
about how to be a man
than his presence ever did

ADRIENNE CHRISTIAN

Dog in a Dead Man's House

I was
a dog in a dead man's
house. I was
a tooth in a dead man's
mouth. I was
a rat in a family's
den. I was
a hog in a horse's
pen.
She spoke
to me when she wasn't pissed
off. She got
pissed off when she looked at my
face. I got
my freckles and nose from my
dad. He was
a man set on being a
rat.
She was
a girl with her head in her
hands. She was
a girl who just couldn't make
ends
meet up
with no support check from my
dad. I was
the blood and the pain with no
pad.
She said

your dad needs to take care of
you. *He* needs
to feed you and buy you new
shoes. *He's* got
to learn to provide for his
kids. I ate
the roaches I found in the
fridge.

MARY CATHERINE LOVING

Babel

Recent blessings fritter attention from faithful virgins.
The once gay air dusty now: progress, its pursuit
upstages infatuation; rivals courtship's silly, exact rules.

Brides forsaken for construction efforts
steal pennies twice-blessed by nuns;
tender sacrifice in dark prayer;
surrender all in return for a lover's notice.

                  . . . Then the undoing.
Workers rail against the loss: would-be wives, lies
scattered across a hundred lands. Unfamiliar tongues,
strange faces greet them. Everyone.

Nothing is ever recovered.

KEITH WILSON

On Spring

I am not deceived, I do not think it is still summer
Because sun stays and birds continue to sing.
> —Gwendolyn Brooks, "A Sunset of the City"

and winter's been alright. i mean,
loving a person is a misnomer, right, because

you're being expected of your heart's opinion
on a sentence that is never completed

as you're having it. and then it's an example, a grammar.
and then what? i mean,

i love some of the things we appeared to have said
back there about the way our hands seemed

to have fit like gradients, like choosing
the colors of a kitchen that might become our daughter

or our son, and the ellipses, at the time, were merely
or especially

eggs and coffee was the only thing that kept us
as we made ourselves

watch rival movies and made forever of our hands like pancake batter
from the heat of our skin, when, outside, then, even as now,

the whole damn world was secretly and differently alive
under all that snow

DASHA KELLY

Bitter Winter

Forgiveness hangs flimsy between you
and the raw truth you've come to know:
Resentments do come home to roost, to peck, to force you
into navigating fatherhood from your knees. There are
explosives undetonated on your tongue, tasting
like guilt, goddamn, and gunpowder all swirled together
You teach yourself to swallow, to repent, to deny the
flames licking from your chest. Arms crossed, she bids you a bitter winter.

DAVID BUBLITZ

Suicide One

the first time
my sister and I
stayed briefly
with my second grade
teacher and her family
while doctors on base pump
wet pearl strings of pills
from mother's stomach
father disappeared
after she shrieked
I'll kill myself
and he replied
Go ahead
but I know he kept
letters we sent
him in combat
mother sealed
the envelopes
Don't let them down
black and blue ink
wrote her own
tangled cursive
the theater of war
to beg my Soldier father
live as Christ would live

Lovely Love

(after Gwendolyn Brooks)

At the funeral, inside a chapel hall,
I first saw you. Your eyes were closed. I thought
of her young death. *CF.* The organ sought
variations of Mozart's rise and fall.

When she and I were six, we'd prop a box
to climb on horseback, clicked then kicked. We'd kiss
parents goodbye. Two years since she died. This
afternoon we drift among the shocks

of bluebells. You propose. What do we know of love
or death? Will there be a birth? Maybe one,
if any? Goldfinches take wing above.
On the Fox River below: walleye run.

She lived thirty-eight years. We now stand here,
during ice-melt, this crackling atmosphere.

Sweet Stalk

(an elegy for Gwendolyn Brooks)

hereafter
we cool to grace

chase gray cares
above washed prayers

stroke the heaven place
hunt the night to breaking—
      no sleek smoke
      no crazy light

only the old
      sad quiet
I must kiss
every milk sense
through wild color

leap across tiger sleep
to climb home
through long black
& pillow your absent
          face

Genetic Codes

We spoke a secret language
through our skin. Hieroglyphs
hidden in pigment. Genetic codes
to survive genocide. Evolve and
elucidate. We whispered prayers
through our pores. Mantras of fables
unique like fingertips. Mother tongue
dipped in melanin to give it flavor.
Now every movement is a Testimony—
each word etched on skin marking Kin;
each toe on our feet keeping Beat;
each sway of our hips crying Ships—
Bopping Blues of an ocean that drank
a people, we Hip-Hop etymology
through our Lucid Lips, Vogue the
subtleties of neck rolls. We Ska
the air with eye-lashes Whipped upward
like the Naps on our Crowns singing
Spirituals to Jah, Jazzing with Sun Ra.

The Samaritan Woman

The sun shouted hot words and the desert glared disgust. Her sandals shuffled, the parched sand pressed down by the weight of wooden buckets straddling her shoulders. Her robe, dark as well stones, draped her arms, hid hands once smooth and olive-brown, now cracked with self-reproach. Rich bronze eyes, refulgent in the sun, spoke a pittance.

The Jew went to her, broke the prejudice. He reached deep down into the well with a rope and bucket, transcending heat. Offered her the water. She sipped an everlasting sweetness, cool and lingering. Yet the ancient wellspring from Jacob's Mountain could not clean her guilt. But when he touched her worn hands, warmth flowed, as if waters from Siloam had refreshed her skin; washed her soul; laced her heart, broken from so many lovers who had failed to make her whole.

There was something about his eyes . . . it was better than any kiss.

Part 4

You need not die today.
Stay here—through pout or pain or peskiness.
Stay here. See what the news is going to be tomorrow.
—Gwendolyn Brooks, "To the Young Who Want to Die"

Look Behind

The road ahead shimmered in autumn. Lost in their own thoughts, they barely noticed the trees, crowns blazing like women with their heads aflame. Historic Route 66 twisted through sleepy towns with names like Shirley and Lebanon. Places Jeremy didn't remember from his own journey west some twenty years before. It had been winter then, a different landscape.

Some of the circumstances had been similar. Leaving Chicago in a sudden rush, a duffel bag hastily stuffed with T-shirts, jeans, a toothbrush, a few changes of underwear. Pieces of fruit and bottles of water tossed into a brown paper bag, then left forgotten on the kitchen counter.

Jeremy hadn't thought to grab his collection of road music this time, though it wouldn't have mattered. Saraya's ancient sky blue Honda didn't even have a CD player.

"I'm from the cassette era," she'd warn whenever Kenny tried to plug in his iPod, "and so's this old Betsy. We don't do MP3s."

The recollection sawed through Jeremy. The most innocent recall could catch him that way, a scab of memory ripped open once again.

He could pass the kitchen sink and clearly remember Saraya hunched over in reading glasses, washing off collard greens leaf by leaf. Or opening the middle dresser drawer and finding her collection of earrings that had lost their mates. I'm an orphaned earring, Jeremy thought, both disgusted and fortified at the surge of self pity.

He switched the radio to Saraya's favorite FM station, though he didn't care for the announcer's snooty British accent. Jazz followed them nearly out of Will County before fading into static. He changed it to an urban contemporary station, which was good for another 200 miles. From the Missouri border on it was soft rock, country music, and farm reports.

Kenny stirred from a three hour silence, taking out his earpiece and turning toward the driver's seat.

"Kidnapping is a federal crime, you know."

"Not when the 'kid' is messing up, and the 'napper' is his own father."

"You mind telling me where we're going?"

"The Land of Look Behind," Jeremy gently punched his son's shoulder.

"I ain't in the mood for no riddles, Dad."

Jeremy resisted the urge to correct him: *I'm not in the mood for any riddles, Dad. And I'm not the mood for your thug pretensions, Kenyatta Davis. Your mother's an English professor, for God's sake. Was a professor. If you want 'hood, buddy, I've got stories to curdle your bourgie blood.*

"Who says it's a riddle?" Jeremy forced a smile. "Look Behind is for real. You know about the Maroons of Jamaica. They had to pass through Cockpit Country, so pitted it was nearly impassable. Runaway slaves had to rustle their donkeys and ride in twos."

"Please, Dad. Not another lecture."

Jeremy ignored him. "One faced forward in the saddle, the other looked behind. A person never knew who was gaining on them."

"Let me get this straight. We're *driving* to Cockpit Country."

"Something like that." Jeremy's wink glanced off his son's smooth face, already turned back toward the passenger window.

"In a *car*, Dad?" Kenny addressed the passing landscape. "Not a plane or boat, but a fricking car?"

"Precisely."

"Going west when Jamaica's at least a thousand miles to the east."

"More like two thousand, actually."

"This crap is totally bogus." Kenny fitted the earpiece back in and sulked for another sixty miles. At least he hadn't tried any fake ghettoese that time. *Bogish* is how young men in the mentorship program pronounced it. When Jeremy was coming up in West Garfield they called it whack. *Man, this shit is straight whack, yo.*

Ever since Kenny tried to bolt from the moving car when they passed his grandmother's exit on I-57, Jeremy had been keeping a close watch on him. When they stopped for gas or a fast food drive-through, he double-checked the childproof lock. At a pit stop outside of Kankakee, he'd kept a grip on Kenny's upper arm all the way to the urinal, shrugging off the stares of passersby.

"This is embarrassing," Kenny whispered, trying to pull away. "They might think you're a marshal and I'm a felon."

"They might," Jeremy admitted.

"Where I'm gonna run to? We're in the middle of nowhere."

"True, but we don't want to take any chances."

Jeremy was careful to keep it in the collective pronoun. It was we, a joint project. Father and son on a road trip together. Still, Jeremy didn't let go until they were safely back in the car. He was nearly two decades older, half a head taller, and twenty pounds heavier than his fifteen-year-old son. Besides, Kenny had been doing track since the sixth grade. Given a running start, Jeremy would never be able to catch him.

He didn't hold onto Kenny at the next rest stop, but walked closely behind him. Jeremy used the facilities, washed his hands, listened for the toilet to flush in his son's stall then waited for him outside. There weren't any windows in the restroom, so Kenny couldn't escape if he tried. Jeremy told himself they were building trust.

The setting sun burnished his son's eyes a cough drop-colored bronze. He had his mother's eyes, that curious hazel so startling against her dark skin.

Kenny didn't put the earpiece back in, but fiddled with the dial and found a PBS station out of Oklahoma City.

"I'm hungry, Dad." He sounded like a little boy.

Jeremy's heart clenched. He almost forgot about the handgun hidden in a hollowed out geometry book, the burnt roaches in Saraya's Fiestaware saucer, the anger-bitten boy who didn't cry at his mother's funeral. The threats of retribution against unknown enemies when a stray bullet struck his mother on her morning walk.

Jeremy resisted the urge to lean across the console and kiss the side of a cheek that hadn't even started to sprout whiskers yet.

"I think there's a McDonald's coming up ahead."

"Not Mickey D's. I want me some real food, man."

So Jeremy decided to build trust at the next roadside diner. He didn't even follow Kenny into the bathroom. Finally, with veggie burger and fries reduced to crumbs, the side of steamed broccoli voraciously consumed (Kenny had always liked his vegetables), and a slice of peach pie half-eaten, a pair of reproachful hazel eyes regarded Jeremy across the scuffed Formica table.

"If you won't say where we're going, at least tell me why."

Jeremy sighed, reached for Kenny's pie and tasted it. It was sugary and stale, crumbly against his fork. He pushed it away.

"Remember when we used to live on Marquette Road? You were forever trying to bolt across the street to the playground. Your mother and I would have to watch you like a hawk."

"So what? I was four years old."

"We were trying to keep you out of danger, son. And now, I'm afraid . . . I see that . . . " Jeremy faltered.

No, that wasn't the right way to say it. Kenny was no longer a child who had to be watched in busy traffic. He was almost a man, if Jeremy could keep him alive long enough to become one. His son was all he had left now.

Kenny cocked his head in curiosity. "What do you see, Dad?"

"I see you headed down the same road I traveled on. And if I hadn't turned away, I wouldn't be here talking and you wouldn't be here listening."

"Why?"

"Because I'd be dead at nineteen and you never would have been born."

* * *

Saraya Kadeem Nelson had long been disillusioned with the rotten cabbage of faith she grew up with, pious on the outside, wormy on the inside.

The leadership preached purity, but fornication was the sin most frequently atoned for in showy public ceremonies. The mosque's prominent males were rarely banished, unlike some of the women they bedded. If the men wouldn't marry them or take one on as unofficial co-wife, the girls would have to leave the community to have their babies in secret.

Saraya asked her mother if it was true that the imam had fathered three children out of wedlock with two different teenaged girls.

"No virtuous woman says such a thing, Saraya! She doesn't even think it."

Later on she'd overheard Muhammad and Leroy Triple X discussing the matter. Saraya was fascinated at the rough language coming from the half-open door of her brother's bedroom.

Muhammad lay in bed playing a video game with the sound turned off. Leroy XXX stood with one hand braced against the ceiling, bouncing a basketball with the other.

"Don't fool around and get dis-fellowshipped," Leroy warned. "That imam of yours preaches against video games. Doesn't he call them, 'a plot to rot our young men's brains and warp their morals'?"

"Man, fuck the imam," Muhammad snorted. "A little *Tron* ain't never hurt nobody."

"'Fuck the imam?' Shit, I'd have to stand in line. The man got a sho' 'nough white liver, the biggest fornicator on the South Side of Chicago."

Muhammad wagged his head, like he hadn't just uttered an oath against him. "You know his wife is barren. A great leader's got to pass on his seed."

"Pass on his seed? That's what you're gonna call it when he comes for your sister?"

"Saraya's a righteous woman, not like those whores you sleep with. Leave my sister out of it. Don't even let her name pass your filthy lips."

"I wouldn't dis' my own wife," Leroy teased, turning to the half-open doorway and giving the thumbs-up sign. He must have known Saraya was out there listening.

She flounced off in a huff. Saraya hated to be referred to as Sister XXX, even in jest. Long, tall Leroy had come from a small town in Kansas to live with "a good Muslim family" while playing basketball for a local Catholic college. In his spare time he served on the imam's private security detail. Saraya couldn't figure out when he had time to sleep with so many different "whores."

Saraya was eavesdropping again one day and just so happened to catch a group of women chopping vegetables in the kitchen. According to Sister Maryam, men who spread their seed too freely ended up with female offspring. Depleted stores of X chromosomes and stuff like that. Maryam was a registered nurse so she must have known what she was talking about. Saraya wondered if Leroy's children would all be girls.

After much fornicating, their fearless leader, the one with three daughters young enough to be great granddaughters, had finally produced twin boys. By then the imam had already been to the Kadeem Nelson house.

That Saturday morning her mother had wrapped Saraya in veils and her father lent Leroy XXX a wedding band. To avoid the impropriety of unmarried, unrelated people living together under the same roof, the imam had come to perform a provisional marriage.

Muta'a was a wedding of the spirit, not the body. No one expected the sham marriage to take, though later they lived together for a time. Saraya had just started her junior year in college and Leroy had finished two lackluster seasons in the NBA before changing his name to Shabaka and taking a job coaching high school athletics.

He had been Saraya's first, no telling how many women he'd been through by then. He now wore a beard and had grown out his crew cut into matted dreadlocks. He was beginning to look, act, and probably smell like a wookiee, that tall, hairy thing from *Star Wars*. She had started thinking of him as *Chew*bacca, though she'd never say it to his face. He'd given Saraya an antibiotic resistant STD and left her for a white woman before the year was out.

It was just as well. The man had been growing slowly and steadily paranoid. Mohammed said it was from all that weed he'd started smoking. Shabaka had moved up to the North Side, then back to Kansas, convinced that the preteen sons of the now-dead imam had put out a fatwa against him. Any day now they'd be sending their minions to execute him, "Just like they did Malcolm." Saraya was never clear what he'd done to deserve a death sentence.

The day she'd met J-Dawg and Laquita was her twenty-first birthday. A college graduate for all of seven months, she was legal to drink if she wanted. But she didn't. Even though she'd been away from the faith more than four years and had been shed of Shabaka for two, she still moved through the world like a Muslim woman.

Daddy had said she should have been married off straight out of high school before the world ruined her righteousness. Mama complained it was that fancy private college and all those world religion classes that made her lose Allah. Even so, Saraya still wore long, loose skirts and always kept her head wrapped.

The Muslim-woman wardrobe was her spirit armor, protection from the stares of strangers that would strip her bare.

* * *

Now, that was a do-rag lady for sure. Long-sleeved dress practically dragging the ground, just like it wasn't hot as hell out here.

Laquita had seen ones like her waitressing at the vegetarian restaurant on 75th Street, as meek and obedient as puppy dogs. She pitied them the nappy edges peeking from beneath their head-ties.

It was ninety-seven degrees in the white-hot heat of July. She and J-Dawg had gotten off the Red Line train and were walking through the shopping center to reach the movie theater on the other side.

"Look at that do-rag lady," Laquita whispered. "I bet that hair is wild as weeds under all that yard goods."

"What I care about some damn do-rag woman?" J-Dawg growled, loping ahead to walk two steps in advance. Apprehensive about reaching the theater, he was sweating up a storm. The piece tucked into his waistband slid up and down against his clammy back.

Laquita began singing at the top of her lungs. It's what she did when she was pissed off but didn't feel like fighting.

"Nasty, nasty boys. Don't go to church."

"I got your nasty for you." J-Dawg jostled his crotch. "Right here, baby."

"Sittin' in the movie show, thinking nasty thoughts. Oh, you nasty boy."

J-Dawg was nervous, understandably so. There'd been a scuffle the last time he'd come to this movie theater. Ten members of a rival street gang had roughed up him and three of his road warriors.

When the management put them all out, his crew had to scramble in all directions, their enemies in hot pursuit. While J-Dawg darted through the empty field behind the railroad tracks, one of his friends crossed 87th Street and ran into the Jewel supermarket. Teddy Bear tried to make it to the Red Line station on the Dan Ryan Expressway. The Desperados caught up with him on the overpass and stomped him to a pulp.

All J-Dawg had wanted that day was to watch a movie with his boys. All he wanted now was to see one with his girl. He wasn't looking for trouble, but if trouble came he wouldn't be bleeding from the eyes in some emergency room, not if he could help it. The handgun tucked behind his T-shirt told him that he could.

J-Dawg glanced at the woman coming abreast of them, light eyes set in a dark brown face. She wasn't dressed to turn nobody on so he was annoyed at the unexpected stirring below the belt. The woman was darker and a whole lot thicker than Laquita. He could see that even with all those clothes, the loose-fitting dress looked like a costume. Her breasts were large and those full hips gave her a sauntering gait.

The woman was loaded down with grocery bags. He thought about offering to help but decided against it. He hadn't carried bags in years. That had been his childhood hustle, carrying people's groceries for whatever change they felt like paying him. He learned it was more profitable to work the intersection at 79th and Stony Island with photocopied fliers and a coffee can, collecting to buy uniforms for a Little League team that didn't exist.

A black SUV cruised past them, music thumping with heavy bass. It slowed down alongside Laquita, still singing and swinging her arms.

"*I don't like no nasty car, I don't like nasty food . . .*"

"Ride with me, redbone," the driver called. "Take you anywhere you want to go."

Laquita stopped singing. She giggled in embarrassment and smoothed down her freshly permed hair, scampering ahead to grab J-Dawg's sweaty hand.

"I'm going to the movies with my boyfriend."

The driver was middle aged. He had two gold teeth and a bad case of adult acne. Pimples drifted down his chin like drops of drool. He let down his window and leaned out. J-Dawg felt the blast of air conditioning.

"Nigga, if you can't keep up with your woman," he snarled, "I'll snatch that girl right from under you. I'll buy me a bitch today."

J-Dawg reached back to fondle his weapon. He could blow the dude away before the next word came out of his mouth. A bigheaded joker like that, it almost made him laugh. Old enough to be his damned daddy, talking about taking his girl?

But J-Dawg wanted to see a movie with Laquita that day, Brandon Lee's last film before he died. He froze for a moment, torn between fight and flight.

The sultry wind reached out a finger as Saraya passed him, lifting his shirttail to reveal what was hidden in his waistband. She stopped and turned back, reaching out a hand to touch his shoulder. Despite the heat of the day, her hand was cool. Confused at the gentle, insistent touch, J-Dawg shrank away.

"What you think you doing?" Laquita demanded, staring at the dark brown hand. Another woman's hand on her nigga's shoulder? Oh, hell no.

"Don't do it," the woman said. "No shame in turning away."

"Don't do what?"

"That man taunting you, he wants what you've got. Your youth, your fresh life, your freedom. Your girlfriend. I'm assuming this is your girlfriend."

"Damn straight," Laquita spoke up. "We been kicking it since way back."

When the do-rag woman turned to smile, Laquita smiled back though she didn't quite trust her. She looked like one of those veggie burger Israelites, but acted like a Jehovah's Witness or something. Laquita wondered what kind of salvation she was selling.

Bass rhythms throbbed in the air as the SUV idled alongside them, inching into reverse and nearly hitting an old man wheeling a shopping cart across the parking lot.

"Looka here, sweet thang." The man leaned out his window, thrusting forward a wad of folded bills. "I got this and more besides. What that little nigga got?"

J-Dawg glanced at the thick fist stuffed with greenbacks. He wondered how far he'd get if he'd grabbed the money and took off running. "What I got for her? A strong back and a hard dick. How long since you had one of those, grandpa?"

"Just turn away," Saraya murmured. The hand on his shoulder squeezed it lightly. "That's an empty shell you're looking at there."

The man with bloodshot eyes didn't look empty at all. He looked full, seething with something thick and hot, like lava. *He hates me*, J-Dawg realized. *He hates me and I never even seen him before.* It wasn't even like the Desperadoes or K-Town Killers, people he had beef with before. *What have I done to make him hate me?*

"You have everything to lose," Saraya answered, just like she could read the thoughts running through his mind. "And this one has nothing. Can't you see that?"

J-Dawg glanced at the man in the driver's seat. Oh yes, he had something to lose. An expensive SUV and a handful of money, and J-Dawg could help with that. He tried to psyche himself into being angry about it, but all the fury he should have felt was draining out through the cool hand that lay on his shoulder. J-Dawg shrugged it off.

"All three of y'all can suck my dick," the gold-toothed man hissed. He slammed into drive and zoomed off, screeching from the parking lot onto Lafayette Drive.

"You ain't got nothing to suck, old man," J-Dawy hollered after him, not sure whether he could still be heard.

"Here," Saraya said. She reached into her purse and pulled out a bill. It was a twenty, far less than the wad he might have grabbed.

"What's that for?" J-Dawg asked suspiciously.

"For you to practice living and being happy. Too many of our young men leave this earth before their time. Take your girl somewhere and buy her lunch."

When J-Dawg continued to hesitate, Laquita eased the bill from the woman's outstretched hand. "Thanks. We're fixing to go see a movie."

"Wonderful," Saraya smiled, hoisting her grocery bags from one hand to the other. "Be young and happy and love each other."

The bags looked heavy and it was hot outside. He really should have helped her out, but J-Dawg didn't.

Laquita snickered as they walked away. "Be young and happy and love each other. That do-rag lady was straight up whack."

It couldn't have been much more than ten minutes later, fifteen at the most. Saraya had stashed her groceries in the trunk of her car, conscious of how quickly the fish could turn in all this heat.

She went into the Avenue and searched for something to wear that night. Something modest enough to drape her generous curves but fetching enough to knock a man's eyes out. She rifled through racks of cheaply made dresses but found nothing suitable.

Saraya was headed back to her car when she heard the footsteps pounding. She turned to look behind her. J-Dawg zigzagged wildly through the parking lot, dragging Laquita by the hand.

"Hey, lady," he shouted. "Wait up."

Fear clutched at her throat. A voice whispered in her head. Leave, Saraya! *Go, go, go.* She edged gingerly toward the car.

"What do you want, more money? That was the last cash I had on me."

"I don't want your damn money," J-Dawg shouted then lowered his voice when he saw her flinch. "No disrespect, ma'am. Matter fact, I'll give back what you gave us. Laquita, where's that twenty?"

The girl opened her fist with the crumpled greenback still inside.

Saraya frowned at it. "I thought you were going to see a movie."

"Got some fools coming for me, but I'm 'bout to handle my business," J-Dawg answered. "Ain't tryna mix you up in no mess, just don't want Laquita around when it goes down. Can you take her away from here? Please."

Saraya surveyed the faces before her. One, open and frightened. The other, clenched and determined. She surprised herself with her response. "Okay, I'll do it."

Shouts echoed from the far end of the parking lot. A group of young men were headed in their direction. Not running, but strolling, looking purposefully around them. Maybe they hadn't seen him yet. J-Dawg grabbed Laquita and Saraya by the arms, forcing them beside the car, down into a crouch.

"I'll do it on one condition," Saraya whispered. "You and her together. Either you're both coming with me or I leave both of you out here. Your choice."

She took sullen indecision as an answer and clicked open the doors of her sky-blue Honda, the first hybrid on the American market. It was financed, foolishly according to her brother Muhammad, with a down payment from her first paycheck.

"I ain't no punk," J-Dawg grumbled, but he crawled into the back seat, slid across it, and crouched there out of sight. Laquita followed suit.

Saraya took them to a Roseland address near the edge of the city, even though it was miles from her North Kenwood apartment. Even though she had ten pounds of greens to wash and pick, five pounds of whiting to dredge and fry. And still had to find something in her closet that didn't make her look like she'd been dumped for a white woman. And was expected at an old boyfriend's potluck in four hours—a fundraiser for a boot camp for urban youth called The Land of Look Behind. Not to mention that her gas tank was running dangerously low. Yes, it was a hybrid but she still didn't trust the technology.

"Hold up a minute." Laquita demanded. "I gotta go tell Granny there's somebody with me."

As Laquita disappeared into a ramshackle frame house, Saraya watched the young man's face through the rearview mirror.

"I'm Saraya, by the way. And your name is . . . ?"

"J-Dawg!" He might have been a real dog, the way he barked it. "J-Dawg Davis."

"*J-Dawg?* What's your real name?"

"What are you, the Five-O? Giving me a ride don't give you the right to get in my business. J-Dawg Davis is all you need to know. I'm outta here."

Though Laquita hadn't come back for him, he got out of the backseat. He knew how to make it back to West Garfield, though he wasn't sure whose territory he might be moving through along the way.

Saraya reached into her purse and thrust something at him. "Here you go, J-Dawg."

"Lady, I already told you. I don't want your money."

"Just take it," she insisted.

It was a white business card with embossed green letters grouped beneath a picture of a pine tree. *Saraya Kadeem Nelson, MA. Adjunct Professor of English, Chicago State University.*

"You a professor for real, for real?"

"I am. In a college that's three quarters female. We're always looking for young black men with a decent head on their shoulders. Have you finished high school?"

"No, but I got my GED." J-Dawg remembered Chris Rock's joke. *Good Enough Diploma.* He also recalled how he used to tell Grandma Junie he'd be a lawyer when he grew up, either that or a firefighter and a football player. "Thanks, but I ain't no kinda college material. Been hustling these streets way too long."

He tried to hand the card back to her.

"You're all of what? Eighteen years old?"

"Nineteen, going on ninety."

"Well, give it some thought. My shop is right up the road."

J-Dawg watched her drive away. He thought it was funny that a big-time college professor called where she worked a shop.

Laquita came out shaking her head. "Granny says she ain't having no hard leg boy up in her house, sniffing around her girls. You gonna have to leave."

"What?" J-Dawg protested. "Without my sugar? You betta give me some of that."

He pulled her close and sang into her ear, big hands roaming her slim curves. *"Give it to me. Gimme that stuff, that sweet, that funky stuff."*

"Ooh, Laquita!" a little girl squealed, watching them from the front porch. "You finna get it. I'm telling Granny you out here doing it with a hard leg boy."

Laquita pushed J-Dawg away. "You better go before Granny catches you."

He snorted, kissing her neck. "Girl, you're tripping. What's your old granny gonna do to me?"

"Granny got a gun, J-Dawg. A big old crazy shotgun."

He crossed 103rd Street and walked toward Michigan Avenue. Right down the middle of the street, the better to look behind him. Moving cars were nowhere near as dangerous as moving feet.

A group of boys several years younger than he is hooted three times from a front porch on Michigan Avenue, throwing up hands in complex gestures. J-Dawg strolled past, ignoring them.

"What, you ain't representing?"

J-Dawg looked over his shoulder, tilting his head in a quick half-nod. "Whas' up?'

One of the boys snorted as he passed them. "Don't you know you on 103rd Street? Wild Hundreds, cousin. You better come correct."

The kid was obviously from somewhere Down South. He pronounced "street" like "skreet" and hundreds as "hunnids" and cousin as "cuddin." J-Dawg resisted the urge to laugh out loud. *"Naw, cuddin, you the one need to come correct. Learn some language before you step to me."*

He attempted a gesture, a series of half-hearted hoots that boys weren't buying.

"Shit, this nigga ain't on nothing. We oughta waste his narrow ass, for real."

J-Dawg twisted sideways, feeling the weapon hard against his back.

He could easily reach back and slide it into his right hand. He remembered instead the light touch of a woman's hand. A voice seemed to murmur beneath the rustle of trees, the grumblings of porch sitters as they left their perch to move down creaking steps.

No shame in turning away.

He saw a sky-blue Honda stopped at a traffic light and sprinted for it.

***

But if I hadn't turned away . . .

J-Dawg shrugs off the woman's cool touch, fingers itching for the comfort of cold metal. He pulls the weapon from his waistband and shoots away a gold-toothed grin in an acne-pitted face.

A woman in long skirts screams. She drops her groceries and backs away in horror. Broken eggs splatter his feet; fresh blood splashes Laquita's face. The faceless man jerks at the wheel, the gear jammed in reverse. He plows down an old man wheeling a shopping cart behind him.

Or it could have happened otherwise.

They've bought their movie tickets when J-Dawg notices five Desperadoes hanging out at the video arcade near the concession stand.

"Step off," he whispers to Laquita. "Now!"

"But why?" she whines. "I wanted some popcorn."

A Desperado catches sight of him, a split second of recognition lighting his eyes before he leans into the circle of homeboys. He could have turned away but he does not, and neither does J-Dawg. He ain't no punk, he's a warrior.

Enemies surround him and Laquita too, though J-Dawg tries to push her out of the circle. He reaches for his gun and fires it into circling men, once, twice, three times before lead slams into his own chest. He hears Laquita holler his name as he pitches forward. He doesn't know if she's screaming because he's shot, or if she too is hurt.

Or he might have made it out to Roseland.

He crosses 103rd Street and walks toward Michigan Avenue. A group of boys younger than he is hoot three times from a front porch, throwing up hands in complex gestures. J-Dawg strolls past, ignoring them.

He looks over his shoulder, tilting his head in a quick half-nod. "Whas' up?'

92

One of the boys snorts as he passes them. "Wild Hundreds, cousin. You better come correct."

J-Dawg turns back, singing out his own native song. His hands flash out the contours of his home territory.

"I don't represent shit but West Garfield." He thinks of Teddy Bear blind in his hospital bed. Jermaine shot dead and buried at seventeen. His little cousin Donnie twisted in a wheelchair, the five-year-old victim of a summer drive-by. All of them felled by enemies like these porch sitters moving toward him.

"Shit, this nigga ain't on nothing. We oughta waste his narrow ass."

"Waste my ass? Here, I got something for every last one of you," he coos, pulling the gun from his waistband and blasting the surprise from their scowling faces.

When a man gives into the freedom of fury it blazes a white-hot trail across his heart, searing the skin from his emotions.

And if he relaxes into regret, the hours of reckoning crawl like a colony of fire ants. To turn and look back upon what was done parches your eyes into a crust of tears, freezes your body into pillar of ash.

Better then to form calluses, to hide conscience beneath a scab of indifference. People's lives are wasted every day. Always have, always will be.

And the prison cell is dark. The days are long, the nights filled with intimate terrors.

And the grave is cold in its frozen foreverness.

A pimpled chin, a gold toothed grin, the sloping sides of a high-top fade. A man will remember, in the dread of his leisure, the features of another man's face before they've been blasted away.

Deuce and A Quarter

I can't say for sure it was you
Who wore the battery down
Playing the radio which meant
We couldn't go to the beach.

But later that evening
I came out onto the porch
The Buick Electra was gone.
Silly me I still can't decide

Whether we were denied
Sand seashells cotton candy
All for the sake of a few songs—
Or was it just a ready excuse

For Daddy to disappear?
The other witnesses are dead
As the Buick's battery sounded
And today it's your funeral

And we ride in silence
All the way to the cemetery.
But going home we play
The radio, tell stories and laugh.

Convenience

Brady, this boy with a Gaelic name and skin the shade of imported ginger, traces the cracked glass window of his pharmacy. The detritus of the departed lies near a crowded entrance: unfolding toilet paper, slanted or ripped signage, typed instructions from pilfered prescription bottles. He steps over several bought braids, brandished but now banished to the blacktop by some struggling mother. Didn't Solomon give to the most deserving?

The good Samaritans shuffle their feet while moving mops against dirtied linoleum. They'd receive no wages, their sole payment a few seconds of airtime should the camera catch them. Brother, can you spare a broom for Baltimore, clean in a city condemned? Brady dodges the barricade tape across the front door, tape that's become a trademark during the last thirty-four hours. Bright bulbs cloak the word cashier on his turquoise nametag. It almost breaks away to slip into a sea of packing peanuts. Would that be another loss to bear?

Brady recalls the pulse and panic of the former afternoon. The body brims with nostalgia if you let it. Then, his blood percolated every teenage limb, each capillary fighting impulses of control, each endorphin winning the day. Then, his knowledge of daily sales and dairy product contents disappeared with every sneaker that walked by. Then, the discounts seemed to be on a higher plane than before. Neighbors soiled their hoodies with stolen sodas. Floral hair combs, beaded bracelets, the stuff of proletariat proms were gone for more than an evening. Unaccompanied, the scanners weren't touched while women examined their unused food stamps. Brady heard the sirens scream from overuse. All the tear gas, charred cruiser remains, and threadbare tires were too much to cry about forever. Multiple tantrums exhausted Charm City. Peel after cringing peel from nearby police cars stilled Brady. He could only detect the crunch of gift bag tissue, the moans of creased poster boards, the slosh of stolen milk against the carton. The body brims with noise if you let it.

The new neon store sign, now faded, buzzes as Mr. Hao follows a trail of trash bags leading to Brady. Brady straightens his employee vest out of habit even though they won't reopen again. His supervisor's complaints come out mint-scented since Mr. Hao works part-time at a hotel. They don't care to fix anything through laws they might not understand. They don't care to rebuild trust that was never there. These were Brady's reinterpretations of Mr. Hao's differently worded declarations, mental additions that keep his feet rooted to the stained tiles.

"Please tell me you made it home safe," whispers Mr. Hao.

Yes, with shoestrings loosened, hands full, mind empty. Low-fat cookies line the bottom kitchen drawer where his brothers don't look. He may be the single sixteen-year-old with four tiny containers of hand sanitizer next to his basketball. However, this sixteen-year-old knows he's going to use them on the first day he's thinking straight.

"Of course you did," says Mr. Hao, sighing. "Or else you wouldn't be here. Where are you going to work now?"

"I might be a dishwasher or something," replies Brady.

"Well, my wife's restaurant would hire you," says Mr. Hao. "I'll check."

Lily Hao came to Maryland to marry her husband, a bad joke that nonetheless amused both Haos. She never received an education, but Mr. Hao worked three jobs for culinary school tuition. With the store closing, Brady foresees a halt to these plans, more delays in changing anything. He wonders if his mother's soul food recipes would help Lily Hao at all.

The entrance bell signals the arrival of two strangers. Their uniforms, iron-pressed and smoke-scented, earn a darted glance from Brady. Where were they when the aisles weren't jam-packed with fallen baked goods, when a host of lithe fingers went mad for the last iced tea? They came with the tape, not the terror. They could've saved Mr. Hao's business. Or prevented the frenzied thoughts in Brady's brain. Perhaps that's why he really hates them.

"But, first," says Mr. Hao, noticing the officers. "I have to handle them."

Mr. Hao wears a crew cut in memory of his father who died in the Vietnam War. The story of a Chinese soldier living in America and dying in Asia made Mr. Hao cling to patriotism that much harder. He often urges Brady to shave off his dreadlocks, to fall in line, to delight in and devour any chance to be disciplined. Brady wonders if surveillance caught the kinky spots near his neck, the precious part he leaves unattended, when he left his cashier post. That's how his own father wore his hair seven years ago when his head laid on the coffin cushion.

As Mr. Hao goes away, Brady watches his boss' weighted shoulders inch in toward his squared hair. He remembers when the pharmacy opened last year and the corner dwellers christened the bricks with their sweaty backs. Kids sucked frozen Kool-Aid popsicles. The homeless asked for the time of day just to talk to someone. That's why he applied here of all places. Here lay a piece of property that was almost idyll in the inner city, a rectangular refuge among the streets.

He served all his neighbors, maybe in spurts, maybe Freddie Gray once. Only finding a valued customer card would reveal the truth: Freddy was a regular. He would've walked in cool, that forgivable slouch twenty-somethings cherish, ears open to the ever-present hum of fluorescent lights. The water from bagged ice would baptize him when he reached for his carbonated drink of choice. Then he'd strut up to Brady, slide in his card for payment, and leave the safety of this store.

Brady strokes the shelves he stocked where only scuff marks remain. They creak, empty, like rocking chairs with missing grandfathers erudite in the ways of riots. No one including Mr. Hao can explain how to fix these creaks or fully describe how they got there. Brady taps them as if testing them for the first time. The sound travels while he takes in the soaked boxtops, askew shopping carts, and spilled cleaning products.

"Brady!" calls Mr. Hao.

The policemen greet Brady with leisurely smiles. Brady unbuttons his vest when meeting them at the register. Mr. Hao moves a dreadlock when it obscures Brady's vision.

"He locked up that night," says Mr. Hao. "All by himself. This boy . . . "

True, this boy ran in the crowd while the city yelled its discontent, when supplies toppled into the waiting arms of a throng. True, this boy paused to think while considering if this was a solution, yet his feet pattered after his peers.

"You need to check . . . ," says Brady.

"On the restaurant job?" says Mr. Hao. "In a minute, but . . . "

"No, you need to check surveillance," says Brady.

He removes his vest and sets it on the scanner. The nametag joins his surrendered uniform. Mr. Hao views a slouch Brady's earned, wonders at the burden. Brady keeps a steady pace while walking out, this joyless boy.

TONY MEDINA

Anacostia Suite (13 Ways of Looking at a Black Boy)

Anacostia Angel

White berets like wings
    Brown eyes of a brown angel
Kool-aid smile that sings
    Mama's little butterfly
Daddy's dimple grin so wide

Images of Kin

South East Benin mask
    Face like a road map of kin
Brought back from the past
    Resurrected dignity
Flesh of onyx majesty

Little Mister May

My granny made me this suit
    So I could look nice for God
She's always at church
    Her Bible's older than me
It's heavier than can be

Street Corner Prophet

Dreadlock halo crown
  Jesus show up everywhere
In a black parka
  Here in Anacostia
Winter corner crucifix

The Charmer

Between you and me
  All of the girls like my smile
The boys be jealous
  Call me bubblehead and laugh
The girls roll their eyes and sass

Givin Back to the Community

I went to this school
  When I was a shawty rock
Breakin in the yard
  Wanted to be a rap star—
But a teacher's not too far!

Lazy Hazy Daze

Summertime on stoop
  Forehead sweat like ice cream tears
Hiding from the sun
  Wishing for the rain to come
Cool us like johnnie pump spray

My Soul to Keep

We preacher's brothers
    Grew up crawlin' under pews
Splintered as Christ's cross
    While Daddy spit the Gospel
From sanctified porcine lips

Brothers Gonna Work It Out

We righteous Black men
    Patrol the soul of this 'hood
Raise young bloods proper
    To be the kings that they are
Crowned glory of our future

Do Not Enter

Ashes pepper sky
    Over deserted landscape
Of broke down buildings
    And cars that no longer move
Where hope was a place for love

One Way Street/Ticket

Payday don't pay much
    Every breath I take is taxed
What kind of life where
    I have to take out a loan
To pay back them other loans

Broke Bus Blues

Know how many times
    I done missed this broke down bus
Hardly catch my breath
    Knees ain't what they used to be
Broke like this bus leaving me

Cat at the Curb

Sandwiched between curb
    And black radial tire
A cat with nine lives
    Halfway spent contemplates life
Mundane days bunched up like grass

ADRIAN MATEJKA

Sold to the Man with the Mouth

> *Except that Strong Men are*
> *Pasted to stars already.*
> > —Gwendolyn Brooks

Even in these subsidized spaces
    of homemade telescopes

    & bed sheet ladders, busted
    father figures collaborate
in embouchure shapes trumpeting

a whole lot of bad advice.
    Their split-pin maxims

    & Reagan fist-shaking axioms

& walls coming down while
the women around are old adages

    scuttled like empty
tall boys tossed on the side
of newly-plowed roads without

    a running car in sight.
Afterward, somebody chuckles
    through the wall

like a housebound blue jay.

Others, mothers & sons,
watch at angles hoping

their particular father is pulling
into the lot after his shift

or store trip or cigarette
break that somehow took him
all the way to Chattanooga:

Trying to get this money right
for you & no one

believes him—not the son
practicing his macho in the mirror,

not the mustached mouth
exhaling the words to begin with.

Not the mother blinking into
the receiver like a tired astronomer.

Kenny's Friend

She set down the bag of groceries, slipped her key in the lock, pushed the door open, grabbed the bag again, and stepped into the vestibule. Glancing at the slab of mailboxes, she decided to check hers later. She pushed open the second door, tossed her keys into her purse to grip the handrail with her free hand—something she did now since that time her knee gave way and Mr. Johnson on the third floor kept her from falling. Ever since she rounded fifty, she had become more cautious. About everything. Her weight, for instance. Just this morning she tipped the scale at 152. Not bad for a woman five-feet and nine-inches tall. She'd been drinking lots of water too, so she used her sunrise beige powder less and less. Her skin was smoother than it had ever been. She told her boss the other day, "That's the advantage of getting old—no more zits." But she knew it was the water.

She was rounding the carpeted steps to the second floor when she heard someone. He was standing on her landing in front of Kenny's door, 2B. Over six feet, she surmised. He turned. "Let me help you with that," he said as he descended a couple steps to reach her. Was that blood on his white shirt? She brushed him aside and continued climbing.

In front of her own door, she bent and set down her bag, then listened before reaching in her purse for her keys. The boy knocked on Kenny's door again. Bang, bang. She thought of gunshots and turned. His back was to her. His pants hung low on his waist. Kenny told her they called that sagging. A white T-shirt hung below his black Bulls jacket and past his butt. The baggy legs of his black jeans lay pleated in folds over his huge red and black gym shoes.

He turned. She spoke, "Kenny won't be home for at least . . . " She hesitated. Although Kenny wouldn't get home from work for another hour, she lied and said, " . . . ten more minutes."

"Dang." The boy said. He was about seventeen, eighteen years old. Very little evidence of facial hair.

"He know you're coming?" she asked, still avoiding her purse and her keys.

"Naw." A pause. "I just thought I'd drop by." She strained to hear him.

"Thanks." Footsteps on the stairs, then the vestibule door closed. Quickly she dug into her purse, located her keys, and opened her door. Grabbing her bag, she slipped inside, and bolted the lock. She thought of Malcolm, her only child, way over on the other side of the world in China, teaching English.

Then a knock on the door. She moved on tiptoes back to the peephole. It was the boy.

"Yes?" she said through the closed door.

"Excuse me, ma'am, but I wonder if I could wait here for Kenny. You said ten minutes?"

"I don't know you, son."

"I'm a friend of Kenny's, ma'am. I don't mean you no harm. I just, I just . . . "

She watched him as he stared around like someone lost, looking for something familiar.

"You—you remind me of my grandmother. Would you have just a minute?" She watched him turn toward the stairs. "Never mind." She thought she heard tears in his voice.

She opened the door and stepped out to catch him before he reached the vestibule. "Son!"

"Yes, ma'am?" She heard him take the stairs two at a time back up to her floor.

Seeing his face filled with tears, she held her arms out to him. He walked into them, this man/boy she reminded of his grandmother. His sobs were audible and she patted his back, her face buried in his chest.

"What's wrong, son?" Her fear gave way to his vulnerability.

He sniffed hard, let her go, and stepped back, wiping his eyes.

"A drive-by," he sobbed, looking down at his shoes. "A mistake." He looked up at her. "My brother . . . my brother died . . . in my arms!"

"Come on in, baby," she said and grabbed his arm, leading him inside.

CALVIN FORBES

Run Johnny Run

I hear Johnny's got a gun
Know where I can get me one
Johnny says I stole his girlfriend
She gave herself to me I swear

She said Johnny set her free
This isn't some old sitcom
Come to mess with my brain
Johnny's a man I'm a man

It's either him me or both of us
Johnny got himself a gun
I got to get me a bigger one
I got a right to defend myself

It's in the Constitution in the Bible
Fellas take you for a chump
If you don't have a bigger gun
Here come Johnny look at him run

I didn't steal his woman I swear
I stole the hundred dollars I gave her
They say Johnny got himself a gun
You know where I can get me one

foun(d) poem

(inside *Negro Hero*)

I have to
fish beneath
glory;

Gold-enize Negro blood;

Black
white man
gun;

Battle demon
noise;

Wild kinder
than. I have to
have loved
drowning men
bleeding of battle;

Kick law
into their teeth;

Stutter promises in order
to save them; Or me.

I have to invisible death daily;

Be fight enough
to chip-tooth a white-
gowned city boiling
and howling about.

I have to.

For I am a gem.
A black
air lying cold.

Silly Stories

Martin wants to lower his head, but his daddy demands that he look at him when he's talking to him, and his daddy is really, really talking to him, so he is trying his best to look at him, but the butter is melting on his pancakes, and he needs to flip the top one over so the bottom one will have butter on it too. Martin likes it when every bite is buttery and syrupy sweet. With a knife in one hand and a fork in the other, he is looking up at his father and trying hard to listen.

"Boy, we don't send you to school so you can sit up in that classroom and write silly stories. You go to school to learn. Fifth grade ain't play time, boy. How many times do I have to tell you that? You ain't in kindergarten any more. You go to school to do schoolwork. If your teacher sends another note home about you writing stories during school time, I'ma come up to that school and embarrass you, boy. You understand me?"

Martin does understand. Whenever a kid's parent comes up to the school, bad things happen: sometimes kids get fussed at right in front of the class, and other times the teacher makes the kid sit by themselves the whole day, and the other kids are never nice to a kid after a parent comes up to school; they tease the kid really, really bad. Teresa Brown started crying from the teasing last week. Kids started teasing her, saying, "T. Brown the clown, yo' daddy got a frown." It was a silly thing to say. But it hurt Teresa, bad.

"I understand, Daddy. I won't write any more stories at school. I promise."

"Ok, boy. No more warnings. Next note, I'm coming up there with my belt."

The thought of his daddy coming up to the school with his belt causes Martin to put down his knife and fork. The buttery syrupy sweet pancakes can't compete with the fear of his daddy spanking him in front of the class. No kid's parent had ever done that. Was writing stories that bad?

His daddy comes from the stove with his coffee mug in his hand and sits at the table across from him. It's easier for Martin to look at his daddy when he is sitting.

"Daddy, can I be excused? My stomach hurts."

Martin sees that his daddy's non-smiling face is saying no, so he doesn't ask again.

His daddy takes a sip from his coffee and says, "I used to draw pictures in school when I got bored, but I finished my schoolwork first. I knew if I played around in school and didn't get good grades, my daddy would come up there and beat my butt. Now, that teacher wrote that when she's talking, you be writing stories. When she be writing on the board explaining stuff, she say you be writing in your notebook and not paying attention to her. Now, that's just no good. She said she took your notebook two weeks ago, but you keep writing stories anyway."

She did take his notebook, and it had four good stories in it; one was about eating pancakes with his daddy on Saturday mornings like they were doing now. When Martin wasn't getting it fussed at, Saturday morning was his favorite morning.

"What you be writing that's so important you can't pay attention to the teacher? What is it you be writing about?"

Martin knows he should answer, but he merely hunches his shoulders.

"Is it the same story or different stories? Sometimes, when I was your age, I would work on the same picture for a long time to get it right. Is it like that with your stories? You be trying to get them right? Is that it, boy?"

Martin still doesn't answer, but he keeps looking at his daddy.

"Well, the teacher also wrote in the note that the stories be good stories."

Martin must not have heard his daddy right.

"What did you say, Daddy?"

"Yeah, she said your silly stories be good. She just don't want you to write them during class time, and it seems like other people think they good too because she also sent home a form from the *Chicago Defender* for me to sign . . . giving them permission to publish one of your silly stories."

"What does that mean, Daddy? 'Publish?'"

"They want to put one of your stories in the newspaper, boy. Yeah, and they gonna pay you for it. $300. Your teacher sent a story to the *Defender*, and they gonna put it the paper and pay you."

"They gonna put one of my stories in the newspaper?"

"Yeah, boy, they are."

"But Daddy . . . suppose somebody sees it and reads it. Suppose one of the kids in my class sees it and reads it."

"What? I don't understand you, boy."

Kids get teased for doing stuff that's different. Martin knows that, and writing stories is different, so different that he tried to keep writing them a secret from the other kids, and he had until Ms. Peterson took his folder.

"If they put my story in the paper, people will read it and stuff."

"So?"

"I don't want nobody to read them because I wrote stuff I be thinking about, and stuff I made up in my mind, silly stuff that I was thinking about, just me thinking."

Martin sits quiet looking at his daddy; he never thought about anyone reading his writing.

"Well, boy, your teacher read what you wrote and she liked it, and the people at the newspaper liked what you wrote too. Don't you want people to like what you write? If you want people to like it, they got to read it. I draw and paint because I like doing it, but I like it when other people like what I make; it makes me happy."

Martin wrote stories because he liked writing them better than doing schoolwork, and sometimes he wrote because nothing good was on television, and a lot of times he wrote because the boys on the block weren't doing anything fun. Reading and writing stuff he wanted to read and write was always fun. He didn't care if other people liked what he wrote; he liked writing.

"They are my stories, Daddy, and Ms. Peterson should not have took them and read them, and she should not have sent them to the newspaper."

His father reaches over and pulls the plate of two pancakes from Martin, and without standing he swivels around to the counter and opens the door of the microwave and places the plate inside it, "And you should have been doing schoolwork instead of writing stories in school."

Martin watches fifteen seconds click by on the clock without saying a word. When the timer rings his father pulls the plate from the microwave and places it in front of him. Martin smells the butter, and the pancakes becoming appealing again. He reaches for the syrup.

"But Daddy, the other kids are gonna find out I write stories." He flips the top pancake over allowing the bottom one to be buttered. "And . . . "

Martin stops talking and sticks the fork into the pancakes.

"And what, boy?"

"Aren't they gonna think I'm weird, Daddy?"

"Boy, what kids in your class read the paper? And besides, they might like your stories. Your teacher liked them."

"Ms. Peterson likes a bunch of stuff that kids don't like. She likes giving homework and kids don't like that." Martin pours syrup over his pancakes.

"Do you know how much money $300 is? Of course we are putting $200 in your college fund, but you can spend a hundred on whatever you want."

Martin cuts into the pancakes, "Anything, Daddy?"

"Whatever you want, boy. Well, whatever your mama says is okay."

"Can we go to the show and buy stuff there instead of sneaking stuff into the show to eat? I mean can we buy a big bag of popcorn and put a lot of butter on it, and buy some of those big candy bars that cost too much? Can we do that with a hundred dollars?"

His daddy laughs out loud, "Yeah, boy. We can do that."

Martin fills his mouth with the sweet buttery pancakes.

"Daddy, I won't write anymore stories at school, I promise, but I can still write them at home, right?"

"Yes, Martin. When you are home, after your schoolwork is done, you can write all the stories you want."

So what if some kids found out he wrote a story for the paper, he was going to the show and he was gonna eat some show goodies.

"Daddy?"

"Yeah?"

"Can I have some milk?"

"Yes, son. You can."

His father gets up from the table to get the milk. When he gets to the refrigerator, he turns around and says, "And boy, I'm proud of you."

Martin is smiling and chewing.

Dying of Laughter

your father was not about to be the father of a gay boy
& he said this with his empty gun holster & deputy
sheriff shirt unbuttoned & a can of beer in his left hand
& his father told him he needed to not be left handed
& not have such long eyelashes & this is when _____
you decided it was all peaches & cream & you decided
you neeeded no father & you had your bears
& you told me this while you were left nostril-ing cocaine
& talking shit about goldilocks & we had a conversation about
uncomfy beds & things people take & when you showed me your
h.i.v. meds you laughed & said *now this is a motherfucking*
cocktail, bartender! & i couldn't remember a time we
laughed so much or so hard or so fuck it & woe (in this way)
& you promised to visit & said we would paint the town
because that's what close cousins do & i kept my paintbrush
close & waited—until the paint dried. & when they told me
you committed suicide all i could think to say was: too hot.
too cold. just right.

DAVID BUBLITZ

Sleep Smoking

When I find him
he's a bony thumb pointing
one direction, he's relaxed
his spine against the couch
a forearm across the thigh
of each leg, his feet resting
on the soft spot of his heels.

This is the way it happens.
Not with a gunshot, no uniform,
he's waiting in the dark
his eyes close, a cigarette
burns down to the filter
and smoke still hangs
in the air above us

Five belly buttons

My father has five belly buttons.
They look like dull copper coins on
a clear belt, riding high up his girth.

He did not get them—the surplus ones—
on a treasure hunt. My father steamed
the globe with the Navy. He was on

tour in a theater where he was
an extra hiccuping through fire. He
was harried out of his line. He

remembers wet purple—a stippled
curtain, a blind billowing in
a volley of claps. He soaked up

the hard, staccato applause—clutched it—
in his gut. The world still howled out of him.
My padre was prayerful, not hungry;

he bowed, anyway, gnawing sand
and grappling dust. He kinked into a worm-
hole. Medics sealed him up.

A skipper would pin valor on him. O,
my father has five belly buttons.
In winter when he pulls himself out

of the whirlpool, shoulder by shriveled
leg, his Navy navels blacken—clouding
over like fish eyes at the loss of moisture.

Yaakov's Jackets

When Yaakov
walked out of Auschwitz,
he went to a great pile of clothes,
hoping to find a jacket
to cover his skeletal body.

 He tried on jacket after jacket.
Some were too short, some too long,
some sleeves came to his wrists,
some fell past his fingers,
so he took several.

Later, in his new country,
he bought clothes that fit properly,
but he kept the old jackets
in the back of his closet.

Many years later, he cut off the stars
and threw the old clothes away.
His son, my grandfather,
told me the story, embarrassed
that his father took anything at all.

I saw his photo, and imagined him
furtively slipping away
head down, eyes darting to right and left,
inching into a new and fearful day.

JERICHO BROWN

The Hammers

They sat on the dresser like anything
I put in my pocket before leaving
The house. I even saw a few tiny ones
Tilted against the window of my living
Room, little metal threats with splinters
For handles. They leaned like those
Teenage boys at the corner who might
Not be teenage boys because they ask
For dollars in the middle
Of the April day and because they knock
At ten a.m. Do I need help lifting some-
Thing heavy? Yard work? I wondered
If only I saw the hammers. The teenage
Boys visiting seemed not to care that
They lay on the floor lit by the TV.
I'd have covered them up with rugs,
With dry towels and linen, but their claw
And sledge and ball-peen heads shone
In the dark, which is, at least, a view
In the dark. And their handles meant
My hands, striking surfaces, getting
Shelves up, finally. One stayed
In my tub, slowing the drain. I found
Another propped near the bulb
In the refrigerator. Wasn't I hungry?
Why have them there if I could not
Use them, if I could not look at my own
Reflection in the mirror and take one
To the temple and knock myself out?

mama gwendolyn kiss(is) uncle ruckus on de forehead

Sometimes their passings are even more painful than ours.
It is just that so often they live till their hair is white.
—from Beverly Hills, Chicago

on a school day in bronzeville de blk boy want(s) to unpeel himself from him body dat ache(s) him flat & hard of seein. him want(s) to feel a girl inside(s). him tire(d) of emergency room spinnin. him mouf(s) him brudda(s) name(s) durin spinal tap(s). dey name(s) him prayer(s). jee-sus aint in him beleef cavity. no bible verse(is) either. him jus(t) got volume(s) upon volume(s) of brainstorm(d) suicide-him-not(s) memorize(d).

on a school night in a hospital room de blk boy want(s) him mother to tell him her cant no mo wif him back & forf tween earf & glory & finally lose de heavy those word(s) make her throat. him want(s) to tell her its alright not to luv him as hard as de other(s) cause eventually him wont come back home. & when dat become(s) dat day in bronzeville him want(s) him father to stan(d) above him & speak of all thing(s) soccer & poem(s). but de blk boy know(s) him father will weep. de blk boy know(s) him father a box of tissue.

tonight in a dream. inside de blk boy. inside a bed. inside a home. on a street. in bronzeville. de blk boy will fin(d) a super suit so him can lay still wif no head pain worry to keep him eye(s) hard of seein.

civility

the first time a friend from high school
called dad by his first name, neither
    of them were troubled. neither stifled

        extension of hand, smile of long knowing.
        when we were young he was mr. myles.
            fifteen years gone, those teenage clowns grown

men, middle aged testosterone. my friend
freshly knotted, my nuptials looming. dad
    wrinkling toward casket. it was an odd sting

maybe the okie twang which i never harbored
nor appreciated. six years since daily tongue
was this country music, reminder of one-way

ticket, $23, a folder of poems. but this remains
home for them. *good to see ya, j* as they grip.
would never call his pops john to his face

or his son's, my closest homey from 1981.
i ask about his father and call him sir when
we meet. is this culture, privilege or bad

manners. my big city black fertilizing
weed where wheat and alfalfa grew. are they
dubois and me booker t.? i stand in the front

yard with men who have informed my sight.
one black, one white. i swallow. dad goes on
his way.

REGGIE SCOTT YOUNG

Tribal Differences

(A Bluesville boy visits his Bronzeville cousins)

they said
"welcome to
alkebu-lan"

the sign said 79th and
cottage grove

they offered me their out
stretched palms, but
i couldn't shake
our grasps were not compatible

they introduced them-
selves: abu, abdul, akim,
kareem, haki, barraka, chaka, chabaka,
johari, hodari;
i said my name is Slim

it was suggested i read fanon
and mao, nkrumah and marx,
to allow the correct ideo-
logical perspective to set in,
i said "naw"
pulled out my copy of

Mules and Men

quickly,
i was bansished from alkebu-
lan as a lumpen-
head, told i had
a deficiency of blackness
so i left them to their meal of
millet
and lentils
and sunflower seeds
and honey
as i walked away munching ribs
washed down with wild irish wine
not feeling real black, but
feeling fine.

CALVIN FORBES

Players Online Dating Service

I was the brother leaning against the wall
Waiting for the slow jams to begin the night.
As the lights dimmed and the music spun
I would make my move and ask for a dance.

I could always run a few unfamiliar words
Together especially if the Thunderbird
Was flowing and my boys busy in the corner
Had my back in case some honey's man

Got jealous and wanted to start a fight.
Even my mother says I was born talking junk
And I got the pick up lines to prove her right.
Once at a party a bully threatened a friend

And I said touch him you got to deal with me.
And the dude quickly punched me in the mouth.
I may not be a hero but I am my father's son.
He never praised my book learning but he dug

All the fine ass women I escorted around town.
I might never be a player or playboy in this lifetime
But like the men I studied growing up I am myself.
And I got money in my pocket and more in the bank.

mr. oscar brown jr. goes to heaven

(for Oscar Brown Jr. and Oscar "Bobo" Brown III)

I.

a jump and the buick spits a phlegmy tune
a pink-skirted sista asks *who got shot?*
youngbuck by the car is quick and numb
sirens wail black mama on my block

evans ave. begs & pleads for quiet
midnight sky grips a heavy truth
black people gather like some kind of riot
should be, but it's just spilled blood of youth

crackhouse next door is twenty-four seven
door knocking, wolf calling all night long
i kneel, pour libation to oscar in heaven
and wonder how would he tinder this song

from my front stoop (not my window) miles i see
roadmaps carved on stone black faces
the hardlust jones of living almost free
our hearts, our souls and other empty spaces

the air is dense with murder, lies & hate
blacks, lacking love, kill what looks like them
it's now memorial day, the sun is late
still the buick coughs up more phlegm

II.

i remember first your great bear hug
yes! you all are doin it! you said
after our set at some chicago club
bo thumpin bass til his digits bled

nate on tenor sax and doctor watts
keith & me with syllable and sound
lovely mama jean lovelied the spot
the funky wordsmyths were in the house

hard hittin black poetry in song
our mantra, our call to page & stage
your smile told us yes we did belong
go tell stories of black love and rage

III.

minister farrakhan, at your service,
said he did not know you but he knew
the rappers brought to the precipice
through stubborn earth you broke new

then the minister put out a call
for rap emcees to bring your words to life
afro blue instead of *kill them all*
signifying monkey's afterlife

JACQUELINE JOHNSON

Looking for Venture Smith

Imagine the surrey empty and rusted.
Your favorite blue and white plates
in hundreds of pieces; one of
Chloe's shoes unbroken on what
used to be your living room floor.

What would you think of your old office,
once filled with shillings, pounds,
where Solomon kept his ledgers and
small bottles of rum and port, now
site of nuclear silos and electrical fences?

What survives a life is an eclectic mix:
Hanna's perfume bottles, smooth stones
of your private wharf; outline of a
blacksmith's shop and a half dozen old nails.
Those scientists who play in the dirt
say stones of pink crystal and tourmaline
are remnants of your Nkisi left by the door.

Venture, myth was you were six feet tall
and six feet wide lifting stone or
oxen like blades of sweet-grass.

You were larger than life
using your prowess with money
to free your wife and children,
purchase land, freedom of others.
Brother, you were so cruel, they say

some went back to their masters
rather than work for you. Were so frugal,
swam clammy cold, Connecticut River
rather than pay for a ferry.

Abraham the local historian asks, "What
is the position of your water wells?"
"Black people," he says,
"built small wells in these parts."

CAROLYN JOYNER

Sonnet for Gordon Parks

He says he's lived in so many different skins,
he can't be claimed by any one. Attempts
to keep him trapped inside himself all failed—
he danced the lyric of Olatunji's drum,

drank deep the cool of Blue Nile waters, then launched
those proud, undaunted journeys into "every
tool shop of his mind." The sixties' riots came.
When asked why this, he simply said, "I'll show you."

And so he did, with photographs and oils,
journalism and concertos. *The Learning Tree*
and *Shaft*. Poetry. This man—a well of all the arts,
of making beauty—his patron goddesses,

long-searching, devotion to his restlessness.
It all started with a camera someone had pawned.

JACQUELINE JOHNSON

Oriki for John Oliver Killens

(after Ted Joans)

You with the brass map of Africa
Owner of ancient wisdom of Oshogbo
Word warrior from Ouagadougou
Clever trickster from the dog gone Dogon
Nkisi of the village of Brooklyn
Oba of Medgar Evers
Keeper of Youngblood clan
Swiftest of the long distance runners
Owner of "Black Man's Burden"
Oh you of Kikongo mask.
Yoruba's benevolent one.
Oh you, a grandmother's freedom dance.
Carrying green bag of fresh thoughts.

Oh you who heard the thunder.
Oh you who saw the lightning.
This is the morning of your dreams.
This is the morning of our dreams.

Part 5

Here is some sun. Some.
Now off into the places rough to reach.
—Gwendolyn Brooks, "To the Diaspora"

Remembering Gwendolyn Brooks

When I was a boy on a Utah farm,
I listened to Chicago blues and dreamed
of the city's big shoulders and wide arms
and the roads leading up from the Delta
old bluesmen escaping poverty's chains.
And watched on TV the "troubles Down South,"
the clubs, vicious dogs, and water hoses
blasting people down the streets. Horrified,
I couldn't shake those images for my life.

In nineteen-fifty-five they killed a boy
who was just my age, and his mother
showed the photographs, the brutality
of what they had done. I swore I'd not forget.

Years later, I marched with many others,
one step at a time, against violence,
against the big machine that grinds people
into fodder, into shame, into hate.

Gwendolyn Brooks was in my mouth and ears,
and I can hear it still—my voice shaking,
rising, as I read to an audience
her poem about the bean eaters, through tears,

trembling, her "Last Quatrain of the Ballad
of Emmett Till."

Quatrain for Emmett Till/Trayvon Martin/ Michael Brown/LaQuan McDonald

(inspired by Gwendolyn Brooks' "The Last Quatrain of the Ballad of Emmett Till")

Inside me
A boy
whose feet
have never touched
the ground where
I lie down to rest
On a mat made by
My mother's hands
Weaving the tall
Green sharp grass—
Of her childhood
She would weep
remembering
How things had come
To pass—
The incidents that
moved her and her family
To Bronzeville.
Secrets passed to me
From her womb
Cut into my eyelids
Images of men
Still ripening
Black
Walking quietly
down hidden paths

Past midnight
With nothing
But the light
From faraway stars
and a dagger
of a moon
They glance
over their shoulders
More than once
Ever watchful
Peripherally
Wondering what follows
Wiping the sweat stained face
Expressionless
Not wanting to betray
The heart
racing—
Wishing to
Stop
the shadows
quickly closing
the distance
from behind.

My swollen belly
Rising and falling
Underneath a shade tree
Where above gazes
a Cycloped-eyed sun
My son gnawing my insides
feeding on memories and
history.

Many Sons, Many Mothers

(after "The Last Quatrain of the Ballad of Emmett Till" by Gwendolyn Brooks)

When a boy named Trayvon is shot, Emmett's
history is not a distant, removed story. A mother
fails to reverberate hollow in chests. A woman is
stoic, vigilant, when she should be proud, doting—a
parent with lullabies for children to come, pretty-faced
affirming nods to the future, dollops of hope, not thing
nor animal unless in front of a gun that dims, dulls the
dusk across a boy's cheeks, matching the tint
of his untainted eyes that whistle falsetto, the song of
bittersweet. Loss has yet to be mined, but it is pulled
from his clockwork heart sped by fear, snatched like taffy
in shoplifter's greedy pocket. When the mother is left, she
becomes banshee in a soundproof bandshell. A wailing sits
at the top of a range of fury. The sharp piercing within
sparks the dead boy's face. There is nothing but a
sea of heads shrouded in hoodies. There should be red
still pulsing in him, as he chews candy, sips tea with room
left for dinner. Instead, there is a mother alone, drinking
water. She cannot eat. She replenishes conviction, a coffee
that keeps her purpose clear. She knows exactly what she
must do. If she cannot open the casket, she testifies, kisses
the memories of many sons gone, not just the flicker of her
days extinguished, found waterlogged or unidentified, killed
despite his screams that ignored a spark who was called son.

A Depraved Indifference 2 Human Life

What did they look like?

I mean, how did they C them?

Could these killers

look their victims in their eyes

& even C eyes

or were they imagining monsters

the dark demons that dwelled

in their closets and corners as children

haunting their hallways

when their parents weren't home

Creepers

creeping out of the shadows

after the lights had gone off

& the moon reflected all types of

oddities

N2 the quiet room of a child's

imagination

Kill the creepers!

Kill the creepers!

Kill the creepers!

Make them go awaaaayyyy

How did they C them?

these victims

who dared 2 commit the crime of

breathing the wrong airspace

at some particular period of time

How dare U B Black?!

Nigga!

How did they perceive these human

beings

already socially reduced

2 something less than human

beings less than significant

a type of primitive people

whose actions rely more on instinct

than conscious thought

"Lash out

at these overgrown insects"

"Swat these flies!"

"Burn the ants!"

"Burn the ants!"

"Spray these ants!

with this police issued Raid"

"Raid their centers

their businesses

their organizations

their hideouts

their parties

their homes"

"Raid wherever U little Black insects

skitter or exist!"

"Crush these seemingly insignificant

ants!"

They look at us with blurred vision

"Crush the ants!"

"Crush the ants!"

"It doesn't matter

They're just ants"

How did they C them

The victims

B4 erasing away their future existence

How did they C them

B4 they found toys

& barbecue lighters

& cell phones

threatening

How?

How did these beasts in blue

sworn 2 protect the very lives

of those they have forced 2 live in fear

view the victims

3 seconds B4 fatally firing

firepower that snuffed the firelight

in fearful eyes

& then

in the next breath

rationalize their actions

as the stress they work under

Have U ever wondered?

Has it made U want 2 lash out?

Scream and question what this is all
about?

Lash out

& strike them down dead

with the fury

that the victim's families must've felt

when they found out that their child

was dead

that their spouse

is dead

that their parent

is dead

Lash out

& they'll call it murder

No justice would find our actions

justified

but when they lash out at us

they creatively call it

a depraved indifference 2 human life

When they menacingly massacre our

men, women and children

they call it

a depraved indifference 2 human life

But we'll be charged with murder

Death sentences given

whether U've done it or not

Life in prison

versus losses of pension

A depraved indifference 2 human life

Murder masked as something less

serious

but it's not

Call these cops

Killers

These killers

employed as cops

with a legalized license

found joy and just cause

in the killing of Jews, Blacks, and gays

blessed

2 manifest the melanin within them

Call these cops

these predatory expungers of brown

people

these federally funded gangs

with the governmental go ahead

4 head bashing

& trashing our positive images

killers

Killers

Not unlike the great Constantine

Who murdered millions of Muslims

in the name of Christianity

who crucified countless coloreds

4 refusing 2 convert

Killers

Not unlike Adolph Hitler

who in the name of God and country

found joy and just cause

in the killing of Jews, Blacks, and gays

Killers

Not unlike Nathan Bedford Forrest

Confederate major general

who road N2 Fort Pillow

& massacred 300 Black men, women, and

children

yelling, "Kill the god-damned niggers!

Kill all the niggers!"

Killers

These cops R killers

consisting of great white sharks

& sell outs who haven't figured out

U can't serve Satan

& the Savior

at the same time

Sooner or later

they'll all have 2 choose

or lose their soul

shooting down another sister

armed with a cellular phone

Our moans go unheard

because all we have R words

condemning these unconscionable killers

These killers

with a depraved indifference 2 human
life

A depraved indifference 2 human life

Not unlike Jeffery Dahmer

the cannibal with a taste 4 coloreds

Like Ted Bundy

whose outer beauty

was but a distortion of his inner demons

that ravaged 100+ women across the

united states.

John Wayne Gacy

the carnivorous clown

David Berkowitz

The savage Son of Sam

Richard Ramirez

The nefarious night stalker

How unlike those serial killers

R these officers

with serial numbers

attached 2 badges

which R flashed

from the chest of bulletproof vest

just B4 we R harassed or blasted

A depraved indifference 2 human life

What was it

that first made someone recognize it?

What was the first sign

that gave it away?

How unlike Joseph Stalin

Jim Jones

Alexander the Greek

Cecil Rhodes

The South African police

R

the Chicago Police Department

the LAPD

the NYPD

the DC police

the U.S. State Troopers

the FBI

the CIA

the UN Occupational Forces

How unlike human violators R they?

& they will call us

criminals?

I cop no pleas

4 guilty criminals truthfully accused

but I ask please

of the cops

not 2 accuse me

when they R the guilty

Where can we find justice?

When will we C true justice?

Maybe it should be left 2 just us

Maybe it should be left 2 just us

Maybe, just maybe

it should be left 2 just us

Rulers write history and the law

the conquered just accept it

Inspired by Tanya H., A. Diallo, Donald M. (of E.W.F.),
& any other who has ever fallen in the face of police brutality.

ROGER BONAIR-AGARD

The Short Answer

wait. how many times did they kill him? i mean . . . shoot him? (Uma, aged 9)

You were right the first time
You are asking the right questions
You want to know what the value of the human body is
You want to know what the value of the Black body is
You want to know what the power of the Black body is
You want to know why it must be killed exorbitantly
You want to know how brown your skin is
                how brown your brothers' skins are
                the weight of their forward motion
                how many bullets it will take
You want to know the nature of your already committed crime
                        of your body's forward motion
You want to know if you'll someday birth something
so formidably killable   You want
to know if your Tito Roger is in danger
                or Tito Elgin or Tita Dayo
You want to know the value of any love you'll ever have for Black
bodies   You've already said you will
not birth anyone   Perhaps
you are wise beyond your years   Perhaps
you already know what you will unlearn by building
and birthing and loving someone to watch her become
made entirely of lead
watch your own house become
a wailing wall

How many times do you kill a God?
How many times do you kill a ghost?
How much iron do you need to kill Ogun?
             to resurrect him?
How much lead do you need against Shango?
             against his extravagant sex?
How high to hang Oya? Is she ever extinguished?
How high to build a wall between America and Mexico?
                   between America and Englewood?
                   between America and the Lakotas?
                   between America and any History that shakes
a fist   at it

You want to know the collective weight of the bodies
             of the children your mother works with
             and loves   You want
to know how many hollow pointed bullets
on average
are required
to stop those young and supple
young and angry
young and distressed
young and Black
young and Brown
young and Black
young and Brown
young and poor
young and young bodies

You want to know how many have been stopped since we've been here
You want to know what arithmetic lends you and Akilah and Zora
and Simone and Tita Rashida one knowledge
and the police a completely different one
             You want to know how many times the boy was killed

which is to say you want to know where
along the firing timeline the death occurred
where along the trigger squeeze timeline the deaths
metastasized   You want to know what kind of Gods
require consistently ten bullets, six bullets, forty-one
bullets, fifty bullets   to put them down
You want to know what demons require such firewalls
against reincarnation or what demons require
such an ecstasy of noise to pray out of suburban
nightmares   You want to know what algebra
solves loose cigarette sales for death by choking
You're a nine year old intimately acquainted with death
enough to understand the question is no longer
whether or not the boy's body or the girl's body
was expendable but how expendable You're nine
so you've begun to recognize intimacies of scale—
how much do you love   how much do you love
how much do you see how much do you mistake
how much do you dismorph the bodies of Black
until we're all the writhing, demonic, super powerful
tormentors of good white people who require
extraordinary measures for extinction You want
a statement made on this 21st Century
Trail of Tears Uma, You want to know
which treaty we signed and lost You want
to know a History your schools will not teach
You want to know Reconstruction songs and lynch
postcards and the sound of disallowed drums
and the song of running North and the rhythm
of factories that looked like Oz but tasted like graveyards
You want to know what costume your father can wear
to camouflage his own murder   You know our cathedrals
offer us the promise of a cannibal's grace   and maybe
this is why you cry when your brother is on his way

Maybe this is why you protest your mother's
question of more babies. You have seen the cellar where
they make the bullets You have seen
the cellar where they make the bullets
You have seen the cellar
where they make the bullets You
have seen how many bullets
they might use You do not know
how many it will take.

a neighborhood boy

i live quite near to a boy
who kills people

he is fifteen years old
or maybe closer to fourteen

young enough for me
to remember when he
in the fourth grade was
the most wonderful poet

you could see his brilliance
shining with the dark energy
of a universe expanding

he neatly filled both sides
of the lined newsprint sheet
as he took the color black and
dressed it in all the possibilities
his nine-year-old mind could imagine

it was magic and sleek
it was thunder and song
alive and powerful
and yes it was
beautiful

he wrote his poem
and then asked
to read his words out loud

voice strong and clear
purposeful and steady
each line emerged rich
with rhythm, rhyme
color and sense

he shone brightly then
brighter than so many
of his classmates

some of whom
he may now shoot at
some of whom
may now shoot at him

youth together taking
the majesty of the night
and turning it into
sirens of misery and blood

i live quite near to a boy
who was born a poet
who turned black
to the sound
of semi-automatic rounds
clattering across the mall
a pop, a whistle
a death wheeze
a mother's sobs
a tear dropped into oil

who was it then
who taught him black
as nothing but
caged and uncaged
field holler whip groan
bar clang lock nod
shake em up
shake em down
crack that back
bend and spread

who took his smooth obsidian
and ground it into gunpowder

ANASTACIA RENEE TOLBERT

Rite of Passage

you bundle the cub
& send him off to the woods
to be eaten
by the big bad wolves
(on purpose)
you want him to learn early
how to keep it moving
despite a rip in his genes
or five-hearted worms crawling from his eyes
show him how to give them raw meat
from the left hand
& pet them with the right
learn the scales of self p(reservation)
how it all comes down to
which parts of the body to preserve
& which parts to eat yourself
you bundle the cub
& send him out into the woods
with big bad wolves
(on purpose)
watch the white ones gnarl
his skinny backbone
from bottom to top
when he bleeds
bark at him to drop/stop/   cop
& give you twenty
tell him there will be no mercy

for his black ass
just a few olive branches
& crisped up fallen leaves

KEVIN COVAL

we real

January 2, 2013

The Glory Boys
on house arrest
at Grandma's

we real. we
steel. we
still here. we
no fear. we
know school lame. we
dope game. we
know gangs. we
Jeff Forte kids. we
jail bids. we
broke, bitch. we
capitalists. we
jupiter gassed. we
murdered fast. we
unseen we
wanting we
something we
more than one thing. we
eastside. we
southside. we
westside. we
on the block, we
high noon. you ravinia picnic and air condition. we

fire hydrant & fire, cracker. we

hot hell in June. you nap noon. you spoon. we

rap. we

die, soon

NILE LANSANA

Roots

At a soccer tournament in Oak Park
Brooks scored 7 goals in an 8-1 win

As we rushed to the restroom
A group of young white boys
Were scattering and scampering around a public park
All armed with fake guns
Hiding in wooden bunkers and behind inflatable barricades
Dodging death with a dash to the nearest tree
All I could think about was how their ancestors hung mine from branches
They break off to block BB gun pellets from hitting their skin

Stood in the eye of this storm
Of little children who haven't had
BANG BANG lullabies
Haven't stepped over shotguns to get home safe
watching older brother tote a .45 to get $45

Couldn't ignore the phenomenon on display
At this birthday party
Looking cousins in their pupils
While pointing pistols, then rewarded with cake
Black blood is ingrained in the soil of these United States
In return, our men are targeted, our babies killed, our women raped

One seed in an Oak Park playground
Can grow to a Zimmerman in Sanford, Florida
A Wilson in Ferguson, Missouri
A Van Dyke in Chicago, Illinois

A Loehmann in Cleveland, Ohio
Where you can carry a firearm in plain sight
From a sidewalk to a supermarket
So when Loehmann and his partner pulled up on a playground strapped
They were just following orders

Didn't want my little brother to believe
Those boys have the same reality
Not much older or taller
All about the same speed
But one would get a warning
While another would get a coffin
Why is there peace at a pistol party
Where little white boys are playing dead
But no pulse with a black child on a swing minding his own business
And the police popped bullets into his chest in two seconds
Before they even checked to see if his gun was fake

When did it become ok for the police to persecute and shoot
Before they protect and serve?
One rotten officer should not be overlooked
Another breathless black baby
Is worth more than a two minute segment on WGN
And Al Sharpton at their funeral

I yelled at Brooks a few weeks ago
He waved at a police officer from inside the minivan window
Couldn't erase the image of
Those suburban seeds
Growing with guns in hand
Breaking off tree stumps like the officer would break Mom's neck
Smiling every time he earns a kill
Don't want Brooks to be his next victim
He doesn't know that his smile might not keep him safe in these streets

Kindness and cooperation might not keep him from getting killed
My love and correct care might not have been enough for him to grow

I guess Brooks' selfishness on the field is ingrained in his roots
Knowing that he'd only have so many opportunities to thrive
Before his growth would be stunted
How could he know death before he gets to know about life?
I hope it's not too late to tell him

MARY CATHERINE LOVING

news item: Police seek African-American Man

last seen wearing cornrows
and a brown bomber jacket:

that stench is the smell of black men
burning brown bomber jackets
in alleys and on dark roads
they hide from night's never blinking eyes
avoid unlucky meetings
when the cavalry comes

seeking black men. Found guilty
of wearing brown bomber jackets—
last seen running
from justice
wearing cornrows:
black man running
kill him. kill him. kill . . . them.

that rustle is the sound of black men
undoing cornrows, their rapid-fire fingers
scratch selves free of identity
they hide—whether in dormitory halls
or side-street bars
black men
last seen. Running.

History of Static

Selective deafness one learns from dad like taking out
        the trash.
For practice, dial up staticky talk radio and tune out
        the human voice,
savoring only wavelength buzz—a talent the kiddies
        soon perfect,
so chit-chatting, yours will be the tuned-out voice.
        Hear me?

My father wielded newspaper box scores as Achilles
        did his shield,
fending off the day's pinko-commie yammering. So I'd
        fret the Reds
dropping doubleheaders while my war's Vietnamese girl
        ran newspaper-napalmed
to our house on Lincoln, who emancipated those still not
        free.

"Everybody's talking but no one hears a word," sang Lennon
        before his bullet.
Still not. A staticky rapping lit Detroit's flames, language
        of the Strike-Anywhere riot,
unboxed speech of the quick-flicked match and those
        billyclubbed heads
rapped for H. Rap. Those marches across bridges burned,
        and sermons heard

but not, "peace talks" that brought neither. Still.
       Those villages
bombed by jet and churches KKK-kaboomed—all that
       so after football practice
we black-and-white showered together but didn't speak
       on street.
A folded newspaper's all *blah blah blah* to the puppy,
       and cops will go

ballistic at "yo' mama" as others will at The Man.
       Just what
hath daddy static wrought? Selective deafness necessitates
       practice,
as does talking trash. Static palaver's perilous to (un-)
       learn,
no matter the Declaration's lyrics and our inner ears'
       blended shades.

MARY CATHERINE LOVING

East Texas Blues

Here, the voices of ghosts meander down alleys
filter through screen doors with tepid breezes
settle in parlors, on front lawns
travel on the thin veil of air
that sighs from paper fans
to taunt you,
wrack your body with brittle memory—

I have not heard those voices;
I am not witness to their work.

Absent my experience, these voices exist
only along the edge of knowing
washed away in the cool water of forbidden fountains
vaguely recalled in the outline of a child's foot
on a simple, bag brown—
framed in understandings borne of habit and reason.

When to reclaim sanity from East Texas cotton fields
is to heed the voices, the cries that sing
beneath red dirt, for renewal may yet be found in these thickets,
in these fields lain fallow in shame.

Hear now those voices!
O, hated horseman of the night!
O, bloody cry echoing from each shadow!

Remind stem and bone of its own bloodthirsty deeds
revealed in the innocence of play: children track red dirt

into crumbling homes, invite the ghosts in with them,
give weight to the voices that swallow me, tie my tongue, swell my senses
until I am confused by understanding.

Not merely forefathers who plead, cushioning me in the false security
of folktale and myth, lies born of understanding —
Not merely forefathers who screech their warning
too late, too late.

Mock me in prayer, East Texas. Cackle your danger to my marrow,
call from cotton fields tinged with hope and blood
call in metaphor, mistaken for song.

MARY CATHERINE LOVING

Robert's Hill: San Augustine, Texas

Sundown sinks into country roads,
heightens the scratch of men
scurrying to safety beneath sway-backed porches.

Mothers whisper caution, dip rags in turpentine,
soothe sore gums of teething babies,
fan mosquitoes—

keep alert for crosses,
suddenly aflame in the quiet night.

we real

(after . . .   )

they come through   cool
hood-
     id eyes   slow
no boy moves quick
here in the Cook County Juvenile Temporary
Detention
Center only the eyes
          panic

I was a boy
   like this once there
but for the grace
                  and books and another
country. history.

I'm an old man
now—behind the daps my own slow
crawl   these boys
doing
     what they can   with what it do
asking the world
                  of Chicago—we Real

Black   by which I mean
reading poems   looking
for prayers to offer the Judge

they read   hang themselves
on line
        breaks—stay Real
hard
wanna know   not for nothin
if we   gon be here
        nex week   they leave. We
nod   dap up—only
the eyes   panic.

WWW2015

Each day I awake too late to know peace
Fresh ichor dances upon my nostrils,
Bombs over Baghdad still on repeat
Decade and a half, who thought probable?

Yes love in the heart of broad shoulders
No love in hearts of those under attack
Bullets a coming from every way
And from every way bullets sent back

My hands are up officer, please don't shoot!
What have I done? Why treat me this way?
Bang, Bang to the head, lil piggy lies dead
From a rooftop quite far across the way

The World Wide Web gave birth to World Wide War
World Wide Wickedness never seen before

The Tragedies

It's best to admire the police from afar,
all that badge glint and the clip-on tie
safe for wrestling guys bad or good
to the unceremonious pavement.
O, sartorial fakery, your dapper clip-on
winged me free of knotted hours' indenture
mirroring my father's sandcastle hands.
In song Jimi Hendrix laments what befalls
all castles made of sand e-ven-tu-al-ly,
waves lapping syllables as they do ankles
in my desktop vacation photo. I'm flaunting
the inflatable canoe my breath made whole
on Huntington Beach before its Titanic
maiden *voyage*, which I first misspelled *voice*
while channeling Jimi's, and those clouds
scudding as Wordsworth's always do,
tranquil above the cop's blueberry-cherry-top's
Tintern Abbey. Allen Ginsberg dropped acid
at the Abbey, so good thing he's not here
to get busted naming what can't christen itself,
say, the Carolina chickadee or my backyard's
budding bleeding heart that I've dubbed Ruby,
or the masterful *diacope* of this cop's baritone,
"Your hands, your hands, let's see your hands,"
the phrase echoing Richard III's horse-wish
before a sword punctuated the kingly comma
of his scoliotic spine. Power's not a thing to do
without, being *without* both cause and measure
tin-crowned upon thy head. Power skewers

even our lionhearted, interring what's left
beneath a parking lot not unlike the one
I'm eyeing now, where black hands rise
from the pavement's opaque rhetoric.

JOHN C. MANNONE

Skin

> skin is the largest organ of the body,
> with a total area of about 20 square feet
> —WebMD.com

Each morning, I slip into my skin
careful not to fold its delicate parts
over my bony brain, yet I want the
thick skin to grow over vulnerable
organs susceptible to all the sharp
words. If you were to walk a mile
in my skin, you'd know why its soul
scrapes the world's anger that burns
my feet.

JODI JOANCLAIR

Keloid Cells

Cells building on cells,
keloids represent rejection—
fragility deferred. I fold over
myself, engulf me in armor.
Fact becomes fiction to survive
the aftershock of slavery. Brittle
as bones devoured, I fight battles
that began at sea when countless
marrow were swallowed whole
and nameless sorrow survived to
dance for freedom. Watch me
Whip. Watch me Nae Nae. Watch
me bleed, suffocate, and get sprayed.
Hose me down with steel
bullets. Riot as I sit stoic.
Epidermis marked as target
practice. One keloid is never
enough to hide four hundred
years of scars passed down
from prison cells to cells,
from cells to prison cells.

TONY MEDINA

Landscape with Chalk-marked silhouette

(for Gwendolyn Brooks)

They real dope. They
Like to smoke. They

Crack some 40s. They
Hit the shorties. They

Hang on the Ave. They
Likes to laugh. They

Shoot C-Lo in the hall. They
Drive-by the mall. They

Play some B-ball. They
Love to shoot hoops. They

Sit on front stoops. They
Watch the girlies go by. They

Bullshit and tell lies. They
Like to stay high. They

Don't ever wanna die. They
Make his mama cry. They

Sit on front stoops. They
Waste a lot of time. They

Watch planes go by.
Planes go by.

ESTEBAN COLON

Everyday Horrors

Fuck your fiction.
        I don't need the ever-present groan of zombies
the air here's still
                    thick with rocking mothers
chalk outlines, the knowledge that things don't change.

We
        don't need to imagine aliens invading,
when
         police officers have torn possessions out of our hands without recourse
when
        drug wars are waged in communities brown and black enough
to assure politicians won't lose any family

Let the werewolves sleep during the full moon
        because claws and fangs would be a blessing
to detainees tortured daily.

I
have stared into the face of sleeping old gods,
beings
        of tendrils and horns with insanity skin
who
shiver at night
whispering of a nightmare that tears itself apart
based only
        on skin pigment.

When Racism Dies

i will nae-nae upon hearing the news
whip it at the funeral
dab at the burial
do the D-Lo shuffle at the repast

the next day

i will footwork
at work
then moonwalk out the office

Tuesday will be a chill day because it always is

on Wednesday night bible study
i'll pour Henny for all who died in flames
either by burning or bullet
then turn up with what's left in the bottle
because black church ain't black church
without being drunk in the spirit

others days i'll still be sad
for the death of racism
doesn't mean the end of grief
but the beginning of it
for all those built-in tears will
pour out of me like a confession

and I will wail.

MARY CATHERINE LOVING

Overheard at tea, near Kensington and DeVeers, London

I have loved the sons of men who owned my mothers.
I have traced their blue-veined fever, watched as it consumed

both sibling and offspring. Then coveted little more
than the stumbling cry: its throttle—

Lust. Danger. Dark seas:
cross your heart, swear to forget.

I have drunk the names of men who may be my brothers,
found comfort in the arms of rapists.

What can it matter? My thighs, Africa
open before them—picked white in the aftermath.

a feast of whispers

elizabeth keckley was nobody's back woods *whisper* She knew that even the clothes-pins sparrow feathers blue glass all *whispered* in the night like the spider unlacing a full moon web She gathered the very blood line of cotton damask silk linen She worked inside of the stillness of the night Knowing that this stillness was deeper than death waiting She becoming more of the notion of free.

each stitch prick between torch flight and night's light knew how to measure a sky of neck hips wrists thighs each stitch taught her how to tell rock from bone each stitch *whispering* bone hangs close to the needle rock pushes slices color pattern like the soles of her feet out racing the notion of freedom.

the unrecognizable sound of her own voice crying for the loss of her son's skin weaves into the dancing sleeve of a white woman on the brink of *becoming* more of the notion of free like birds who fight the shadows of their own wings.

soft dawn *whispers* crown a morning that pushes back the blush of shimmering thread against the paleness of a dancing southern mistress stupefied elegance stretched across drowned indigo-stamped chemise soaked in a music that erases the gentility of surrender.

mary todd lincoln prayed for rain clouds against a bloodstained horizon that would not bend Her only salvation in the hands of her *modiste lizzie* slave bonded as confidante Her words carrying empty potions unrecognizable as the taste of Her own bondage.

the master's tools will not dismantle the master's house . . . lizzie offered a prayer for the prayers unanswered for the torched scorched torn damned soul of her captor Her womb soothed a thousand lashes that wounded the sky the grass the river the fire of her breath.

as the story unfolds beneath her cloth She holds the few strands of what remains of another story hushed folded unwritten like the path from arrival to departure from hem to bodice She sews glass buttons in between the hours that grow inside the desert of her unrecognizable heart.

two women hold back sinister nights drink from the same cup that spills disintegrating the only blank canvas between them They reach for the same light one hand burned the other holds heat so close it frays the lace the landscape of her whiteness so close it becomes an airborne divination.

face to face silhouette to silhouette They feel each other's breath but too many years have stripped them bare of any notion of the freedom they stole from each other They are the reflection of the same offering to a hungry god.

conjuring new skirts for new dancers the prick of the thumb unleashes more than blood stained seams unleashes more than the shrouded dance floors of slaves in unmarked cemeteries more than the unbearable notion of unrecognizable freedom crawling through the very eye of Her needle.

mary todd lincoln wears weary well like an undressed sunrise bulging with veins of poverty throbbing beckoning with the unraveling voice of fallen petals *it becomes her well* She steps out of her skin for an unmeasurable fitting of her soul.

one last lift of muted organza that hugs the waist perfect She becomes her own *modiste* dressing for the dance of freedom dressing for all the denied dances of her mother dressing for all the denied slaves whispering from her unrecognizable voice.

from a rooftop She imagined she saw him but then she never could decipher between bone and stone the smell of *her* abe lincoln still lingering in the bloody fabric pressed hard against her chest flooding parched untamed rivers weighing more than her drooping breasts.

each stitch taught her how *to tell* taught her how to measure the heaviness of her own war each stitch created a forbidden game a forbidden weapon She learned to dress and undress the shadows of her own ladies-in-waiting the shadows of quivering stardust hanging from shackled branches.

(Editor's Note: Elizabeth Hobbs Keckley, AKA "Lizzie," a slave who bought her own freedom, was confidante and personal dressmaker to Mary Todd Lincoln, First Lady. She became a successful businesswoman, civil rights activist, and author. George Kirkland, Keckley's son and only child, died fighting for the Union Army in the Civil War.

In Praise of Wisdom

(after Gwendolyn Brooks)

I.
Birds nest and see—
the heartbreaking fruit aloft
in the trees, their scarred beauty
stealing the moment's notice,
raw silk of the sapling torsos
yielding to their darkly waxed heads,
the real thing in their fulminant roots,
the sure surviving seed,
fracturing sidewalk symmetries . . .

Diviners, their pelts most intimate
with air . . . tree-tall tellers
heralding a truer kingdom,
birds nest and know, theirs
a fine frequency to our
grosser, hurting love,
theirs the wisdom—
no less joy?—to be.

II.
Behold the denizens of anguish—
milkfed, pampered, preening—
  who think they own a world,
    who crave all, the rotten
      parts as much, to covet
        or discard as they please . . .

Or lobbyists of hate—
its ground fertile for terror—
          who are provoked by pin-drop and baby's wail,
                    envious of the groaning,
                              stretching satisfaction
                                        of other tribes,
                    and of nature and minds grown
                              thick-to-bursting,
                                        yet inscrutable . . .

          who are ensnared
                    by what's beyond their reach
                              and so disguise a stingy creed
                                        to disseminate their schemes.

Deconstruction and destruction
their mode—
          breathing confidence into their designs—
                    who fear the rustlings
                              in the undergrowth
                                        and name them enemy—or useless,
                                                  aggrieved by life that flourishes
                                                            where it wants.

But there's a fine blackness
in the screaming weed—
feathery and petal-fierce,
of staunch, avid gaze,
steeled, lucid mettle—yes!
in this bitten and bewarred world,
a neat brilliancy . . .

with untamped hunger for the harvest,
unafraid of no,
astute, aboriginal . . .
  who penetrates—still—the chaos and clamor,
   who crafts our mutual estate.

Editor's Note: The poem borrows or riffs on several phrases found in "Notes from the Childhood and the Girlhood" and "The Womanhood" in Miss Brooks' Annie Allen.

MALAIKA FAVORITE

Halloween

As the children get ready for Halloween
I get unready, deciding where to hide
And pretend I'm not home.

I don't want to see their little marked up faces
Grinning up at me, begging, hoping
I will bless them with diabetes.

In their sugared over grin
I can see their future—fat mommies and daddies
Passing out candy to their fat twins.

This is a holiday for merchants.
No one sees them standing behind the kids
Their sacks open begging:

Buy more than enough
Bless the economy
Bless the children who are blessing me

Who Needs the Stars If the Full Moon Loves You?

Sister was detangling her hair when she heard Faith scream. She put the bottle of rosemary and lemon oil down on the edge of the sink. Scented water dripped down her neck, wetting the back of her shirt and her shoulders. Sister stared in the mirror, her eyes weary half-moons, as if she'd woken from troubled dreams. She stepped over the fluffy blue towel and walked out of the bathroom, a black, wide-tooth comb stuck in her hair, an upturned fist.

Faith lay on the floor on her belly. Her wiry, grasshopper legs were stretched out so far Sister had to hopscotch so she would not trip over them. "What you done did now?" she asked, but Faith didn't answer. Instead, she scrolled down the bright screen, her finger a dark blur casting shadows in the living room.

"I don't want to see any more of your crazy videos," Sister said. "All that foolishness makes my head hurt." She paused and waited but Faith kept scrolling. "I don't see how you can stay on there so long."

Faith only nodded. Sister frowned. It was the silence that worried her. It wasn't like Faith not to laugh or speak. Faith and Sister were *two scars on a dead woman's belly.*[1] Of the two, Faith was the more sociable of their mother's daughters. Faith always had something to say. Now she lay there like a bump on a log. Sister decided that maybe she should investigate, so she dug the big black comb deeper into her halo of hair and peered over Faith's shoulder.

"Who is she?"

"Her name was Sandra."

* * *

Faith put the black Sharpie down and held up two signs. "Justice for _____ (fill in the blank)" covered one sign, with "AM I NEXT?" scrawled in Faith's wobbly handwriting beneath it. The other sign was more plaintive. "END RACIST POLICE BRUTALITY NOW" it said simply.

"Which one?" Faith asked, flashing each sign beneath her chin. Her eyes were night-black lace, dark, defiant. "Which?"

Sister studied the signs, the words in her mind stuck in her throat. She raised her hand to point, but could not move her limbs fast enough. The name, Sandra, spun inside her, and she couldn't keep the young woman's eyes out from her own lids. Sister could see her, the parked car, the concrete sidewalk, and hear her screams muffled in the darkness past seeing. Then the names came. The others her mind had kept in a locked box until this moment. Latasha Harlins, shot in a Korean corner store in LA. Keara Crowder shot by her husband in Memphis. Bettie Jones gunned down in Chicago. Asleep in her bed. Aiyana Stanley-Jones was only seven. Yvette Smith. Miriam Carey. Mya Hall. Tanisha Anderson. Malissa Williams. Rekia Boyd. Tarika Wilson. Eleanor Bumpurs. Kathryn Johnston was shot when policed burst into her home, and Pearlie Golden was shot multiple times in her front yard. Unlike the other young women, Pearlie had been ninety-three and Kathryn, ninety-two, but the litany didn't stop there. Sharmel Edwards. Tyisha Miller. Shereese Francis . . . No woman or girl was safe. The names kept coming.

I do not even know all their names / my sisters deaths are not even noteworthy . . . [2]

"Sister? Are you listening to me? Don't you ever get tired? Spending your life in the front yard?"[3] Sister could feel Faith's sharp words cutting into her, but she could not hear. Her ears were filled with names. "You need to come too this time," Faith said. "You can't ride the movement out in here forever." Disgust, a shadow, covered Faith's face.

Sister tried to look away, but now her hands and her feet were frozen. How to tell her, *I dream of your freedom* . . . [4] that I wished you'd never learn that *black is not beloved*,[5] that the words are pressed up in my throat like a fist, that the tears boil in the pit of my belly, like some kind of strange bitter brew? How to tell her that when I try to drink or eat, all my stomach and tongue desires is poison, hunger, a food for assassins, dirges for deacons of defense?

Her nails raked the dry, patchy skin along her arm. Sister looked down. Inside she was changing.

The whole world was watching, but what did it see?

Sister turned her eyes away from Faith, her fingers covering the black bristles erupting all along her arms, her shoulders, and her spine like ebony spikes.

"Well I'm going to leave without you, if you're just going to stand there looking crazy." Faith opened the door and stared up at the sky. "It's dark out here. I can't see a single star." She said, "Oh, wait. There's the moon." She waited, then sucked her teeth. "At some point, Sis, you gonna have to *do* something. We can't keep going on like this."

"But . . . I . . . " Sister began, but the names kept coming. They hung in her throat, dangled in her belly like a long endless rope. *At first they used a noose, now all they do is shoot . . .* [6] She gasped, unable to breathe. All the water seemed to evaporate from the air. She stumbled and reached for Faith, at least she thought she did. She reached, but suddenly a hundred Faiths swirled in the air around her. They all frowned and recoiled from her touch.

"Ff-ai—" she gasped, her wet hair resting limply on her shoulders. "Ff—ai . . . " But Faith had gone.

* * *

When Faith returned from the protest, weary but hopeful, at least some of her anger spent, she tossed her bent sign onto the dinner table and called for Sister.

"Where you at, girl? You missed it," she said, kicking off her shoes at the door. She placed her boots neatly next to Sister's sandals and pulled her earrings off. A brass hoop got caught in her curls. "So many people showed up. Beautiful people, we spilled all into the streets. You would have loved them. One group had these giant puppets—

You hear me?"

But Sister didn't answer. The TV was still on and so were all the lights. Faith ducked into the bathroom and stared at the hair products scattered across the counter. Sister's bottle of homemade detangler still sat on the sink, untouched. Faith picked up the damp blue towel and hung it up.

"Sis, what's up? You sleep?"

She pushed open the bedroom, their mother's old room, but Sister wasn't there. Her black comb lay in the middle of the floor.

Faith shuddered. She heard someone calling her. She turned, but no one was there, nothing but the ghostly blue TV light from the hall and the full moon in the window. Faith saw Sister's clothes tossed in a corner of the room.

A sense of dread filled the air. Then she heard it again, faint and quiet, soft as a breath.

"Ffaa-ith."

The sound vibrated against her skin, tickling the fine hairs along the nape of her neck, inside her ear. She knew that voice. Her old woman's name, the one mother had gifted her, had two whole syllables—but only in one person's mouth.

She turned and then she saw it.

Just below the bed, in a corner of moonlight, the crazy quilt pattern just barely touching the floor. Faith kneeled, her eyes wide, searching.

It skittered once, then rolled over.

She raised her finger slowly in the air, then gently brushed its little silver back. It flinched and the ball tightened. She touched it again.

It shivered, laughing or afraid, Faith could not tell which. All she knew is that her sister had once reached for her, and she had turned away. Now her sister held herself.

Faith picked up the tiny ball, careful not to crush its curved back or its tiny antennae. She held it in the palm of her hand, brushing her fingertip across its silver-coppery shields, until it slowly uncurled itself, one plate at a time, its tiny legs tickling her palm. Faith held it, the disappointment she felt earlier now a dull ache in her heart. It crawled across her palm, its little pill-shaped body resting on her lifeline. Faith stroked its shiny back, knowing she would

always remember her face
always say her name
"Sister."

1 After Lucille Clifton's *Two-Headed Woman* (University of Massachusetts, Amherst, 1980)

2 Audre Lorde wrote "Need: A Chorale for Black Women Voices" in 1979 after twelve black women were murdered in Boston over a span of a few weeks.

3 From Gwendolyn Brooks' poem "A Song in the Front Yard" (*Selected Poems*, Harper and Row, New York, 1963). Revisit the little girl "Pepita" in Miss Brooks' title poem, *In the Mecca*, conceived in 1954 as a young adult novel, then published as verse in 1968.

4 Lorde wrote "Need: A Chorale for Black Women Voices" for Patricia Cowan and Bobbie Jean Graham and "the hundreds of other mangled Black Women whose nightmares inform these words" (*Undersong: Chosen Poems, Old and New*, Norton, New York, 1992)

5 Lamentation from Gwendolyn Brooks' title poem, "In the Mecca" (*In the Mecca*, Harper, New York, 1968)

6 Sandra Bland (@a_sandybeach) of Chicago tweeted this at 9:43 a.m. on April 8, 2015 with the hashtags #BlackLivesMatter and #SandySpeaks, three months before she was found hung in a jail cell in Waller, Texas on July 13, 2015.

JAKI SHELTON GREEN

Prayer for Jordan

I have come to this new place whose trees have no medicine
barren ground that has never tasted a thimble of blood
where birds fly backwards and sky is afraid of falling
it is here that I meet the man-child who is remembering his true name who
searches for the river where his story was born

the man-child climbs hills that scratch him without mercy
he becomes the balm for the angry ground that refuses to see him
he is without country so he becomes the map of all his ages
he is without eyes so he becomes the compass of his heart

I hear him offering sacrifices to the ocean the wind
to the fires of his uncertainty
not now spirit wails
not now

spirit carves patience grace tenderness inside his palms
between his ribs
the lost ones wait for him
the ones he's been waiting for
pale ghosts running from their own shadows
he is the one they've been waiting for

suicide is never enough for you man-child
it will not feed the dry season in your throat
it will not water the parched soles of the ones who came before you
it is not even the theater you've dressed for

the trees cry out for your medicine
this earth does not need your breath
the earth needs your hands planting and watering new seeds

this place needs the medicine inside your hands

your clan waits for the feast you have prepared for this season of harvest
choose red vibrant pulsating knives that go gently into your bread of life

the trees have no song
muted by ghosts who trod dragging skeletons
dragging undergrowth dragging swords of a sun-bleached confederacy

Part 6

Where it's rough and untended and hungry weed grows.

—Gwendolyn Brooks, "a song in the front yard"

KEITH WILSON

The Corner

it's my job, i say. i dispose of her
loudness, her attention, her tics
and exclamations and loud sudden

coughs. her body
wrapped in black jackets like a well-loved
doll. i'm sorry ma'am. you can't use the phone

anymore. she curses me, curses me again
as if i were her son. but my mother is not
black, i have none like that. she seems

not unhappy. until then—she called me
baby, my mother too, my father is black:
he calls me junior. he rarely calls, i rarely call

and all night she asks for the bathroom, rambles
past sparkling water, sriracha popcorn, ciabatta,
baba ghanoush, paneer and masala, to the back

room which glows gold with freezer light, and talks
like my favorite aunt who used to steal
the nintendo controller and make us watch her play

my father's games, she stays around the corner, customers
say, and what does she like besides trail mix, and she curses
me and returns and narrates to herself and, now, the cold.

MARILYN NELSON

A Deaf Old Lady

Voices have darkened
to a gray peace,
and in silence,
her private room
in the old folks
welfare ward,
she listens for movement
with her slowing eyes.

There are no flights
of birds,
no children
screaming through
the walls,
no bursts of anger
from the street
to wake her.
Only her wild old hair
frenzies around her face.

At night
she lies black
in the stippled darkness
and dreams that she has fallen
without taking leave
toward this small end
the whole of her life.

street woman

a cracked mirror, a red sweater
a bottle that once held perfume
a piece of fool's gold, a torn map
a bar of soap, some thick wool socks
a picture of a boy who could be my son

some things to remind me
that someone somewhere loves me
or someone somewhere used to
a catalog of memories
some blurry and some ice water clear

just me and my cart rolling
from place to place
through the night hours
and across the dawn
from the lake to downtown
you'll see me or
pretend to ignore me

but i'm here either way
pushing my cart, pushing myself
pushing my cart, pushing myself

you'd be surprised how many lives
can fit in one grocery cart
full of bags that are full of bags
that are full of parts of me

Black Woman in Russia 2015

"It's not true that Russians are 'rude.' I encountered curiosity here and there, that translated into puzzlement that a Black woman was walking their streets."
—Gwendolyn Brooks, *Report From Part 2*, 1982

I received an invitation from Christine List, one of my former professors to join a group of scholars and filmmakers. The travelers included Robert Coles, Dr. David Bethea, and Don Winter who were making a documentary exploring the life and writings of Alexander Pushkin. I was not sure how I would get myself over to Russia, but I believed in the project. I'd been introduced to Pushkin seventeen years before as a student of Dr. Bartley McSwine at Chicago State University. He'd roll his shoulders back, expand his chest, fill his cheeks with breath and pridefully allow the name to surge from between his lips: "Push-kin!" And with that release his eyes would soften and the corners of his mouth would stretch into a grin. He'd pause as if suspended somewhere between defiance and satisfaction. I looked at the traveling expenses and decided that I could not afford it, but then the unexpected happened. The ruble dropped, and I was able to scrape up enough cash to get myself to Russia with room and board.

I consider myself to be one who moderately travels. I am accustomed to moving about without knowing "the language". My recipe for communication was usually learning a few words and keeping a pocket translator on my person at all times. In the age of YouTube, I figured I'd find a video or two to arm myself with a few words. My top five are usually *yes, no, stop, food, toilet*. Yes and no were so simple—*da* and *nyeht*. I continued to look up common words and quickly found out that beyond yes and no, one American word equaled at least two and a half Russian words. That seemed to be the rule, two and a half words for one. And the pronunciations proved to get lost somewhere between the back of my teeth and the roof of my mouth. I tried reading Russian one month before, but found myself met with letters that looked like a mixture between Arabic and Greek. However, none of it mattered. If my visa didn't come soon, I would not make it in time to meet up with the crew. And with the haze of mystery around Russia there was no way that I was traveling without knowing that there was a familiar face to meet me on the other side.

It was three days before I was scheduled to leave America. I faced the fact that I might not be able to go. I checked my mailbox daily looking for my Russian Visa—*c'mon*—and finally it came. I opened my passport and read my name in Russian. SHAHARI MOORE, the name that I'd known for forty-one years became ШAXAPИ МУР. A few letters seemed to be missing and it went against the two and a half for one rule, but it was me. So, I grabbed my shiny new Russian visa, shortened name, *da, nyeht*, and got on a plane.

The thirteen-hour flight from America to Russia by way of Frankfurt was surprisingly relaxing. I read more Pushkin, slept, ate, and thought about the work before me. By traditional American standards, one drop of "black blood" made you Black. So by those standards the father of Russian literature was basically a Black man who died as a result of gun violence. Unfortunately as an African American, I can recite the stories of too many lives of black men that were cut short by bullets. We know them by name: Michael Brown in Ferguson, Trayvon Martin in Florida, Kimani Gray in Brooklyn, Kendrec McDade in California, and Ervin Jefferson in Atlanta were all victims of gun violence by police or "security." However, according to Bloomberg Business, over 100,000 Black men die annually in America as a result of gun violence. Behind those statistics are men with lives, thoughts, opinions, pride, loves, and aspirations. In Pushkin, I see a man who explored his identity and place in the world as a person of color. The closer I look at Pushkin I see the parallels between his life and the lives of many Black men in America, minus the aristocracy and access to resources.

I arrived in Moscow around 11:00 a.m. Entering the country was much easier than I thought. In my mind, I'd prepared to be interrogated entering and exiting Russia. As a Black woman who travels alone, that is my biggest fear. *What if I am branded as a terrorist and detained? What if they overlook the fact that I am over forty and sell me to traffickers?* I cringe and plead the blood of my ancestors even as I type those words. *Please never let that happen.* In the event of that unfortunate situation my mother had prepared me. "Shahari, don't go into Russia talking that Black shit." Translation: Tell them that you are studying Alexander Pushkin, but never reveal your desire to unearth and explore his African identity. Thankfully there was no interrogation, just a customs agent who asked me to pull my hair back so that she could see my ears. I complied with a grin, and received one back as she gestured me through. What was it about ears? Were ears the new fingerprints? As I looked around the airport I saw a couple of African families. They were dressed in traditional cloth and moved through the airport with a sense of urgency. I looked around for other people who looked like they could be African American, but there were none. Just as I decided that Russians would assume that I was African a cab driver called out to me, "Americana!" *Americana*? I'd never thought of myself in that way. I walked across the paths of two little Russian twin boys of about age four in blue coats. They stood shoulder to shoulder, close enough to be Siamese. Their eyes grew wide and their blue-hooded heads turned in tandem as if they'd seen a mythical being. In a sea of shouts and hustle and bustle I found the driver whose iPad bore my American name. Glad that I'd pre-arranged a driver through a third party, I exited the airport and got on the road.

Under the cover of a gray sky I listened to jazz as we sped down a road generously framed by towering birch trees. I made a couple of attempts at conversation with the driver who didn't speak English, yet hummed Motown with purpose. He really went in when Marvin Gaye's "What's Goin' On" came on the radio. I tried to read the billboards as they blurred by but the words were too unfamiliar to my brain. In forty minutes Kremlin Square came into view. I immediately fell in love with the swirly candy cane, the onion tops. Something about them reminded me of Moroccan architecture, but surprisingly with a little more color and whimsy. With religious structures that colorful, Russians could not possibly be as stiff as they are portrayed in popular American culture. Actually they reminded me a lot of New Yorkers—straight, no chaser, and passionate about representing their part of the world. I made it safely to the hotel without being trafficked. I rested and met up with the film crew who were still adjusting to the time difference. We ate rich black bread, had surprisingly tasty entrees, drank lovely wine, settled in, and prepared to continue to do the work that my mother told me not to announce.

The next morning we met our guides: Victoria, sweet, knowledgeable, beautiful, flawlessly polite and the other guide, the pushy one whose name I have blocked out. She sucked her teeth and craned her neck when in the midst of disagreement, a special skill that has evolved as characteristic of the Black woman, *Ha!* Sasha was our handsome private driver. The maleness of days of old pushed through his pores. Each day we were picked up around 10:00 a.m. and whisked off to either a Pushkin point of interest or to interview a Pushkin scholar. He always made sure to take my hand as I stepped in and out of the van. A few times I spent breaks between shoots chatting with Sasha, who I perceived to be a little over sixty-years-old. Though I spoke very little Russian and he spoke very little English we exchanged flawed phrases, leaning heavily upon pocket translators. Sasha, "Me, retired. Driving, extra. You, filmmaker?" He applauded. I thanked him by replying, "Spa-see-ba." "You married, boyfriend?" I replied, "Nyet." Sasha's brow furled and he threw up his hands in disgust. "You, beautiful." I replied, "Spa-see-ba." Then he looked into my eyes, "Me, divorced, but girlfriend." I pouted and placed my hand over my heart, and said, "You girlfriend, me sad." He took my hand and placed it upon his chest, "Me have big heart." I gave him a look, letting him know I'm not the sharing kind. He looked at me once more, "Jazz?" I leaned back and smiled, "Dah." He turned up the radio and we smiled at what would never be, but loving the authenticity of the present.

In America we usually have one statue per city that is dedicated to individuals. In Russia, it seemed that Pushkin was interwoven throughout history, integrated into the curriculum from grammar school to college, and reflected in monuments and museums. This man of African descent undergirds Russian culture. During the shoot I learned a lot about Pushkin, but what I found even more fascinating was the reverence that Russians who live in the twenty-first century pay to a man of African descent who was deceased by the nineteenth century. They are absolutely bananas about Pushkin! For sport and for the purpose of the documentary we stopped several Russians—men, women, seniors, and children and asked them to recite their favorite line written by Pushkin. Without fail, they would stop and pridefully recite a line or two. Our schedule took us to several sites dedicated to Pushkin. I was blown away by the fact that there are so many. All of the museums, the lyceum (boarding school), and "Pushkin places" were well maintained. And then we made it to his apartment at Moika 12, where he died. It was full of his personal effects: of course a writing desk and a plume well maintained and guarded with ropes. Unlike Irving Stone, a colleague who travelled to Russia with Miss Brooks in 1982, I dared not ask permission to sit in Pushkin's chair or to hold his plume.

Alexander Pushkin was born on June 6, 1799 and died on February 10, 1837 from injuries related to a gunshot to the lower abdomen. As a poet he ushered in a new era in Russian writing. Most Russians consider him to be the father of Russian literature. His writing reveals a fascination with love and folklore. Like Gwendolyn Brooks, he wrote in an accessible manner that resonated with both the masses and the elite. His writing is romantic, dramatic with glints of humor and adept wit. He influenced many writers after him like Gogol and Dostoyevsky in the nineteenth century and Mandelstam, Akhmatova, and Tsvetaeva in the twentieth century. During his life and later in the Soviet era he gave Russians a means of free expression through words.

Miss Brooks:

Before I embarked upon a plane I read your essay, and I thought of you while I was there. I thought of you and the way that you've used words to translate the lives of Black Chicagoans to the world. You have made us into flowers that push through concrete. You have influenced too many writers to name. I've seen your bust, but never a statue. Does one even exist? May our words and expressions of the consciousness of being serve as a requiem.

Artwork

These images were chosen for both their excellence of craft and their Gwendolynian elements. Some of these are portraits of the artist at various stages of her life. Others engage in either delicate or deliberate dialogue with specific themes, works, and titles of Miss Brooks' oeuvre.

Felicia Grant-Preston, "Sink or Swim," Oil on Canvas, 8" x 24", 2008 series: Sapphire and Crystals: BEyOND Race and Gender." From the collection of Dr. E. Renee Garrick. The brilliant color palette, the natural elements, and the forthright body language in Grant-Preston's silhouetted image of a young girl emerging from sun-lit waters evoke Miss Brooks' personal, political, and literary coming of age.

Joyce Owens, "More Than Cool" (a portrait of the poet laureate), 2016. Acrylic and collage on canvas 30″x12″x2.5″. Mirroring the poet's use of nature imagery, Owens surrounds a portrait of Miss Brooks with free floating pearls, clouds, birds, and flowers, along with text from Miss Brooks' iconic poem and her title as Poet Laureate.

Malaika Favorite, "Kitchen Dreams, Ironing the Collar" © 2013, Mixed media 28 x 12 x 3. In this narrative image by artist and poet, Favorite valorizes the fierce and the feminine elements of Miss Brooks' work.

Arlene Turner-Crawford, "Cosmic 3" Cosmic Community Series: the Healers, 2000, Acrylic paint and mixed media collage, Ancestors pictured. Turner-Crawford's abstract composition evokes the spiritual, the ancestral, and healing elements of Miss Brooks' work.

Adjoa Jackson-Burrowes, artist "To Disembark (Revisited)," Mixed media print 5.5 x 8.5 in. 1981 and 2015. This reprise of the cover art from Miss Brooks' 1981 collection, *To Disembark*, Jackson-Burrowes captures the complexity of black life, youth, African origins, and masculinity (see artist statement, page 296).

Arlene Turner-Crawford, "Pass the Iron, We Live! (Portrait of Gwendolyn Brooks)," Acrylic. 28" x 30" 2005. Collection of Dr. Patricia Lassane. This piece inspires a reflection of political themes in Gwendolyn Brooks' works, presenting a portrait prominent against an African-inspired design, with imagery and text reminiscent of the Black Arts Movement.

Satoki Nagata, "Sunday afternoon, Chicago 2011," From series of Cabrini-Green; Frances Cabrini Rowhouses. This image from Nagata's photographic series set in a black Chicago community reflects Miss Brooks' interest and examination of place and setting.

Malaika Favorite, "Hand in memory of Gwendolyn Brooks," 4 x 8 mixed media, 2014 (includes the poem "Sadie and Maud" by Gwendolyn Brooks). Created as part of a one-person show at the Furious Flower Poetry Conference, Lisanby Museum, James Madison University, Harrisonburg, VA in September 2014.

Rose Blouin, photographer (clockwise from top left: Henry Blakely, Haki Madhubuti, Miss Brooks, Nora Brooks Blakely; Henry Blakely with Miss Brooks; Angela Jackson, unknown male; Haki Madhubuti with Miss Brooks; Mari Evans with Miss Brooks; Sonia Sanchez with Miss Brooks).

Roy Lewis, Gwendolyn Brooks portrait, © Roy Lewis Archives. Roy Lewis' portrait of Miss Brooks sporting her newly minted Afro is said to have been a favorite. Lewis would go on to chronicle Miss Brooks' life and career in photographs for the next three decades.

Rose Blouin, photographer. Miss Brooks reading from *Say That the River Turns*, a 1987 collection of essays about the impact of Gwendolyn Brooks on a new generation of writers.

Part 6
Continued

REGGIE SCOTT YOUNG

Recollections

I take a walk through Bluesville,
eyes visiting old corners now vacant
asking them to tell me their poems,
but all their metaphors have been exploited
and sentimentality won't resurrect old stone.

There's a house across Ogden on Sawyer
where I received fifty-cent haircuts as a boy,
decayed and full of tombstone weeds
nothing seems to work there now.

It's strange growing old, cherishing
things not cherished in youth
not knowing the value of what was once had.
In Bluesville there grow dandelions,
to the world, Bluesville's flower is a weed,
but being from Bluesville a person knows
a dandelion is a ghetto rose.

OPAL PALMER ADISA

Urban Couple

(after Gwendolyn Brooks' "The Bean Eaters")

where the heater and
washer/dryer are kept

they rent a room
in someone else's house

they crawl in through a side
gate that's not really standard

size or legal but they have a
roof over their heads

and they are together so what
is there to complain about

every friday they line up
with many others at the church

where they get a bag of groceries
often too many onions but they

eat them like delicacies
and the gas they produce

offers occasion for laughter
and a game of whose smell

is worse or is louder or detonates
no matter they still sleep spooned

and she often catches him
and he often spies her

eyes lit or a gentle smile

The Tenant

"We are things of dry hours
and the involuntary plan,
Grayed in, and gray."
— Gwendolyn Brooks, "Kitchenette Building"

or like coffee, the privilege turned down; the curtain
that hangs like an odor

above the door, or the bed bugs like beats
burst upon the wall. it is all

peanut butter straight from the jar and nothing
else. the raccoon,

wily as a founding father and impossible to convince
from the wall, though the cage is slim and white as a promise.

of course anyone who won't leave is an artist
and the neighbors here are too, and the mice and the cans

that wouldn't be cans if everyone got real
jobs and stopped pretending in fate though that too is a social security tax

or a lottery ticket that only makes it harder in the moment
to eat

PATRICIA SMITH

Meanwhile, a Lawndale Girl Burns Cornbread

(After Gwendolyn Brooks' "A Bronzeville Mother Loiters In Mississippi.
Meanwhile, A Mississippi Mother Burns Bacon.")

My mother bled moans for hours before I was born, the tortuous labor enough to shake her belief in a merciful Jesus. I pummeled the air with tiny fists, already expecting enemies in my first anxious days. "You came here fightin'," my daddy said. "Wudn't nothing to do but lay there and be a baby, but you didn't trust it."

Patricia Ann, my painfully plain name, was in vogue before the rampant tacking on of 'nishas and 'ellas and 'essas and 'nikas. I was a black girl born in Chicago in 1955. My sisters and I were the first daughters. Our parents loved us, but urged us to conform, disappear. *Don't talk to no white folks. If you do, say yes sir and yes ma'am. Don't be so sassy, girl.* We were rooted underneath what could be seen. But whole lives would grow from us.

The children of migrants, we were told that our history held shame. When I asked my mother about her life before Chicago, she'd say *Girl, what you wanna know 'bout that stuff for? That's down there stuff.* Her seat on that northbound Greyhound was as far back as she wanted to go.

"You just worry about what goes on *here*," she said. "Here, right where you are."

Her idea of introducing me to the world? Keeping me away from it. I was protected and coddled to the point of mystified ignorance. People disappeared, locations changed, relatives wept without explanation. My grandmother went away in the night and never returned. No one bothered to explain. She just never came back.

If my mother's mother had lived longer, I would have learned my southern blood. Instead, my mother clogged my scalp with grease, used fire to sizzle my hair straight, instructed me in the painful silk of little white girls.

And she kept pinching my nose. Without warning, she would reach out, trap my nose between thumb and forefinger and crush, hard enough to spark a cry of pain. The mashing was a morning ritual for years.

My mother also medicated me incessantly, whether I was sick or not. Particularly terrifying was the daily dose of Doctor John's, a stomach-churning blend of cod liver oil and sluggish sugary cream. Thick, nut-brown Castoria was for my non-existent bowel problem, because, according to my mother, everyone had a bowel problem.

"Did you make boo-boo today?" she'd ask.

"Why?"

"'Cause you got to stay regular."

"Why?'

"'Cause otherwise that stuff builds up inside you."

"What stuff?" I was beginning to conjure the image of hundreds of unboweled movements crowding my heart, my lungs, making me fat.

"Girl, stop asking so many questions, and take this Castoria. Then go sit on the toilet until something happens."

You see, as a little colored girl, I wasn't quite right. My skin. My bowels. My color. My hair. My nose. I would sweat, that hair would crinkle. Nightly slatherings of Artra Skintone Cream couldn't tackle my blue-black. My mother moistened a washcloth with Lysol and feverishly scrubbed the back of my grimy neck, hoping to remove a layer or two of black. And my nose was broad, too inescapably Negro. I was way too much of what she had been.

She saw salvation as my only chance. Every Sunday, I was snapped into pinafore and patent, and escorted to a thunderous Sunday school lesson. If I lived my life according to these kiddy-sized sermons, I would sit perfectly still and be perfectly silent.

After Sunday school, I joined my mother for the regular service. Enthralled, I watched an aged preacher burst the bounds of his body, serving up gospel in tones both guttural and meteoric. Thanks to his locomotion, the dramatics of an unflappable choir and a thick wall of organ wail, "the ghost" would descend and many would, in Pilgrim Rest Missionary vernacular, "get happy."

The phenomenon was fascinating. Eyeglasses shattered, matrons howled, eyes rolled back, garters popped. Elaborate Sunday crowns were flattened. The chosen ones wailed in syllables urgent and heated. Every Sunday, more and more folks swooned, fainted, bellowed, jerked, whinnied, boogalooed, chatted in tongues, and earned their passport to glory.

I wouldn't be right unless I joined the ranks of the possessed. Until the Ghost jammed His hot hand into my head, I was, for all practical purposes, a transgressor.

So one Sunday, I pretended—hoping my performance would convince the deity that my intent, if not my heart, was pure.

The Rev. Matthew Thomas' face writhed as saints and demons battled for control. The organist timed chilling chords to the reverend's whoops. Fans fluttered, righteous heat arose, the newly-saved collapsed.

Glancing sideways at my mother, I buckled and kicked, yelping, "Take hold my soul, Jesus," plus a few unintelligible syllables. Blur. White-gloved hands.

Sounds of grateful weeping. Insistent tambourine. I wasn't sure how long to go on. I didn't want the congregation thinking I was born to lead them.

So I eased out, avoiding my mother's proud gaze, as well as the blue-eyed glare of the Jesus in the crucifixion scene spanning the pulpit. He didn't look quite as pleased.

Although she was often "touched," my mother was no saint. She played Tyrone Davis 45s, wore tight skirts, knew how to spin on a barstool, lusted for things. Of course, I preferred my mother's sinful side.

My mother was staunch, orderly, maddeningly upright. She Cloroxed everything. Every room was bleached to such a shimmer your eyes would tear. Every night, she religiously scrubbed that day's underwear threadbare on a rippled washboard. Nothing soiled saw the next day.

But she wasn't just a cheerless domestic goddess. There's a very sensual black and white photo of her perched on a barstool, circa 1963, doing her best come-hither, gold tooth winking in the neon splash. It was like looking at an alien.

The threat of my mother kept me in line. She was not above utilizing tree branches, douche bag cords, clothesline, ironing cords, or jump ropes to lay down the law. I was often required to be a participant in my own undoing.

"Get your butt cross that street and bring me back a switch."

"Huh?"

"I know you heard me. And you don't want me to have to go over there and get it myself."

Most colored children my age remember the ritual none-too-fondly. After misbehaving, I was ordered across the street to the park—there was *always* a park across the street—to snap a switch from a bush and deliver it to my mother so that she could whup my ass with it.

"Bet' not be no skinny switch, either. Or I'll send you back to get another one, and I'll beat you twice as long."

Desperation would set in. Stupidity would follow. "Mama, what I do? I didn't do nuthin.'"

Everyone outside witnessed my endless trek across the street. The beating would come. They would wait.

No one met my eyes as I turned back toward home, clutching the knobby switch. I could feel the heat coming from my mother as she filled our apartment window. I slowed down.

"Girl, you get hit by a car, I'm jes' gon' let you lay there, you hear?"

The walk up to the third floor never took long enough. The window was open while I entertained the neighborhood with my screams and her running commentary:

Girl, didn't you hear me tell you 'bout being so fast? Bet you gon' think twice 'fore do something else, ain't you?

Didn't.

I.

Tell.

You.

Not.

To.

Be.

So.

Fast?

The gaps between each word were filled with the beating of me.

Afterward, she would coddle and coo, thoroughly confusing me. Her face would untwist and become the comforting countenance of EveryMama. *You made me have to do that. You don't give me no choice. This world is too bad, you gotta learn . . .*

The next day, my friends marveled at the welts crisscrossing my thighs, calves, and my arms—where I had tried to fend off the blows.

Despite my mother's attempts at discipline, I was a ball of sass, imbued with my father's ain't-this-the-shit view of things. I wasn't merely tempted by the worldly, I was committed to it. The more she kept me away from the world, the more I wanted to jump my whole self in and wiggle.

Instead, I spent lots of time inside, face smashed to the window, watching other girls beat the pavement with their Keds, swell their muscles with Double Dutch, get gloriously sweaty. Me, I read books. Mary Poppins thrilled the hell out of me.

I loved mama, like you love what steadies you. But I was so in my father's orbit that she became something to overcome. She was stiffly and infrequently affectionate, a rule-setter, an expert at avoiding conversation that veered toward intimacy. I felt a little guilty at the ways I complicated her life. I confused her. And when I joined forces with my daddy, she almost gave up.

My mother and father were like an ill-matched sitcom couple thrown together for laughs. I still can't imagine them in the same *room*, let alone exchanging a heated touch. I never thought of them as married.

My daddy, Otis Douglas Smith, was tender, hyper, and slight, daily overjoyed at the sight of me. He was such a gleeful rogue, a cackle, a winking eye.

He was a storyteller, crafting worlds I wanted to crawl into. His favorite protagonist was Homer, a country-bred colored boy lost and bewildered in the big city. My mother was absolutely horrified by Homer, who was exactly the kind of shiftless Negro she hated. Daddy would adopt several voices and sometimes imitate Homer's loping gait.

In his most memorable exploit, Homer wanders into a fancy department store to buy a pound of hog jowls. Stopping at counter after counter, he's ignored and sniffed at by snooty white folks. Finally, a clerk hisses, "This is a very exclusive store. We don't carry any part of the hog in question. Even if we did, no one would help you. Look in the mirror, and you'll see why."

Homer skedaddles over to a mirror. He is blue-black, unkempt, shoeless, one buck tooth rotting, and unbrushed.

"I know!" he exclaims. "I forgot my hat!"

After his storytelling, 'round about bedtime, daddy would grow restless. It was time to roam.

During the day, he folded into the rigors of factory. Then he ate and played with his daughter. When the night said, *That's enough of that*, he'd tip out for some shit talk and poker playing.

Every corner of my neighborhood was populated by slumping men loud-talking their dying dreams. But Daddy never expected the city to save him.

His dreams started out simple, and he was living them. A job. His daughter. Light flashing in a woman's sad eyes.

A pig-tailed little buffer zone, I was the reason my parents stayed together. Some of my friends didn't even know their fathers—so I needed mine to be somewhere close, every day, or I would lose everything.

My Murphy bed was in the living room, right by the front door. When daddy came home late from a night of whooping it, he'd whisper for me to let him in. He had a key, but a chain latch kept him out.

My mother would be waiting. "Gimme one good reason why I should let you in this house."

"Woman, I live here." I prayed he'd be able to douse the little laugh lurking in his voice. "I pay the rent."

"You didn't think that when you was out in the street. Go on back out there. Let your other women take care of you for a change."

"Told you I was going out to play cards. Now open the door."

Hands on hips, my mother glared at the door. Then she'd turn on me. "If you let that man in here, I'm whuppin' your butt." She'd leave me there right there by the door, with the person I loved most in the world on the other side.

Torn and powerless, I'd cry, and Daddy would whisper "It's okay, baby girl, it's okay." He could have pushed the door and snapped the chain, but fury wasn't his style. I'd hear cards slap as he passed the time with solitaire. Then he pounded on the door again, knowing my mother hated folks in her business.

"Annie Pearl, let me in! This don't make no sense."

My father pacing right beyond my reach drove me crazy. Soon, with "See you in the morning, baby girl," he'd skip back into the night. My mother was a fool for sending him back to where she didn't want him to be.

Increasingly resentful of the bond my father and I shared, my mother was determined to break it. One day after I had again crossed the line with her, she decided he should be the one to exact punishment. My father had never laid a hand on me.

My mother discussed my misbehavior with him in low, dramatic tones. Our eyes met briefly. *Let's get through this.*

He said I shouldn't have done what I did. I nodded solemnly. He laid me across his lap and paused, like a doctor looking for the best place for an incision. He popped me once, twice, on my left thigh. I remembered to yelp for my mother's benefit. But once I realized he had actually spanked me, I cried in earnest.

He pulled me to my feet and immediately left the room. Not satisfied with the lukewarm punishment, my mother yelled at me a little more: *See? You done made your daddy mad!*

I just wanted my father's arms to undo what had been done. When my mother and I went into the kitchen—her to badger, me to forgive—he was at the table, weeping into his hands.

It was a sound like the world shredding.

I will never know how I survived a love so huge. My mother wanted me to be a proper northern lady. My father flaunted his flaws, giving me permission to have my own.

I chose his world of blue notes, bopping language, a sense of the possible rising from the impossible. We talked out what mystified, angered, and fascinated us. While my mother bleached the world into order, my daddy and I met in the kitchen and cooked. We heated our mouths with slivers of hot pepper and Tabasco. We got drunk on buttermilk and peppery things.

The first thing I ever cared to cook was hot water cornbread, because my father taught me. It was thin and crusty bread good for sopping potlikker, soaking up butter, or crunching with steamed greens. The recipe was simple:

Corn meal, hot water. Mix till sluggish, then dollop into a sizzling skillet. When you smell the burning begin, flip it. When you smell the burning begin again, dump it onto a plate. You've got to wait for the burning and get it just right.

Before the bread cools down, slide some butter on it. We would slather it with salted butter. Crumble it into a bowl of buttermilk, or in some collards with sweet pickle juice.

Daddy and I licked our fingers while my mother watched *Bonanza*, muttering how stupid it was to be burning that nasty ol' bread in that cast iron skillet. When I told her I'd cooked my first ever pan of hot water cornbread—and that my daddy had branded it glorious—she sniffed and kept mopping the floor over and over in the same place.

One day, long after that day, somebody killed my daddy. He was shot in the back of his head. But that's a story for another time, a story for an older woman. I'm not even sure why I wrote it aloud. We were talking about a little girl and her father. We were talking about hot water cornbread and the making of it.

You take that bowl with the blue flowers and only one crack. Put the cornmeal in it. Now turn on the hot water while you tell me that secret again about the boy who kissed your cheek after school or 'bout how you really want to be a reporter instead of a teacher or nurse like mama says.

And daddy said, *You will be a wonderful writer and you will be famous someday and after you get famous, if I wrote you a letter and sent money, would you write about me?*

Now run the water slow into the bowl, until it moves like the mud moves at the bottom of a river. Then you turn the fire way up under the skillet and you pour in the mix that looks like quicksand, like mud moving at the bottom of a river, like a slow song sounds.

That stuff kicked something awful when it first hit that blazing skillet, and sometimes Daddy and I would dance to those angry *pop* sounds. He'd let me rest my feet on top of his while we waltzed around the tiny kitchen and my mother huffed and puffed on the other side of the door.

When you are famous, will you write about dancing in the kitchen with your father?

I said, "Everything I write will be about you, then you will be famous too." And we laughed and dipped and spun, but then he stopped and sniffed the air.

The thing you have to remember about hot water cornbread is to wait for the burning so you know when to flip it, and then again so you know when it is crusty and done.

Then eat it the way we did, with our fingers, our feet still tingling from dancing.

But remember that sometimes the burning takes such a long time, and in that time,

sometimes,

poems are born.

BETTINA MARIE WALKER

R. Taylor's Project Girl

I've stayed in the front yard all my life.
I want a peek at the back
        —Gwendolyn Brooks

I am supposed
to be immoral
with no GED or
high school diploma
to be ebonically correct
not *parle un peu de français*

Others will see me
to be a menace,
produce brown babies,
have common law husbands,
and stay sky-blue striped Link

I was not supposed to know
the Black Panther movement
with Bobby Rush firsthand
nor their free breakfasts,
sickle cell screenings,
and daycare programs
coupled to yellow water
stained hallways
with heroin addicts
—my front yard

I was not supposed to know
the gifted hands nor artistry
of my big brother's
glow in the dark
Afrocentric murals
one story high
painted on caged porches
and project gangways
of 4352 and 4331
displaying proud naked men,
women, and children
chained and bathing
in the Donkor Nsu Slave River
or kneeling
at knee-high tree stumps
to carve words
of grief and good-byes
with blood flecked fingernails
to their families

I should not be able
to recognize true love since
I was not *married to the bed*
but pinned to a mattress of shame
assaulted by Kennybell at 13
This unexpectedly blemished
my depth
maybe for life

I should not have seen
my mother on Channel 7 news
saying that I was kidnapped
from the playground
by a man in a black Cadillac

with yellowing newspaper
covering its rear window
when I disappeared because
I could not cope
and allowed swift wind
to carry my shoes
running away

I should not have been valedictorian
nor given the speech to my peers on
how *We have only just begun*
instead, I'm supposed to be
turmoil turned suicide,
sexually indiscreet
and not know that AIDS was the
serial killer in my neighborhood
that snatched mamas from babies
disguised as pneumonia
on life support

I should be statistically improper
connotatively negative
A project girl—with a backyard view
that once held the world's
tallest building captive with
its antennaes stretched upward
tuned to White Sox's bursts
of red, white, pink, and green
kaleidoscopic speckles interchanging
on orange dusk sky
to celebrate a home run
While fall crept stillborn
on asphalt playgrounds
signaling summer's end

ADRIAN MATEJKA

Final Frontier

Big eyes & abandoned sleep over here
east of the bridges potholed like empty
tempos, unnamable hubbub of rusty axles
jumping the bad concrete. Wheeze & cough
at the furnace start up add to the tremor
& might sound less like a closet monster
if my homemade tent staked a backyard
instead of a drafty townhouse. If the tent
was made out of polythene, not run-down
towels & the neighbors' same-old, same-old
aggravating the in-between plaster & particle
on the way another break up to make up.
Listen: being broke is what it is & every
smashed plate & hair-pulling yelp flows
around that scant fact to the nervous middle
of the week when meals get skeptical
in the gangly days before payday. No quiet
rooms while the neighbors come & go—
anxious in unison, open-nosed & red-eyed,
couched in front of a projector TV, *Star Trek*
reruns every Saturday at 9:00 p.m. We have
a brown couch & a TV stand with wheels,
dining table with a wobbly leg & two chairs.
Curtains, too, & behind them: spine up
against a metal chair leg & towels as exoskin
between me, the slick-skinned Dracos & Ursa
Minors skulking around campsites & after-
school centers on after-school specials.
My mother's exhaust sparks little suns when

she finally pulls up to the curb. The neighbors
cut & bag themselves in wide-brimming motions
at the same time Voyager finally gets pictures
of Saturn's bluer parts. The neighbors
sound like a planet zipping its curtains.

KEVIN COVAL

Gwendolyn Brooks stands in The Mecca

I wrote about what I saw and heard in the street.
There was my material.
      —Gwendolyn Brooks

blocks of brick. floors
& floors of Black bodies.
everyday people here
fighting & fucking
& struggling to make it.
sometimes they didn't.
she slang snake oils
at 19. her small hands
moving love potions
out bottles for some kind
of doctor. stalking halls
listening to the masses
speak, stuffed in kitchenettes.
nose ripe with onion fumes
rising like the peoples'
will in the warpland.
she took rich snapshots
of the poor. some rhythm
rattling around her head.
each sound an ornament:
a key turning the tumbler,
faucets praising the body
with lukewarm water,
the laughter of kids
& criminals. the ghost

echo of Pepita, the lost
girl. she kept count
of them, each syllable
stuck in a handbag
in her head, waiting
til she got home,
waiting to give birth
to everything.

The Last Supper

Julia stood half concealed behind the bathroom door. She held a black skillet limply at her side. She watched him, the Good Reverend Doctor Bing, sitting in a tub of suds, singing.

"Precious Lord, take my hand," he bellowed between puffs of cigar smoke.

She hated him and all that he was: philanderer, false prophet, and preacher of sermons he didn't write, believe, or follow.

"Lead me on."

Her side ached; her eye, now purple and oozing, pulsated from indescribable pain. Her good ear heard Little John's wheezing intensify with each pull the Reverend Doctor took on his cigar.

Julia knew Little John hid behind the storage room door, not far from where she stood. She felt his eyes on her, as her eyes were on the Good Reverend. Together, their eyes formed a binocular-like observation of the crooning man.

Julia waited patiently for the right moment. The moment that had come and gone a hundred times before when the Good Reverend Doctor would sing himself to sleep, stupefied by liquor and narcissism.

She waited, vaguely aware of the smell of fried chicken, spaghetti, and cold water cornbread wafting through their third floor walk-up.

She waited with the stillness of dense, musty air. She waited with the glower and intensity of a lioness lingering for the right time to kill. Little John watched, expecting her to deliver, not food, but peace.

Julia glanced over her shoulder, struck by Little John's bulging eyes. He'd been abused most of his young life. Maybe tonight he could sleep in peace, instead of having his innocence stolen one penetration at a time.

Pounding noises from the apartment above reminded Julia she and Little John weren't the only occupants caught in hell.

Every family in that tiny walk-up seemed intent on playing out their own personal tragedies. That tiny walk-up where every apartment door opened onto a dank, rectangular hallway, leading to the living room, leading to two bedrooms joined by one bathroom and across from it a storage room sandwiched between a wall showcasing Jesus, Kennedy, and King to the left and portraits of once happy families to the right.

The elongated hall spilled into a square kitchen with just enough room for essentials. Cast iron skillets, a refrigerator akin to an ice box, a tabletop stove, plus a small dining table with a gray marble top bordered by rounded, ridged chrome that never dented no matter how many times her head hit the edge.

Angry voices emitted from all of the little apartments where tenants worked at some kind of destruction brought on by an emptiness pitted like plum seeds deeply inside.

Julia's neighbors fought with the ferociousness of animals. Just last Friday, May stabbed Harold between his heart and a main artery. May meant to kill Harold but failed. Harold, simmering in revenge, had not pressed charges when the police arrived with the ambulance to take him to the hospital. After the doctor stitched him up, he returned home to do what he did—beat the crap out of May.

That fool burst his stitches whooping her ass from one end of the apartment to the other. He never stopped to investigate the stickiness pasting his shirt to his chest, pounding away as the red blot spread on his wife-beater. Finally, exhausted, the need of a fix seduced him away. May said that fool tore up their place looking for enough money to score.

Julia imagined Harold scratching, rocking from foot to foot, screaming like a woman—the bass stolen from his voice by the heroin he injected, sniffed, and rubbed on his gums. She closed her eyes, seeing terror reserved for strangers in May's eyes. May, who often wondered aloud where was the man she married, the one who sang to her when their first child was born, the one who worked a duo shift and rushed home to drive her to work at the hospital where she was a nurse's aid, the one who picked up report cards, the one who prayed with the entire family circling the bed, the one whose dignity was stolen when a felony as a teenager and instant unemployment resulting from Acme Steel moving its operations overseas closed all other doors he tried to open until he stumbled upon the Candy Man.

Julia and May shared the same secret, hugged the same pain though caused by different men. Through it all, both women strove to keep their families whole, praying often that their men would rise to the worthiness of their sacrifices.

Unlike Harold who was caught up by circumstance and bad luck, the Good Reverend Doctor with his mother-of-pearl skin and cat gray eyes, the by-product of a black mother and white father, was pure evil. He stripped her soul bare then stole what little spirit remained by damaging their son. Julia tried to understand how and when the Good Reverend became so toxic. She tried to remember what drew her to this man who was kind and caring until the day she said, "I do."

She knew the Good Reverend often wrestled with anger and humiliation because the people he idolized treated him like a footstool. His intense disappointment became tangled with grief each time his parents and siblings made it clear he could never be what they wanted him to be, so he punished and ostracized those who dared believe in him, expected better of him.

The Good Reverend Doctor Bing came from educated parents with strong morals and high aspirations. Sent to the right schools and a seminary, he completed two years at Northwestern University, majoring in philosophy before squandering the remainder of his college fund for fun and a mail order divinity school from the Galapagos Islands where Darwin coined the Evolution Theory.

Julia discovered her husband's omission at a picnic, two years after they married, when his mother let the cat out of the bag.

"Bing," she drawled, revealing her Arkansas roots, "When you gon' be a good boy and finish up at Northwestern? Your siblings have respectable professions and live in nice neighborhoods."

The Good Reverend's eyes darted quickly to his wife who knew not to react.

He rolled his eyes in her direction. "Go on and get me some more chicken and potato salad."

Julia obeyed, never once asking her mother-in-law, "What do you mean? There's a diploma from Northwestern hanging right behind his desk at the church."

Having earned a Crane High School diploma and a Unity Business College certificate of completion, it never occurred to Julia that successful doctoral students received degrees, not diplomas. His mother's slip helped Julia see the irony of her husband's terminal degree with the word "diploma" stamped in tall, block letters above his name, though she knew better than to alert him that she'd made the distinction. Either way, he'd beat her later for witnessing his unfurled lie.

Making his third plate, Julia reached for a pop in a nearby bucket, brushing past an ice pick. She fingered the ice pick's tip, allowing the chill of the metal to captivate her.

"What you waiting for?" The Good Reverend snapped, shoving her thoughts.

"I'm coming." Julia raced over to her husband, balancing a mountainous plate of food.

Continuing, her mother-in-law dismantled her husband's facade.

"When you gon' leave that horrendous West Side and stop squeezing that ol' dried up lemon for more juice," she said, winking at Julia.

The Good Reverend leaned back in the small lawn chair, his thighs spilling over the edges. He loosened his belt and sucked his front teeth before popping a toothpick in his mouth. "Mama, my flock is on the West Side, so that's where I need to be. Besides, they take care of their pastor."

"They take care of you," his father taunted, his gray eyes sparkling. "I suspect Julia does a lot of taking care of you, too. You are our only child who won't earn his keep."

Thinking back to that day, Julia thought of all the folks who'd taken care of the Good Reverend Doctor, a man who invited his lovers to their wedding and recruited the same women to be church missionaries, who wore white though their souls were red. He forced his congregation, members with quarters as wealth and buses for transportation, to buy him a Cadillac that Julia only rode in on Sundays. When she asked for rides to work, he'd drawl, "I plucked your ass from the projects. Ain't y'all used to toughin' it out?"

Admittedly, Julia spent her early years living in Rockwell Gardens. But later her parents moved to a house not far from the Gardens to stay near family and friends. There was nothing wrong with the projects; a lot of good people raised their families there. Besides, Julia remembered little about her first home. She did recall her father telling her she looked like her namesake, the first Black Barbie doll made in Diahann Carroll's likeness. Shaking her head, Julia wondered how she went from a father who treasured her, to a husband who despised her.

Maybe she was biased. Sometimes after he laid hands on her real good, he'd cry a bit, getting on bended knees to hug her around her waist as he begged her to promise not to make him hit her again.

His regrets were short lived and didn't stop the Good Reverend from striking Julia again or forcing her to use the money earned as a nurse's aide to pay the rent, purchase groceries, cover the utilities, and put gas in his car. Meanwhile, he used his church salary, bilked from his impoverished flock and forced love offerings, to buy sky blue suits matched by sky blue shoes and socks, set off by midnight black, collared shirts topped by a sky blue ties.

While his clothes spanned the rainbow, he also had an affinity for pinky rings. He had one for different occasions. At weddings, he wore the ring with the square diamond face. At funerals, he wore the onyx ring. When he hit her, he wore a round-faced, 24-carat gold ring. He still had it on, though the beating was over.

Julia rarely reacted to her own pain, humiliation, anger, and frustration of being treated like a punching bag, but he would have to pay for making their son a receptacle while complaining that if he had a *real* wife who satisfied him the way God planned then he would have to *go that way*.

The muscles in Julia's arms tightened as she watched the Good Reverend balance his cigar on the side of the tub before reaching for the glass of Jack on the floor. It wouldn't be long now. He always fell asleep after the Jack was gone, but before the water cooled. Tenement water heaters had little capacity or intensity to supply a steady flow of steaming water, so she routinely boiled water to keep his bath hot. He beat her if his bath cooled before he disembarked or for overflows if she poured too much.

The Good Reverend stirred, but the Jack held him in place as Julia watched until she became mesmerized by the smallest things, the condensation forming from of the moisturizer in his Jheri curl on the inside of his shower cap, to the greatest things, the incessant, deepening grate in her baby's wheeze. The latter reminded her of the urgency for removing their cancer.

Shaking her from this reverie was her neighbor Benson who stayed in the doghouse with his girlfriend. Every evening around this time, he begged her to open the door, like now: "Hey Jac-ka! Throw the damn key down, girl."

Benson's blast sharpened Julia's senses; the time had come.

The Good Reverend's head rolled to one shoulder and then forward to his chest. His cigar fell to the floor. She stomped it out as she usually did, leaning forward to search his face for alertness.

"No second chance this time," she chanted, wiping away tears at the thought of the white picket fence dream that never quite materialized the way her father had promised and the realization this *right* deed could surely land her in prison for the rest of her life. Julia couldn't allow herself to care about anything but her son's future.

Stepping back, she lifted the skillet over her head, bringing it down sword-like with such force that the Good Reverend's head burst like an exploding pumpkin.

Julia stepped back as his body drifted slowly down, down. Bubbles popped up, burst, and dissipated in a pool of red. She would not make May's mistake, so she waited another ten minutes with the skillet poised like a tennis racket to hit him again. When it was clear the Good Reverend would not be resurrected, Julia laid the skillet by the tub and walked out of the bathroom toward her son—his wheezing had stopped about the time the bubbles disappeared, though she suspected the puffs of Albuterol she'd heard during her vigil helped, too.

Julia rubbed Little John's back, kissed his forehead, and escorted him back to the kitchen. Two plates were already set. She filled each with chicken wings, spaghetti, garden salad, and cornbread. Julia and Little John sat down, reciting, "Jesus wept. Amen," into clasped hands before eating their last supper and dialing 911. She made a second call to her parents.

Finally, as she nibbled her food, she looked into Little John's large brown eyes and said in a whisper rasped by tears, "Did I ever tell you my father named me Julia after the first black Barbie Doll? He always treated me like a queen. Now, I expect he'll raise you to be the king you were meant to be."

Little John nodded as Julia reached across the table to squeeze his hand. She held on tight even as the knocking at the door intensified.

second ave. ceiling

```
                    the                          floor 7
who     occupies        ceiling         on       the top floor of 123
the whole floor                collapses         the whole building
the corner of                                    the   street   the
second  avenue                                   in new york city
can only handle                                  so much licking so
much  heat  on                                   walls  that  were
built  in  1886                                  they  are  orange
they are  brick                                  they are  burning
and alight how                                   many  people  will
hear it before  the                     floor 6  they cave in they
fall before the        ceiling         on        landlord is called
before a tenant                collapses         on floor six in 121
takes a gun to                                   his wait no it is his
phone   to  his                                  head  to  tell  the
landlord  smell                                  the  gas  leak  too
late to be fixed                                 smell it burn up a
knock  is  the                                   first call the pop of
the  fuse  the                                   phone line is split
is  stifled  in  the                    floor 5  fumes the gas has
been  leaking          ceiling         on        since a month or
so ago breathe                 collapses         in the damage to
our  lungs  and                                  respiratory system
from the heat is                                 orange thick on the
fifth  floor  an                                 addict his kid and
a locked  door                                   between      them
which  one  is                                   warmer  on  his
terra cotta skin  the                   floor 4  between the heat
and his fix and        ceiling         on        terra cotta walls
he doesn't even                collapses         notice the fourth
floor     below                                  heat rises up it is
hotter than him                                  heat rises rising up
heat from  the                                   fourth floor tenant
is running  to  the                     floor 3  the   third   the
second    floor        ceiling         on        the   first  floor
people   down                  collapses         123 121 heat rises
the   ceilings                                   coming  down  the
building    has                                  gone up in flames
in  new york  the                       floor 2  everyone is scared
when        a          ceiling         on        building starts to
fall again it is               collapses         hot it is fire like
the gas ignites  the                    floor 1  from the knock is
the first call the     ceiling         on        pop of the fuse and
phone line split               collapses         in fumes and the
fourth floor is                                  running the third
floor is running                                 the second floor is
running    the                                   first floor is on fire
                           the floor caves in
```

229

Steel canary

Cowering in the encroaching basement
betwixt filaments of slashing lighting
and the humdiddy bumdiddy gnashing of thunder,
we catch, in our own chests, the short-breath groan
of an airplane, its choked, trembling flight edging closer and closer.

We roll up our fear like an old music poster clasped
with rubber bands. We feel our way through murk
upstairs, nervous to have a look at that gasping sound,
to hold, with our eyes, that steel canary,
moaning through whiptail water.

The pilots must have been circling for hours
and, running low on fuel, decided to put down,
thunderstorm tornado or no. Our faces press
against the pane but we cannot see beyond it;
everything begins to hum and vibrate. Glass breaks

into our vision, filling our cheeks with speckled diamonds.
The hollowness blinds us, the sound leaving us mute.
We stumble up, rushing to tend new initiation marks.
In the mirror by candlelight, we grasp keener empathy
for grasshoppers in lawnmower blades,

for krill, caught in the exultation that is a sperm whale's blowhole,
for fleas braced on an elephant's tail when digestion
gives way to a sated boom.

REGGIE SCOTT YOUNG

Crime in Bluesville

On the West Side,
no one complains about
the heat: there
isn't any; but
folks do be trying to grab
a little warmth.

People naturally
don't want to freeze,
but sometimes
that's a little more
than they can afford.

Sometimes,
we light the oven,
those of us with gas,
or turn on an old electric heater
after running an extension cord
next door,
we even burn old wooden chairs
in the tub, or
bring a garbage can in and
let it be our fireplace.

We know not to relax in—
to comfort in
the winter of the night,
we might get drowsy and
go to sleep.

Too often
we are the burning story in
the morning news.

Eating in the Afterlife

After he had refused
A last meal on earth and after the hunt
For a vein to wreck after a vein was wrecked
He stood at the left hand of the gods and was
 welcomed, a never-ending feast of lumped potatoes
And sauerkraut, fatty beef and rye sprawled before him which
He refused with certainty and wondered
Which was worse:
The achy solitude of the living body
Or arriving at the afterlife only to find
Nothing worth eating, nothing to prolong
A second death before the bitter settled on the first.

Hotel Hades

Cynthia admitted to being an unrepentant sinner. She took the name of the Lord in vain. She bore false witness against her neighbor. She coveted her neighbor's husband and then did more than covet.

Cynthia drank vodka by the bucketful. She inhaled cocaine when she had the means and smoked rocks when she didn't. She was known to turn the odd trick, more for fun than profit. She gobbled plates of fatty food, fire-spiced to singe the palate.

"Don't let Cynthia bring nothing but beer to the barbecue," friends and family warned. "She seasons the pot with Satan's own hand." She always carried a bottle of scorpion pepper sauce, 700 times hotter than Tabasco. Anything less would be bland, and she despised blandness beyond all else.

Cynthia lied with such flair, if she were in Hollywood instead of Englewood she'd have an Oscar. When caught embroidering one untruth, she'd stitch another around it for protective covering.

Wallets poking from men's back pockets, handbags dangling from women's shoulders were so much fruit waiting to be plucked. One old lady chased her down and demanded back her property. After bopping old girl upside the head with her own handbag, Cynthia discovered house keys and loose change, just enough for carfare.

"A big-ass bag with nothing in it," she hissed, tossing it to the trash. "Who does that?"

Her belief in the afterlife never prevented any transgression. "Grab what you want and the devil take the hindmost."

Cynthia saw no contradiction in being a practicing Catholic and a practicing sinner. Those lurid tales of torment were custom-made for reprobation. Like Maria Goretti, who died rather than letting herself be raped. What if the man went and got some after the girl was gone? If Cynthia could rewrite the catechism, Maria would have wasted old dude instead of letting dude waste her. That's what Cynthia would have done.

She *had* killed a man once, though it hadn't been deliberate. Driving from a bar in a blizzard, she squinted at a shape in the road. She slammed on the brakes and fishtailed into a man struggling in a snowdrift. As she steered around him he struggled to his feet, and bang! Down he went, and this time he didn't get up. Waiting for the cops wouldn't bring him back. Cynthia kept on driving.

At the end of life she was curiously unbothered by prospects of Hell. A priest was called in for Extreme Unction. She refused last rites though her daughter worried her immortal soul would be damned.

Yes, Cynthia had birthed a baby girl she sent to the father as soon as the kid was out of diapers. Neither man nor child ever forgave her. It was just one in a long list of sins, venial and mortal. It wasn't even the worst of them.

Cynthia had lived hard but didn't die young. The mourners agreed that the undertaker had crafted them a fairly good-looking corpse.

"Don't Cynthia look just like herself?"

"Yes, she do. A she-devil."

Why dread ending up where devils dwelled in fire, brimstone, and eternal agony? Presided over by Lucifer, magnificent and merciless, it all promised to be anything but bland.

Cynthia followed the darkness instead of the light, slipped through a cleft in the cave. She blinked in disbelief at manicured lawns and picket fences and cookie cutter bungalows. Birds tweeted and a lemony sun shone overhead.

Hell was a middle class suburb. Everyone obeyed the speed limit. The damned were mannerable to a fault. Lucifer looked more like a principal than a fallen angel.

A welcome committee of Stepford wives bore down upon her with trays of sugar cookies. Cynthia was convinced she'd been mislead, had caught the up escalator instead of the down. Oh no, they assured her. She was where she was meant to be.

"We've been expecting you," the Stepford wives chimed in unison.

Lucifer held a Welcome to Hell reception in the lobby of the Hotel Hades. A medley of Abba tunes serenaded the gathering. An array of white foods made up the menu: boiled potatoes, Swiss cheese sandwiches on Wonder

Bread, iceberg lettuce with ranch. Scoops of vanilla ice cream topped thin slices of angel food cake.

"Isn't it ironic?" Lucifer proudly surveyed his handiwork.

Cynthia reached for scorpion sauce and found it transformed into mayonnaise. That is when she knew that her daughter was right. Cynthia was damned to her own private Hell, and there she would dwell all eternity.

CORTNEY LAMAR CHARLESTON

Lincoln Cemetery

This is where we go when we die.

When body breaks down. When heartbeat, when health
goes south, so do we. And far. And west. The exact address:

12300 South Kedzie Avenue.

We drive there in a long line behind the dead of us; white folks
get out of our way, just like old times, still flighty as ever.

This is the place they left behind for us—some
back entrance to heaven, a neighborhood of bones.

Grandma's address is here. Grandpa just recently
moved in; I hope she introduces him to all of her friends,
that he can find drinking buddies and a good reason.

If our folks are to rest here, let them make the most of it;
there is little difference between a casket and a kitchenette,
where their great migrations often ended: to have
enough space for laying down is to have enough space
for making love, for inviting love around.

The grave tight-lips this secret, doesn't snitch
on our departed despite that interrogation lamp of a moon.

Even in death and its darkness—and always
in blackness—there's itch to celebrate like only
we know how: a people whose grief did grow

on trees, like fruit, so we had no choice
but turn that bloody notion upside down.

Gwendolyn still writes poems for plain black folk;
Mr. Abbott prints them in his paper in defense of joy
and all the jazz that keeps the cemetery alive.

                                    That is, until

four, five o'clock morning time when fresh water finds
itself on freshly cut blades of grass and His sweet chariot
swings low and through to carry our skinfolk home to

                                    the big Chicago in the sky,

the one they dreamed of but, in humbled lives
both long and far too short, didn't find.

ROHAN PRESTON

The blinking Apple

To the little girls whose squeals tapered off
into frayed tittering between the canyons of towers as they
hopscotched and double-dutched through downtown,
Manhattan has never had sky, just gray and blue
portals fleeing, like the slate sun, through a lattice

of antennae, escaping from sidewalk to deli
awning to rooftop with the day—shadows that swallow
arrowheads and raised pyramid tips in their way.
Then the needle-points borne on bad breeze punctured

the city, blew it open like curtains, peeled it
like a can, rolled it back like an extra eyelid.
We squinted salt. The blinking Apple took on

the plash of a marine graveyard, its gleaming
obelisks soft as seaweed, its scrapers undulating
like kelp. My city of green spires and gaunt gloom,
of sharpened pencils with rubber to the ground, writing
up—my New York of mamacitas leaning off

fire escapes and fire hydrants whitewashing
memories, the capital of furtive subway
spooning and a million hustles looked up that
morning to find a firmament the color of chalkboard,

with cursive smoke curling against a new sky.

& Later,

one of the star-eyed neighbors
spills white all over

the carpet again & somebody

>   leans into it like sniffing
>   a fish's ear.

The other neighbor
is Pisces reclining,

>   So & So on the couch
>   in Atari's glow.

All these habits brought back

>   from Vietnam, blamed
on Agent Orange—

>   heroin & gunplay
first, cocaine came after.

Not every fatherless black could
object to war like Sun Ra did.

Not every fatherless black could
skip Vietnam, more violent
>   & conscientious

than this circle of Section 8.
      Vietnam is about as far from

this space as anybody will get.

Listen: the neighbor's cigarette
      is about to burn into
      her hair violently

      the way it burned
a socket into that unfortunate
shag rug in their living room.

Listen: we have to get
      off this pock-marked planet.

RITA DOVE

Geometry

I prove a theorem and the house expands:
the windows jerk free to hover near the ceiling,
the ceiling floats away with a sigh.

As the walls clear themselves of everything
but transparency, the scent of carnations
leaves with them. I am out in the open

and above, the windows have hinged into butterflies,
sunlight glinting where they've intersected.
They are going to some point true and unproven.

ANASTACIA RENEE TOLBERT

Cedar

the cedar tree could not comprehend
the crime could not comprehend a leaning
                                a lynching a love gone wrong
how it spilled across its branches like memories

or fog or floating truths
& the cedar tree decided
there has to be a better way to root yourself
                                when the humans spend their days
pulling you this way & that way
when the wind is a bully
a thud a raised hand

& the cedar tree took it(self)
& yanked it(self) out of its soil &
let its body become a sanctuary
how the church goers loved the cedar smell
how it flooded their nostrils
                                like good times like holiday like
                                surprise holy ghost
on a wednesday bible study afternoon.

LENARD D. MOORE

Fun in the Backyard

My childhood lingered in the backyard.
I knew what waited in the front:
bushels of corn, pans of string beans,
red potatoes that needed tending.
How a boy built brave hands.

I need to go in the backyard again,
hear marbles clack
against each other so solid,
and sing rhythmic games.
I need to play with my siblings.

Our mother would tell us
to stay outside and not track dirt
inside the house
while the sun was still up,
painting us a flawless bronze.

Day 4, Somewhere between Athens and Serifos, Greece

On the slow boat, we translate Gwendolyn Brooks' "We Real Cool" into Greek. We are talking loudly, laughing and having a good time. Several passengers get involved giving their opinion on the best way to say "lurk late" or "strike straight." I learn the Greek word for "jazz" is "jazz." Later that night, we listen to Carolyn read her poems from the balcony of one of the apartments where she has taken shelter from a flash rain. Many of her poems are elegies for poets she has known. They are both sad and beautiful. Just before the reading my mood is dark but like the sky my shell of a body makes room for a whisper of light, suddenly turning a marbled blue then gold.

In the far, cymbals
A sudden gigantic boom
The sea rising, falling

MONICA HAND

June 9, Serifos, Greece

Today I compose my first Greek translation, "The Cyclamen" by Yiannis Ritsos. More accurately I render the poem in English from a literal translation from the Greek provided by A and Y. From this one literal translation, each one of us (the five participants in the translation workshop) writes our own translation of the poem. We then share our translation with each other in round-robin fashion, like musicians soloing in a band, each one riffing off the other, each one showing off their unique insights, and aesthetics. What is the right verb for the act of translation? Willis Barnstone calls translation the art of revelation. I like this. The act of translating teaches you valuable information about the source language, poet, culture, and society while revealing something previously hidden by the mask of language. Translating in collaboration is wonderful—creating art together is community building at its best. As each one shares something of themselves and their view of the world, something new and surprising is created, something beyond the one's lonely vision, something like a potluck.

Fluttering flower
Dancing in chains it becomes
a smiling bird, song

JOHN WILKINSON

Blackbirding

Scuttled on a manmade lagoon, set to work
according to their serials,
branded at the neck—
              breaking from their compounds
webbed with paths night has re-trodden,
sociality in dream, on a floor of earth,
in architectures of bread, spit and curing air—

faint web on shackled legs
faint web on water jugs . . .

Webs of stone that rise out of the rubble
dumped by the insatiable chain & bucket
dredgers,
              retrace interior stars, nebulae
within veined pits, the sunsets are propped
against days cut officially,
              tree branches
scribbled into foam, and in coral, vascular,
                            hardening in dream

mottle drawn out in silver
mottle under veils of marble . . .

Blackbird sails in innocuous consignments,
"pressure vessels,"
Project Babylon unpacked on the quay,
screwed together, calibrated,
              booming out of night's waves

a nacreous reflection, fan-vaults,
scalloped spandrels,
                each of these having been machined—

words roam in snatch squads,
seeking birds or darting rodents to trap—

so labour modules/are they/distorted out
of paperwork/form the twisted shell-like
spire and from wooden crates
carve the screen that is actual and vibrant,
gluing it against a shocked sky
The blackbirds shall be fledged/will they/
will have taken shape
not laid out in the instructions,
shred *cartes de résident* with bone picks,
                cross-hatch earth in their frequencies

Under the lantern filled with daybreak,
                                mass new Maroons
flaunting veins in gold wire, in tourmaline,
veins stitched along loose sleeves:
                And soaring through a clerestory
rebuffing furious waves and military
advisors,
liberated songs break from their compounds
                and will fly home to roost

mild colours of a polluted sky
mild colours on a copper torso

                Scattering light . . .

Editor's Note: "Blackbirding" is a practice of kidnapping and forced labour associated with Australia and the Pacific. The poem also references Saddam Hussein's supergun Project Babylon.

QURAYSH ALI LANSANA

seven years

eight hundred miles away for two thousand
five hundred and fifty-five days blanketed
in the melanin rich cocoon of the south side.

jacob squatted in hollow of tree for one hundred
sixty-eight hours til slave catchers passed. only
duppies, good and ornery, vex me here

where it is possible to function, to dream
and never interact with a person of non-
color. more black owned businesses in

my neighborhood than my hometown. can
be thug, threat, teacher, artist, arse, poet
professor, writer, worrier. but sad nigga

in enid, my view obscured by headstones
prison and ferguson. the fools gold of distance.
damp musk of time. grief decomposes on I-44

weather lovely, the politics fucked. fracked up
earth twitches, spits greed. we drive by anyway
led by dollar signs. an uneven stretch of lonely road.

Part 7

I shall create! If not a note, a hole.
If not an overture, a desecration.
—Gwendolyn Brooks, "Boy Breaking Glass"

RITA DOVE

Testifying: A Tribute

How does one begin to convey the influence Gwendolyn Brooks has had on genera-
tions—not only writers, but people from all walks of life? How can one describe the
fiercely personal connection her poems make, how can one chronicle her enormous im-
pact on recent literary, social, and political history?

There is a tradition in the black church: we call it Testifying. It is the brave and
humbling act of standing up among one's family, friends, and neighbors to bare one's
soul, and to bear witness by acknowledging those who have sustained and nurtured the
testifier along the way.

Here, then, is my testimonial honoring Gwendolyn Brooks:

Standing in front of this literary congregation as a grown woman, a woman
who has entered her forties, I feel very strange thinking that when Gwendolyn Brooks was awarded the 1950 Pulitzer Prize for *Annie Allen*, her second
collection of poems, I was not even, as people used to say then, "a twinkle in
my daddy's eye."

I was born two years after Gwendolyn Brooks was awarded the Pulitzer.
She was the first black writer to receive this highest honor in American letters.
And it wasn't until seventeen years later—when as a gawky adolescent I spent
the whole of a muggy midwestern summer combing the local library shelves
for something that might speak to me—that the poems of Gwendolyn Brooks
leapt off the pages of the book in my hands and struck me like a thunderbolt.
These were words that spoke straight from the turbulent center of life—words
that nourished like meat, not frosting. Yes, I was struck by these poems, poems
with muscle and sinew, poems that weren't afraid to take the language and re-
vamp it, twist it and energize it so that it shimmied and dashed and lingered.

From that summer on I read everything by Gwendolyn Brooks that
I could get my hands on: First I went back to her early books, *A Street in
Bronzeville* (1945) and the Pulitzer volume *Annie Allen*; then there was *Selected
Poems*, which came out in 1963, followed by *In the Mecca: Poems* in 1968 and

Riot, published in 1969, the same year she was selected to succeed Carl Sandburg as Poet Laureate of the State of Illinois, a position she still holds. And most recently I admired her *The Near-Johannesburg Boy and Other Poems* (1986) and *Blacks*, collected poems, published by the Third World Press in 1987.

Gwendolyn Brooks also ventured successfully into prose. *Maud Martha*, her moving novel, came out in 1953. The autobiographical remembrances and reflections *Report from Part One* and *The World of Gwendolyn Brooks* were both published in 1972, and in 1980 *Primer for Blacks* appeared.

But Gwendolyn Brooks not only spoke loud and clearly through her books; she made herself heard on numerous disc recordings, in trenchant interviews and through books about her life and creative work. Honors for her outstanding achievements include, besides the Pulitzer Prize and poet laureate position, grants and awards from the likes of the Guggenheim Foundation and the National Institute of Arts and Letters.

As someone who, as a Black child, was educated in a literary tradition that seemed to have little use for my existence except as a caricature or in servitude, and who, as a young person, came of age in a society where the discourse of the melting pot effectively translated into: "Disappear into the mainstream or else," I knew that Gwendolyn Brooks was among the few who gave me the courage to insist on my own story. *And though I never dreamed of following in her footsteps as far as the Pulitzer Prize, her shining example opened up new possibilities for me and generations of younger artists.*

Thank you, Gwendolyn, for your invaluable contributions to changing the face of our world.

OPAL PALMER ADISA

Language of the Unheard

(for Gwendolyn Brooks)

because you took words
under your hat
and made a song

because you stood
unmoved against
the canon and wrote

about how we are
cornbread and songs
feed our cravings

the belittling words
we learn to brush off
then stomp in the ground

i found you
and in finding you
i found my tongue

CLIFFORD THOMPSON

Jazz June

When I was fourteen and nearing the end of eighth grade I developed my first serious crush. The girl, named June, was in ninth grade and about to graduate from the junior high school we attended. Given where my crush ultimately got me—that is, nowhere—June's impending departure, a source of grief for me at the time, was unimportant. June herself, actually, was unimportant. I mean that as a comment not on her worth as a person but on her being the object of my affection, which seems almost completely arbitrary. I was of an age and inclination to make one person the center of my can't-sleep-at-night, can't-focus-on-my-homework longing; along came June, hardly gorgeous but pretty enough, nice if not preternaturally sweet. She fit the bill. I had all I needed to be miserable, which I quickly became, not admitting to myself, possibly not even understanding, that my crush was its own point.

June played the violin. I never heard any of her performances myself, but I heard a lot about them. My friend Big Darryl Greenfield, also a ninth-grader, said about a musical number June played at their graduation, "I don't usually like the violin, but she was tearin' it up." I borrowed Darryl's yearbook so that (I didn't tell him this) I could gaze upon and occasionally kiss June's picture, which showed her smiling in her graduation cap. June was part of a group of musical friends to which I was connected tangentially. To have a stronger tie to those superior beings, I signed up that spring of 1977 for summer clarinet lessons with the DC Youth Orchestra Program—not to be confused with the actual DC Youth Orchestra, the program's elite, of whom June was one.

The program had three levels of bands and orchestras, and I got the unspoken message that the orchestras, with their stringed instruments, were considered more important. While I spent that typically sweltering DC summer riding two buses to my lessons, squawking and squeaking through quarter- and eighth-notes, June went away to a music camp, adding physical distance to the other forms of distance separating us. And as I waited that summer for the promised postcard from her, which never arrived, June—and, by association, the violin—came to represent for me an unattainable ideal.

* * *

June itself, not the girl but the month, has something about it of the unattainable, the unfulfilled promise. That is, paradoxically, because June, at least in the cities where I have spent my life, is the only reliably spring-like month. Spring officially arrives in late March, finding a lot of people still wearing their winter coats; April and even early May sometimes carry a chill. But in June we can venture outside, where green leaves and flowers are, contending neither with the cold nor with the heat of that long march from Independence Day to Labor Day, that season of commuting in sweat-dampened shirt collars over gradually shortening days. June brings freedom and those wonderful extra hours of sunlight, June whispers that anything is possible, and therein lies the ache: as its days fly by—it is, in the end, just another month, and one of the shorter months at that—we may feel a vague regret over what we have yet again failed to achieve, a hint of sadness for what was promised but not delivered.

There is an answer for this, one that has something in common with my long-ago crush on the girl June: a focus on the feeling itself rather than on where it might lead. In my adopted home, New York City, one way that I revel in the feeling of June, of spring, is to walk across the Brooklyn Bridge, particularly at night, when the Manhattan skyline is lit, each of the many brightened windows in the silhouettes of those tall, tall buildings suggesting industry, energy, creativity. The sense of possibility this inspires, the belief that we can *do*, that we can at least try, may lead somewhere; but it is also a wonderful thing all by itself.

* * *

Among her many other poems, Gwendolyn Brooks wrote "We Real Cool," perhaps her most famous work. The poem adopts the viewpoint of marginalized black boys who shoot pool together. Miss Brooks explained about the passage "We/Jazz June" that these boys, effectively locked out of mainstream society, gleefully attack its cherished symbols: to June, that month of

257

wedding announcements in newspapers' society pages, the boys bring jazz, originally the music of the low-down. ("Jazz" was once a verb, synonymous with "fuck.")

I may have read that explanation in a textbook, but it's possible—and this is the version of events I prefer—that I heard it from Miss Brooks' own lips, on the cringe-worthy occasion when I met her. This was in New York in 1991. I was a freelance (read: unemployed) writer of twenty-eight, scrounging for a living, and I had signed on to write a young-adult biography of Miss Brooks. In ninety-nine cases out of a hundred, such books are cobbled together with information from secondary sources, but I saw in the newspaper that Miss Brooks was giving a reading in Manhattan, and so I went, hoping to infuse my project with insights that only the poet herself could provide. To my delight, one of the poems she read that night was "We Real Cool." After the reading, while Miss Brooks greeted friends and signed books, I lurked late, waiting for my chance to speak to her. Finally, noticing this silent young stranger, she turned to me, curious. I explained what I was doing, and she asked what she could do for me. And then, God help me, I said to this Pulitzer Prize–winning septuagenarian, "I was hoping I could buy you a cup of something."

I should add here, to portray Miss Brooks in an appropriately positive light and make myself look like less of a fool, that she later mailed me materials she thought would help my project. (One of them is the book, signed by Miss Brooks, from which I just copied her poem.) In that moment, though, maybe misinterpreting my offer—or, possibly worse, understanding it perfectly—she bent double with laughter; long, loud laughter of embarrassment for me, for us. It's probably superfluous to report that I bought the poet no cups of anything that night, or ever. As she laughed I felt sorry I had said what I did, sorry I'd come at all to see this woman, who seemed to have about as much use for me as did my old schoolmate June.

* * *

We/Jazz June. I have another way of observing and celebrating June: I listen to the late Jaki Byard's solo piano jazz record *Blues for Smoke*, recorded in 1960. Whatever the reason, and it may well be purely subjective, the tunes on *Blues for Smoke*, none more so than "Spanish Tinge No. 1," make me think of soft

June nights, of walking slowly, perhaps aimlessly, through dark streets lined with trees that are thick with leaves, the yellow glow of the occasional street lamp illuminating just enough green foliage to hint at its black depths.

There is also the six-minute title track of Sonny Rollins's album *The Bridge*, from 1962. Prior to making that album, Rollins, a young turk of the tenor saxophone, had found himself being praised by jazz critics even as he sometimes failed to play as well as he wanted. To bring himself closer to what he felt he could do, to pursue what he hoped was possible, Rollins stopped performing and recording for a time and took to practicing his horn on the Brooklyn Bridge. (He eventually settled on the Williamsburg Bridge instead.) "The Bridge," a nod to those days and nights of dogged self-improvement, features contrasts. Rollins plays in a rapid tempo that occasionally slows, possibly reflecting the ebb and flow of traffic on the bridge; and while he often races up and down chords, seemingly playing every note in existence, he sometimes plays impressionistically, blowing isolated two- or four-note phrases, dabs of sound, bringing to mind the pinpoints of light from office windows of the Manhattan skyline. Rollins's practice sessions were not recorded. Still, sometimes during those June walks over the Brooklyn Bridge, I think of those no doubt beautiful sounds, those expressions of feeling, played not long before my birth and heard mainly by Rollins himself. I am happy to be where that music was made, even if it can't be heard, even if, in the traditional sense, it got nowhere.

* * *

I own a clarinet. It was given to me years ago by a friend who found it in the apartment she had just moved into and remembered that I had once played. I don't play anymore. Truth is, I was never very good. There are a number of possible explanations for that—an obvious one, which I don't discount, is simple lack of talent—but an important one may be that I didn't have a model. At age fourteen I didn't know from jazz and wouldn't for years, and so I was without a sense of what was possible on the instrument.

That is not a real regret. I am more than content, today, to be a fan, and to subject my wife and daughters to my fandom. They are good-natured about it. On a recent, chilly autumn day I pulled out one of my oldest jazz CDs, a compilation of the work of the alto saxophonist Julian "Cannonball" Adderley, and played it for my teenaged younger daughter. I have long maintained that the late Cannonball possessed the sweetest sound in all of jazz; I drew my daughter's attention in particular to a ballad called "Spring Is Here," a work my wife once pronounced to be "too beautiful." As we listened to that indeed almost inexpressibly lovely tune, I realized something that I hadn't during the innumerable times I had played this record before, and I said to my daughter about Cannonball's delicate, quivering tone, "He made his horn sound like a violin." And even as, outside, the fall wind stirred brown leaves and deposited them in piles on the wide sidewalks of our Brooklyn neighborhood, I thought for just a moment, hearing that sweet jazz, of June.

to the recorder of history

no ivory tower here if only you could heed
how denizens move in broken iambic,
a fucked up beautiful poem. Language—
a bridge as simple as a fallen log or stone

across a violent river echoing god's nature.
the pigeon-toed strut the scream poetry be
at the corner, the negotiated vagina trade,
a broken english that b not english. a dap

after watching heavy-bottomed women
walk by. two men holding hands, holding
only the love that feels real. this is a place
where timberlands move status quo, where

poetry be hidden out in the open
while ain't nobody looking, listen—

SHARON OLDS

A Note on Gwendolyn Brooks

When I received the invitation to be a part of *Revise the Psalm*, and began to look for a poem of mine which might embody some of the effect of Gwendolyn Brooks' great work on me, I could not find one which adequately represents my immense debt to her. I admire, I love, I am knocked out by, the wild and beautiful power of her poems: the shocking truthfulness; the music; the range of craft—the formal and free verse, the rubbing of the twentieth century stories against the ballad frame; the gift for singing of the individual, with searing feeling and grace, which both carry and transcend the individual; the sense of community. She has been one of the most important poets for me. The riches—sometimes horrors—of the worlds in her poems give profound enlightenment and pleasure to her readers. Her intelligence is impeccable, her imagination sparkly, her ear true. As I looked through my poems for evidence of all I keep learning from her, I couldn't find a poem where it is clearly evident. At the same time, I realized that her work has been like a force-field, pulling my poems a little ways away from their tendency toward the solely autobiographical. Her work has fed my faith in art which nourishes equally truth and community. She has been an example of courage, irony, outspokenness, wit, and gorgeous music and language.

I had the great good fortune to hear Gwendolyn Brooks read, and to meet her briefly, a few times. Her voice had the widest register of any poet's voice I've heard—you could almost score her speaking voice, and you would need to go high up into the treble clef as well as down into the bass. Her voice had a warble to it which conveyed wonder, humor, joy, irony, relish. It was as if she could see every angle of what was being said, and convey the various lights which would reflect off each curve of it. The music of each line and of each sentence was like a tour of, a descant on, that sentence. It was as if more than one person was speaking—or as if she was singing harmony, with no vanity at all, with herself—one aspect of her, of us, singing with another aspect. Oh, she was one person! She was steady as a rock. But she reflected many lights. She contained multitudes.

Such an exemplum of integrity and representation, of the one and the many—without any neurotic warping—gives us an image of the poet as genius and as citizen, of both at once. Just knowing that her work is there makes it possible for our work to move a little closer to it.

I did not know how to say this to her in so many words. I was a little tongue-tied around her. So I gave her flowers, the two or three times I saw her—a small nosegay, with one or two each of several different flowers. I remember the flash of her eyes to mine when she would accept the gift. Her eyes saw a lot! A lot of truth! I felt she understood the tribute and the thanks.

And I'm lucky enough to think of her most days, because when I was walking her back to her hotel from a reading she saw that I was about to step on one of those metal trap doors in the sidewalk, covering some underground stairs down into a basement. Her arm went out in that swift automatic gesture in front of me, stopping me. "I saw a man go down into one of those things, in Chicago," she said, "and he never came back up!" So as I walk in New York City I avoid those cellar doors, and as I write I avoid some of the traps of excess troubled ego, and I think of Gwendolyn Brooks, and I read her poems, and see the best of us.

GWENDOLYN A. MITCHELL

Reading Gwendolyn Brooks

Your words grow with me,
teach talents of life in ordinary
consumption of hours in day.

I live with you now
more than I did in life.
Images of you grace the walls of my home and workspace.
  Your eyes are in a fixed
  watch along hallways;
  you disregard my presence.
  Your smile hides some other knowing,
  a secret I must learn on my own.

Tidbits from your vastness of language
are found in epigraphs for daily living.
I come back to your words, often,
looking for an opening in which to seek refuge,
glimpses of the selves we share.

And then this poem stopped me in my tracks.
Stood up and slapped me in the face
If I can be so bold as to personify your lexeme.

Look at me, look at us
at this time in our lives
older than we could imagine, yet not as old as elder.

I, too, "am aware there is winter to heed."
Cold that will not end inhabits my bones,
cramps my fingers as I manage this surface.
So I look to you again,
consider your urging to find beauty, even in this time of discontent,
and stop to enjoy the sunset.

SANDRA CISNEROS

Letter to Gwendolyn Brooks

I once ran into Gwendolyn Brooks in the basement of the Stop & Shop in downtown Chicago. This was when she knew me as a high school teacher and not as a writer. She was standing in line at the bakery counter looking like a mother coming home from work.

"Miss Brooks, what are you doing here?"

"I'm buying a cake," Miss Brooks said matter-of-factly.

Of course she was buying a cake. Still, it didn't seem possible then that poets of her stature went downtown on the subway and bought themselves cakes. Gwendolyn Brooks was famous, maybe the most famous person I knew then, and I admired her greatly. I'd been reading her work since high school. To meet her at a university or bookstore was one thing. But here she was waiting to buy a cake! She didn't look like a Pulitzer Prize–winning author. She looked like a sparrow or a nun in the modest brown and navy she always wore.

Like Elena Poniatowska, she taught me what it is to be generous to others, to speak to every member of your public as if they were the guest writer, and not the other way round.

This generosity and way of honoring her readers has made me see her not only as a great poet but as a great human being, and this, in my book, is the greatest kind of writer of all.

This letter was written while I was guest professor at the University of New Mexico, Albuquerque.

March 5, 1991

Dear Miss Brooks,

It is what Winnie-the-Pooh would call a blustery day here.

Or what Miss Emily would designate a wind like a bugle. From over and over the mesas, snapping dust and terrifying trees.

I am in my pajamas though it's past midday but I like my leisure to dream a little longer when I am asleep, and continue dreaming on paper when I am awake. I am rereading your *Maud Martha* again, a copy you gave me, and which I am very grateful to have. I remember when I first discovered that book, in the American library in Sarajevo, across from the famous river where the archduke was shot that started a world war. And it was there too that I read T. S. Eliot's collected poems. If you go to Sarajevo and look at the chapter on *Practical Cats* you'll see a cherry stain on one of the pages—because I was reading the book on the opposite bank of the river, under a row of cherry trees in front of my American friend Ana's apartment house, and at the moment I was reading about one of Eliot's cats—the Rum Tum Tugger?—a wind shook a cherry loose that landed with a startled plop on the page. And my heart gave a little jump too because the book wasn't mine. A wine-colored stain against the thick creamy pages.

I mean to teach it one day along with other books that use a series of short interrelated stories. Perhaps with Ermilo Abreu Gómez's *Canek* and Nellie Campobello's *Cartucho* albeit the translation of both is crooked. The form fascinates. And I'd done as much with *Mango Street*, though I hadn't met your Maud yet. Perhaps I was "recollecting the things to come."

Miss Brooks, please know I haven't quite disappeared altogether from the land. I've been migrant professor these past years, guest writer in residence at UC Berkeley, UC Irvine, the University of Michigan at Ann Arbor and now here for one semester. All for the sake of protecting my writer self. Some years dipped low and some reeled to high heaven. But now the days are good to me. I have a new book due out from Random (see enclosed reviews) and I have sold my little house on Mango to the big house of Vintage. Both books slated for this April. And it seems my life is a whirl like the wind outside my window today. Everything is shook and snapped and wind-washed and fresh, and, yes, that is how it should be.

I only wanted to say this to you today. That your book gives me much pleasure. That I admire it terribly. I think of you often, Miss Brooks, and your spirit is with me always.

un abrazo fuerte, fuerte,
Sandra

Nobody Knows My Name

Gwendolyn Brooks' first (and only) novel, *Maud Martha*, came to me as a stack of photocopied pages from a local shop in Harvard Square. The book was out of print and available only in limited quantities, so the class trekked over to the shop to purchase the packet. This was the early 1990s, and the seminar on African-American women writers was led by Henry Louis Gates Jr. The class was filled mostly with young white women who spoke about Octavia Butler, Ann Petry, Nella Larsen, and Toni Morrison with a commanding authority that I could never place. I sat mostly in silence in that class at Harvard, bristling at times at how easily some drifted into shaky political commentary, Professor Gates always guiding the seminar back to the solid foundation of the texts at hand.

Professor Gates called me into his office a few weeks into the seminar, along with a beautiful, beautiful young man of mixed heritage (who was the object of my silent crush). We were the only two people of color in the class. I could look neither of them in the eye, and when Professor Gates sat us down and asked why we were so reluctant to speak in class, I had no answer. On the way out, he said, "I need you to speak up."

It was humbling, to say the least, and Professor Gates said nothing explicitly about the incongruity of a student like me, poor and Chicano, not having a word—not one!—to say about why these women had written about exclusion. From then on, I walked into that seminar terrified, having prepared feverishly for each one, only to come up empty and silent, and watching my beautiful, beautiful crush meet Professor Gates' challenge head on with his own enthusiastic contributions.

My big chance arrived when it came time to discuss *Maud Martha*. While I had respected and enjoyed many of the other texts, Miss Brooks' novel was the first I truly, deeply *loved*. I had been moved by it: a slim novel, it managed an epic arc by the simplest of conceits, the construction of a life via the careful arrangement and presentation of thirty-four episodic chapters. It was an odd novel, to be sure—short, but dazzling, with a reliance on poetic devices that forced me (for once) to slow down in my reading. Maud Martha, a woman growing through pre-WWII Chicago, goes hardly anywhere in the novel and does very little—but her mind! An imaginative person, she is cast by Miss Brooks as a woman who recognizes that the narrative of one's life hardly ever matches what we think of as "plot" in a novel. Maud Martha may be confined, but she can *perceive*, and it is the power of her imagination that allows her to be at once aware of her position in the world, but not complacent in accepting it. She's generous, too, in observing how others manage (or fail) to cope with the same frustrating knowledge.

But I couldn't say a word about *Maud Martha* in the seminar. Already, I was learning that to *admire* a book was to speak first and foremost about its content (not its language, not its structure, and, least of all, not its emotion—a book was not to be loved). All I could do was listen to the discussion of the book's history. It was in this class that I learned why this 1953 novel had fallen out of print, with Miss Brooks failing to get much support from the more visible African-American writers, all male. It was in this class that I learned of Wallace Stevens's caustic "coon" comment*, providing context to her bravery in crashing the old-boy network of American letters. And it was in this class, too, that I listened to my classmates discuss the novel as a failed experiment, as the work of a poet who was clearly a master of language, but who didn't understand the basic structure or demands of a novel.

What I didn't know then was that a great respect is commanded by artists who break rules. What I didn't know then was how revolutionary it was to have a woman of such discernment at the center of a novel. What I didn't know then was that good artists (but maybe not critics) always ask a simple question about formal decisions: why? If a novel is episodic and breaks the conventions of a typical narrative, good artists know the first reaction should never be *This is a failure.* It should be *Why?*

But I failed Gwendolyn Brooks by not defending her, by not attempting an answer to *Why?* I would hate to think of how a creative writing workshop would dismantle her glorious thirteenth chapter, "Low Yellow," in which the point of view seems an abrupt change to first person. It is, in fact, a superbly timed self-assertion, a veiled *I* finally breaking through, all clued in by the slight "Maud Martha thought." But I couldn't explain it then, why this timing was important. Nor could I explain why the panoramic chapter "Kitchenette Folks," with its studied detail of Maud Martha's neighbors, ends up telling us more about Maud Martha as a uniquely gifted observer than the people being described.

A novel built on allusion and narrative cross-current is difficult to assess, much more so when the choice of the central character is a figure so often dismissed in American society. A woman like Maud Martha (meaning, poor and African American) isn't "compelling," even if she is more literate about her own life than most Americans could ever be about theirs. What I, poor and Chicano, understood immediately about the book, was the desperate need for narrative in whatever shape could be wrestled from the life around. But that was the language of a writer (not a book critic or, worse, a book reviewer) and so I stayed silent.

It is no wonder to me that *Maud Martha* was underappreciated in its own time and fell out of print. It hurts to think of how even an accomplished writer like Miss Brooks (a Pulitzer winner in poetry by the time this novel appeared in 1953) could be met with such disregard. Her aim was quite simple: James Baldwin, in the opening essay of *Nobody Knows My Name*, summed it up for many other writers on the margins when he wrote that his investigation of what it meant to be an American was about how "I wanted to find out in what way the *specialness* of my experience could be made to connect me with other people instead of dividing me from them."

Maud Martha, the character, was no writer, but Gwendolyn Brooks had her reach the understandings we expect and demand of novelists. "She watched the little dreams of smoke as they spiraled about his hand," Miss Brooks writes, as Maud Martha observes her husband Paul at a nightclub, "and she thought about happenings. She was afraid to suggest to him that, to most people, nothing at all 'happens.' That most people merely live from day to day until they die. That, after he had been dead for a year, doubtless fewer than five people would think of him oftener than once a year. That there might even come a year when no one on earth would think of him at all."

It might be just too tough for some readers to bear, that a person whom society never regards as the center of anything could hold such inscrutable and powerful knowledge, the creator of a puzzle only she can unlock. Back then, I had been learning to see myself in Maud Martha. But I did not yet have the words to describe what I was beginning to recognize about the power of the unnoticed observer, the bravery and grace of the meek and the small. It would take me years to understand what the novel had long ago shown me: that there is value in even the quietest voice in the room.

* *Major Jackson, "Wallace Stevens After 'Lunch,'" Harriet: A Poetry Blog, The Poetry Foundation, http://www.poetryfoundation.org/harriet/2008/02/wallace-stevens-after-lunch.*

DAMARIS HILL

A Haiku for Gwendolyn Brooks

Lady Dunbar's song.
whiff it, this prayer of wonder.
this fire wet with life.

EUGENE B. REDMOND

Journaling with Gwendolyn Brooks Kwansaba-Style 2016: A Pastiche of Poetic Reports on Her Life & Works

I

Let's climb "organic" blues tiers with Gwen
who ballad-deared & sonnetized our fears.
Went, wince-less, into war, beauty-filling
America's left-over people with bardic noir.
Stood with *Annie Allen*, *Maud*, *Satin Legs*
& *Blacks*. Report'd life-parts hacked by
rail road tracks. Re: begin with Gwen.

II

Some "magic," she said, should balance a
labored "brain." Either case, poetry's grain's immense
& intense: Stay cocked: "ready/to be ready,"
whether in Little Rock or Johannesburg. Sermons
& summons occur in faith or fact.
Long as we're prepped to act in
East Boogie or Chi-Raq, Gwen sends.

III

"Terse" Gwen called Michael
            Harper's *Coltrane* poems "brilliant,"
"blood-stuffed," "black-based and other."

IV

Children headin' home don't always get there.
Some aren't even gotten. But mothers never
forget them—fathers neither. Moon while, Black
boys hang tight & often loose—like
"lynchee/s." Others, raised in pool halls, are

re-raised from pools of blood/s. Still
pooling as Rangers, Nations, Isms—in Hoods.

V
Every back has a yard where dreams
stand guard. But you can only sashay
so far before you stumble upon a
fallen star. Hipsofical poets raise the (corner)
bar: "Black"/blue/"Unknown" birds of song
breakin', healing wings &, like Haki, go
long: Gwen's dens hold writers rebel-strong.

QURAYSH ALI LANSANA

The Weight of the Word

I moved to Chicago in 1989, leaving behind an ugly experience in broadcast journalism and contempt for the state of Oklahoma only natives can truly appreciate. I arrived with two suitcases, a folder full of poems, and big dreams of reinventing myself as a poet in the city that fed some of my guiding lights: Malcolm X, Haki Madhubuti, and Gwendolyn Brooks.

In 1993, while working with the programming committee of Guild Literary Complex, one of the Midwest's most significant literary centers, I was asked to help develop an idea Miss Brooks was cooking up with Complex founder, poet Michael Warr. She wanted to hold an annual open mic poetry contest and award the winner of said contest $500 of her own monies. Not Illinois Poet Laureate cash, but a personal check from her pocketbook. This is how I met Miss Brooks, swaddled in the democracy and generosity of her spirit.

Two years later, while driving her home after the third Gwendolyn Brooks Open Mic Award contest, I mentioned I was considering a return to academia to complete my BA, abandoned in 1985 at the University of Oklahoma. She enthusiastically reminded me that Prof. Haki Madhubuti, her publisher and founder of Third World Press, was at Chicago State University and that I should look no other place. I was reserved about her suggestion initially, remembering my bankrupt attempt of a manuscript Third World Press rejected only a year earlier. Noting my hesitation, Miss Brooks offered to speak with him about school, not my manuscript.

Neither Miss Brooks nor I knew at the time that within a year we would workshop weekly in the conference room of the center created in her honor.

Madhubuti founded the Gwendolyn Brooks Center for Black Literature and Creative Writing at Chicago State University in 1990. He also initiated the Brooks Conference for Writers of African Descent in the same year. I had met Prof. Madhubuti previously, on the floor of his flagship bookstore and African-centered school. He was what many of my Black male friends wanted to be when we grew up: a builder of positive reality.

In Spring 1997, Miss Brooks sat with eleven young poets of varying levels every Tuesday evening for two-and-a-half hours. It was joy. It was torture. It was Prof. Madhubuti who convinced Miss Brooks to lead this one last semester-long poetry workshop. Unfortunately, it was to be her final collegiate class.

Miss Brooks in workshop was a marvel and a wonder. She was an igniter of mind riots. She dropped morsels of ideas: clippings from newspapers, poems by authors she admired, assignments in traditional forms, then sat back and watched us scramble, scrap, and heave. All the while a mischievous, wide grin on her dimpled face, rubbing her hands in delight. She loved instigating, agitating. My work benefited from her firm nudging. It also benefited from her fierce red pen.

Miss Brooks made it very clear revision is a part of the creative process, and clearly her work is proof of that mantra. She did not believe in waste. Hers was a hand of precision, and she often spoke of laboring for months over a single word.

The piece that begins with the short poem by Langston Hughes (eventually titled "baggage") was inspired by the work of my close friend and *The Walmart Republic* co-author Christopher Stewart. What is printed here is a later draft, very close to the way the poem appears in my first book, *Southside Rain*. In one of the many earlier drafts, Miss Brooks commented on the fifth stanza by writing:

"not 'slipping' into? Doesn't an 'orifice' have a wall?
Wouldn't that prevent through—slipping?"

How hard-headed was I? The edits she suggests here fail to manifest in the final version.

On the same draft she wrote the following regarding the sixth stanza:

"rich, fatty soul food is also soft, so
teeth could hardly be cut upon it."

These lines remain unchanged in the draft printed here. However, I finally caught on for the published version:

or would you collect them,
while struggling to remember

the stuff that makes us whole.

Additionally, Miss Brooks and I tinkered with the second stanza of the draft printed here, and ultimately agreed to jettison "the mattresses of mom and dad" for "your parents' mattresses."

Addressing current events in verse was important to Miss Brooks, as any student of her work is acutely aware. "smolder" was born not only of an assignment, but of the evening news hitting literally very close to home.

The years 1995 and 1996 saw a rash of Black church bombings, in mostly Southern states, but a few in the North and Midwest as well. The First Baptist Church of Enid, Oklahoma, located three blocks south of the church in which I was raised, was leveled by a slightly disturbed gentleman who claimed he was simply "copy-catting." Regardless of his motives, he displaced and disrupted the lives of many relatives and old family friends. My people were on edge for weeks. I penned the first drafts (the first stanza and most of the final stanza in the version printed here) in Chicago.

Perhaps a month after the First Baptist bombing I went home for a visit. While sitting in the cluttered, historic landmark that was the living room of my eccentric aunt, the late Marie Adams (we called her Aunt Ree'), I realized the depth of her struggle to forgive (one of the cornerstones of Christianity) this crazy dude who blew up any church, let alone a church in our hometown:

he got a white face
but he got blood
just like mine

Miss Brooks immediately gravitated toward the quote. It made the poem human, personal. Something that was second nature for her.

Her comments on the bottom of the page refer to edits I implemented for the third stanza. In an earlier draft, the poem closes:

while a cross burns
the saints meeting place
she prays for better days
in the ashes of 1996

The draft printed here seems unwieldy, particularly the second line. She compared the drafts, and, after much discussion, we met in the middle for the finished product:

aunt ree has lived
through the mississippi
of sheeted heads
soiling family hands

she say
he got a white face
but he got blood
just like mine
she prays for better days
in the ashes of 1996
while a cross burns
the saints' meeting place

At the conclusion of the semester, the class, now the Gwendolyn Brooks Writers Collective and only nine in number, initiated a tradition by taking Miss Brooks out to dinner. She reciprocated, inviting us to a meal that next Christmas. It was at our Spring/Summer outing in 1999 that her ill-health was becoming apparent. She was very frail, and, uncharacteristically for Miss Brooks, did not have much of an appetite. We worried that she didn't like the restaurant. She didn't, but there was more to it than this. Prof. Madhubuti, who was always very protective of Miss Brooks, was more tight-lipped than usual.

That August, my wife Emily, my two sons (now four), and I went to visit Miss Brooks at her condo the day before we moved to New York City. I had been accepted to the MFA Creative Writing Program at NYU, a graduate school journey Miss Brooks helped initiate and further. She crafted recommendation letters on my behalf and mailed them to Sharon Olds at NYU and the late Michael Harper at Brown. She was weak and clearly in pain, though gracious and playful as always. She loved my sons, and demanded to be either the first or second person phoned upon their births. She was second for both. The photo I shot of her with Emily, Nile and Onam sitting on her piano bench is bittersweet joy. It is one of the last photos of Miss Brooks. She joined the ancestors three and a half months later.

Helping to carry her casket through Rockefeller Chapel was among the most difficult tasks I've experienced. I sobbed with the weight of her, of the inverted metaphor. She held me up, both prior to and after our loveship began, through marriage, births, my first teaching gig, and my first book. The blizzard raging outside the chapel was also metaphor, also very Gwendolynian.

Miss Brooks chose me, and Baba Haki groomed me to become director of the Brooks Center. This was my dream job since attending my first Black Writers Conference in the early nineties. This was the work I was built for since eighth grade, when her poetry and this new art called hip-hop changed my way of seeing. I was honored to help guide that remarkably special space for nine years, and loathe the way it ended. That is another essay.

I led workshops, taught class or held meetings in *her* conference room, the conference room of the Gwendolyn Brooks Center, almost every day for nine academic years. It was both an honor and a chore. But, most of all, I loved to open the door to the Center when no one was in but the two of us.

Baggage

When you turn the corner
And you run into yourself
Then you know that you have turned
All the corners that are left

"Final Curve" by Langston Hughes

[handwritten annotations: "Wasn't this a treasure?! How far-seeing was this guy!" "This poem is excellent + Remarkably well-controlled. The rhythms are exciting"]

what if you woke up one day
and all of your blunders had left you?
your poor judgement calls
your lack of good sense
a lifetime of mistakes
parading around the living room
as you stare in subconscious awe
in your underwear

the money you stole from between ~~mom and dad's mattresses~~ *[handwritten: the mattresses of mom and dad]*
while looking for the true detective magazines

[handwritten: Otherwise you've left "mom" with no possessive]

the distress call you sent out on the cb radio
that hailed ten unhappy truck drivers to your front door

the lie you told your lover
to conceal your other lover

would you feel them departing?
slipping through any available orifice
leaving you lightheaded and stain free?

or would you collect them
while struggling to remember
cutting your teeth on this pain
this rich, fatty soul food

the stuff that makes you whole

Quraysh Ali Lansana

Smolder

smolder

Aunt 'Ree has lived
through the mississippi red
of white sheeted men
staining family hands

she say
he got a white face
but he got blood
just like mine

while a cross burns
the meeting place of her salvation,
she prays for better days
in the ashes of 1996

Quraysh Ali Lansana

→ Glad you added the quotes

I liked your original "pretty much," right?!
I, too, believe the "saints meeting place"
is better. (But is it "saints" or
saints'?)

Part 8

"And remembering . . .
Remembering, with twinklings and twinges"
—Gwendolyn Brooks, "The Bean Eaters"

Reading poetry teaches me about the world, about myself, clarifies what I feel, what I don't know or understand. Reading poetry makes me feel connected to the greater human experience. Growing up, reading Gwendolyn Brooks' poems, peopled with real-life characters like those of my blue-collar childhood, offered insight into how to live as a more hopeful and compassionate human being. For me the writing of poems grows out of the reading of them. I attempt to make sense of life, to make meaning, to connect, to be in conversation with others. Writing poetry is the way I discover and express my humanity.

My poem "A Depraved Indifference 2 Human Life" was written after an acquaintance of mine, Tanya Taggerty, was murdered by a cop. 4 me, it's a vibrant snapshot in time involving addressing the most often inconsequential climate of police brutality, particularly against people of color.

That's what strikes me as most Gwen-like; dealing uncompromisingly with modern issues but, still, in a creative enough way 2 leave the viewer/listener with a lasting impression, such as with her "In the Mecca:," "YOUNG HEROES I Keorapetse Kgositsile (Willie)," and "Riot" works. As I use a quote of hers in my own letterhead, "Truth tellers."

Gwen knew my mom. I don't know how well because she had a way of making everyone feel like an old, familiar acquaintance. But I do know that she knew my mom as the woman with the "big beautiful natural" (that she wears to this day). I used that point of recognition to reacquaint myself with her many times over the years after meeting her as a child. I always felt as if she know exactly whose child I was.

Years later I got 2 talk with her at some length when she visited my college. In the conversation she must've asked me if I was still playing my instrument. I told her, fleetingly, that it had recently been stolen from the dorm room where it was kept. We continued 2 talk while she began writing on a small sheet of lined paper from her notepad. When she finished, she tore out the note and gave it 2 me. The note said that if I would get a letter from my father, a known composer/musician, saying that he would continue training me on the saxophone, she would purchase me a replacement. I was floored. Excitedly, I told my mother that day. I attempted to get the note from my dad but never really followed through. I never got that horn. Soon thereafter, I was doing poetry instead of playing music. I kept the note though. She was an incredibly amazing and gracious woman.

I was never blessed to meet Gwendolyn Brooks while she was alive. It seemed like every time the opportunity presented itself, like at the spoken word events or annual conferences at Chicago State University, I was working. That's why Miss Brooks' poem "Kitchen Building" reminded me of an old tendency I had—to be intimate with life's rigors while a stranger to my dreams and passions. It's an uncomfortable truth, but one I had to face to change. This led to meeting writers who were shaped directly or indirectly by Miss Brooks' passion for words, Chicago, and presenting realities readers could feel in their bones.

I am a prose writer, not a poet, but like Miss Brooks, I write about truths that are hard to swallow but still need to shared. "The Last Supper" is about an abused woman who takes daily beatings from her husband but draws the line when he sexually abuses their son. This story stays with you. You will remember Julia, the protagonist whose father cherished her and whose husband derided her. Hopefully, you will recall her woe and unseemly victory as I can easily recall the women Miss Brooks wrote about in "Mother" and "BRELVE. A Battered Woman." It's haunting to think you can never get past your own harsh realities, like the woman in "Mother" who will always remember ,"the children she got but did not get," or the one who faces an end of love and her own mortality as the man she loves doubles as a brutal stranger. I can only hope my words honor the truth as Miss Brooks does.

What I remember most about the gatherings of black writers in Chicago during the 1980s and '90s was the reverence held by everyone present for Gwendolyn Brooks. She was the Queen Mother Poet and she was ours because she lived and created her poetry on the South Side of Chicago. Though she was celebrated worldwide, here, she was home. And she was accessible. Younger black poets were nurtured by her—Haki Madhubuti among them, and he was her adopted sun-son. He always seemed tireless in his efforts to honor and pay tribute to Gwen. Third World Press sponsored many gatherings of black writers, and always present were Gwen's other adopted sons and daughters of poetry—Sonia Sanchez, Mari Evans, Angela Jackson, Eugene Redmond, and so many others. Her children Henry and Nora always by her side. As a photographer, educator, and African American literature instructor, I relished every opportunity to be at these gatherings with my camera. It was like shooting a family reunion.

The images included in this anthology are from a Third World Press Artists and Writers Conference and another Black Writers gathering during 1986 and '87.

DAVID BUBLITZ

anecdote

For Miss Brooks, for Quraysh Ali Lansana

i met miss brooks through The Mother's love
i met miss brooks through a heritage of poetic craft
cradling my head long-fingered across tumult,
marriage, ache, death, through the meter
and mentoring of mystic turf, her reach, her dna, his dna,
my dna deliberate, angry, gentle, listening
i met miss brooks through a patient discipline,
her reach, unfinished, yes, pain-printed, yes, but carried
proudly, passed to my hands—this is how the truth is to be said
i met miss brooks through her unfinished reach, unfinished
ever-made

I remember Gwendolyn Brooks as a pivotal literary figure from my high school days in Chicago. As a young artist in the seventies I visited the South Side Community Art Center (SSCAC)—that historic art institution that began during the time of the Works Progress Administration (WPA). The SSCAC was an important incubator for writers and artists from the thirties through the Black Arts Movement of the sixties and seventies and beyond. It was there that I met Gwendolyn Brooks and her daughter Nora during my frequent visits for art classes, exhibitions, and National Conference of Artists (NCA) meetings. After obtaining my fine art degree from Howard University in 1979, I returned to Chicago and designed and illustrated book covers for Haki Madhubuti's Third World Press. I was honored to illustrate the cover of Gwendolyn Brooks' *To Disembark*, published in 1981. The photo I incorporated in the cover design was taken in Ghana in 1977 when I was awarded a fellowship to travel and study the work of contemporary African artists in four African countries. The background graphic was from a silkscreen print I created in response to my travels.

My poetry blooms from the seeds the Illinois Poet Laureate sowed in her famous works, "Kitchenette Building" and "We Real Cool." I read these poems at the age of thirteen and have been writing poetry ever since.

"Brooks" culture and literary ambiance cultivated my written and performance poetry.

In 2014, I earned a spot as a semi-finalist among the almost one hundred entries in the Guild Literary Complex's Gwendolyn Brooks' Open Mic Awards competition. This experience led to recommendations for me to participate as a reader of selections from Miss Brooks' *Maude Martha* during the third annual Brooks Day celebration. "My Mother's Clothes" rings true to the essence of Miss Brooks' words.

My piece that appears in these pages, "Dog in a Dead Man's House," has lines inspired by Miss Brooks' famous "We Real Cool" poem. Her poem was one of the first ones that taught me The Magic of the Line, and how the end of the line should not be the end of the sentence.

My mother fed me poetry as a child—Langston Hughes, Paul Laurence Dunbar, Maya Angelou. But somehow I don't remember encountering Gwendolyn Brooks until a class with Robert Stepto at Yale.

I was an underclassman, stomach at a boil from the witch's brew of privilege plus insecurity that one might expect from living in an institution like that, yet looking like/thinking like/feeling like me. The poem was "The Mother." Through her courage to write and publish those words, to give voice to someone society would have silenced, Miss Brooks gave me a model of how to take up space. She demonstrated that approachable language could be profound—not in spite of, but because of, itself. And by unpacking the speaker's ambivalence—and in it showing strength—she clarified that vulnerability did not need apology. It was revelatory.

But not at first; at first I could only stash all that in my luggage. Miss Brooks has affected my life with a slow burn.

More than fifteen years after that class, Miss Brooks reappeared. I'd arrived at the year I would finally claim my identity as a creative writer, by submitting a poem to the Guild Literary Complex's Gwendolyn Brooks Open Mic Award—a contest that she'd founded. Although I did not win, I went home rich with the experience of a welcoming space in which to share my own secret thoughts about being Black, female, human. By lending her name, she created that possibility.

And then the ripple effect. That evening led to my chance to join the Guild's Poetry Performance Incubator, one of the most challenging, inspiring creative collaborations I've ever been part of. The Incubator then led to me serving for a time as the Guild's Executive Director—the definition of "the toughest job you'll ever love." And in 2013 and 2015 I was honored to read among amazing rosters of artists, community leaders, teachers, and others in the Guild's annual tribute to the amazing Miss Brooks.

With this cycle of dormancy, then flower, that Gwendolyn Brooks' influence has repeated in my life, I'm beginning to suspect this all started long before that college class, and will continue long after today. Maybe my mother whispered lines from "Bronzeville Boys and Girls" over her round belly. Maybe someone else will recite "the rites for Cousin Vit" after I'm gone. And Miss Brooks ripples on:

"Oh oh. Too much. Too much. Even now, surmise, She rises in the sunshine. There she goes . . . "

I was fortunate to be invited to accompany Gwendolyn Brooks to a conference in downtown Chicago during the 1980s. As a member of OBAC (Organization of Black American Culture), the oldest black arts workshop of its kind in the US, and a graduate student at Governors State University, I was asked by my advisor to bring Miss Brooks down to a conference where she was to speak. I was delighted. I'd never met Miss Brooks but felt a kinship of sorts since I learned that she and my mother were in the same graduating class at Englewood High School. In fact, my mother and I would muse at Miss Brooks' photo practically adjacent to my mother's in the yearbook. My mother didn't know Miss Brooks, but described her as a quiet student.

The limousine arrived at the University—a long white limo driven by a black male driver. I climbed into the back and spoke briefly to the driver who seemed to be a block away! We made our way from University Park, a suburb of Chicago, and onto Miss Brooks' inner-city dwelling. As we approached, she emerged from her home to join us. I had Gwendolyn Brooks all to myself for the drive from the South Side to downtown Chicago, approximately a half hour. As we pulled away, I introduced myself and fumbled for something to say. I gushed that she and my mother had graduated together. Then after a brief exchange we were silent. Then Miss Brooks turned to me and with rapt attention and said, "I know all about me, Judy. I want to know about you." And Gwendolyn Brooks sat poised on the back seat of that massive limousine and looked into my spirit.

The kind of respect and attention she gave to me was something she was famous for sharing with all younger people she encountered. And it is that caring that inspired my entry into this anthology, "Kenny's Friend." I hope it is reminiscent of the elder reaching out to a young person in need, overcoming the stereotypes that too often can separate us—a fitting tribute to Gwendolyn Brooks' legacy.

In 1998 I was in graduate school at the University of Wisconsin-Madison. I was a proud graduate of an HBCU, Jackson State University, and I was trying to find my footing, not only at a new grad school in the upper Midwest, but as a married and pregnant twenty-two-year-old. On the day that Miss Brooks was to arrive, I was sick and fatigued. I knew that I couldn't miss her reading and Q&A considering my focus was African American feminist literature—it was the obvious expectation.

When she walked to the speaker stand she reminded me of my grandmother, and I tried not to stare at her as she stood quietly, surrounded by movement. It was cold that day and she was dressed heavily in layers. I listened to her and realized I was experiencing our Black greatness, our genius. I was still young and grateful enough to not be as cynical as many of my white peers. I listened like she was royalty—to me she was. I could hardly focus; this was the writer we studied almost exclusively, from elementary to high school, if we studied African American literature. In many ways, she was the voice of all of "us," and I was in the room with her.

After the reading I asked her, rather clumsily, if she would touch my belly. I remembered to tell her I was pregnant because many people just thought I was just fat. She looked at me and said, "Do you think it will help?" and I must have looked desperate as I said, "Yes . . . I mean . . . I would be honored if you would . . . " Looking back, I realized how strange that probably was, but she did it and said, "Good luck, and read to the baby . . . " I considered her touch and her move that day: . . . reading as a diving blessing that day; I didn't mind being a groupie and I still read to and with my children.

Personal Reflection
During a Cave Canem Retreat I attended, Toi Derricotte looked at the circle of writers and said, "Poems are everywhere, you just have to lift your net to catch them." Miss Brooks did not waste anytime observing, speaking as, and

teaching as she wrote about the South Side of Chicago. I have been completely inspired by the way Miss Brooks spoke of her environment with a vast net but with the precision of threading a needle. The works I have included are exclusively about my experiences as a mother of a young black boy and little girl in Kansas City, Missouri. From the location of the elite Plaza to the well known black-owned dance school, I took the city landscape and wrote from a personal place. Like Miss Brooks, I am interested in the push and pull of motherhood, the protection and the release. She is revealing without being too personal, yet she personalizes the macrocosm called Chicago. Miss Brooks writes poetry like a dance, and this is my homage to her work and its impact on me as a poet.

CALVIN FORBES

I fell under the spell of Gwendolyn Brooks' poetry during my time as a student and in the early days of teaching. The feelings I had for her poetry didn't leave me as I moved from New York City, to Boston, to Washington, DC where I had a chance to set eyes on her in person. I heard her read for the first time when she was the Consultant in Poetry at the Library of Congress from 1985 to 1986. I can't say whether her poetry influenced me or not, but I can, without hesitation, report that I have always enjoyed her work, and I still turn to her poems for pleasure and inspiration, however corny that might sound. When I moved to Chicago in 1991 I had a chance to hear her read a few more times. One in particular, at the Borders' Bookstore on Michigan Avenue, was a very memorable experience. It would be naïve or worse for me to suggest that I knew Gwendolyn Brooks, but I will always think of her as someone both kind and firm in her convictions and a poet I will always treasure.

I know Miss Brooks through her words. They have been inspiration for my work. I think every search for identity is a Diaspora. Not a historical Diaspora in terms of the Jews leaving a land not theirs to one that is, or the reverse Diaspora of African slavery as the forced leaving of a land that is theirs to one that isn't. Or the intended Diaspora of Miss Brooks' poem, *To the Diaspora*, as a return to the homeland for a visit. Or the Native American Diaspora as going away from the land as it was to the same land as it is in someone else's sight. Diaspora may not be the exact word in my case. Maybe the word is exile. An exile on one's own land. Whatever the interpretation, I think for most, identity is travel to a place "rough to reach."

What was going on in the backstory of the old photograph in my mother's album is evident in the look on my face. Of being placed on a precarious vehicle held by my mother's hands. Of being a show-piece in the captivity of infancy. I was not happy there. She was white and pretty, and I had the dark hair and olive skin of my father. It would be a long and disputed journey to the mixed place I was from. But "Here is some sun," Miss Brooks tells us in her poem.

JAKI SHELTON GREEN

Reflections: Experiencing Gwendolyn Brooks

Poet Lance Jeffers introduced me to Gwendolyn Brooks in the early 1970s when she was speaking at the University of North Carolina, Chapel Hill. I was a young frustrated twenty-something-year-old, married with two children and literally *writing for my life*.

During her poetry reading, my son Segun, who was just getting into the swing of pulling up and attempting to walk, crawled to the podium where she was speaking, grabbed the bottom of Gwendolyn Brooks' skirt, and gleefully bounced up and down. I was truly mortified, but this sweet woman told us to "let the baby be." The sight of my son (now forty-four years old) bouncing at her feet is forever etched in my spirit.

Gwendolyn Brooks was a beam of guiding light as I attempted to work in my own rock garden of creativity in the darkest of hours. She impressed the principle of honoring and protecting my voice and to always write from the heart . . . even if the heart is dangling from a bloody precipice.

These words by Gwendolyn Brooks continue to chart my flow . . . "We *are each other's harvest; we are each other's business; we are each other's magnitude and bond.*"

I have been reading Gwendolyn Brooks poems since I was a girl. I will celebrate my sixty-third birthday this year. Each time I return to her poems I discover something new. This past year I immersed myself in her work to teach the poems for the first time. I re-read *Blacks* and *Report from Part One* and *Report from Part Two*. What stands out most for me is the universality of Gwendolyn Brooks' work. I especially admire how she uses the interior of the poem as a space for making public the private lives of black people and thereby helps readers imagine black lives and develop an understanding for our experiences. This reminds me of the call made by W.E.B. DuBois in his 1926 address, "Criteria of Negro Art," for the black artist, "To use Beauty, Truth, and Justice as vehicles of universal understanding," and, to counterbalance: ". . . racial pre-judgment which deliberately distorts Truth and Justice, as far as colored races are concerned."

Her sonnets and ballads place her work within a larger literary tradition and you can see her influence throughout the canon. I stand in her light.

DAMARIS HILL

Reflection

I have been raised by women. Women that understand that indoctrination is
a type of subjugation if you be black and sometimes painful. They taught me
how to nurse a hydra. One head was the razor edge of a syllabus that ended in
wounds. The others were books, reading lists of the masters whose tentacles
seemed to end in branches, furious flowers and afro-coiled strands.

Although I came across Gwendolyn Brooks' work in a few anthologies,
I learned her work from the tongues of Monifa Love Asante, Lucille Clifton,
Nikky Finney, Joanne Gabbin, Sonia Sanchez, Natasha Trethewey, and others. To hear them recite her work was like catching summer rain with your
mouth open. It is a way to be wide in this world without fear that something
will scrape you or cut you back.

Studying Gwendolyn Brooks is a study in the masters. Reading her work
has taught me that in order to write you must be a keen observer. In order to
write about black women, people in general, you must love them deeply—in
their inners and their entirety. And from this love, Miz Brooks taught me to
sculpt a poem in a way that is careful to keep the whole.

AKUA LEZLI HOPE

Gwendolyn Brooks Reminiscence

I grew up when the little "like me" was precious, rare, and cherished. Gwendolyn Brooks was not my first woman poet, nor my first poet, but she was my heart star, the AllMother. Her ground breaking claim staking was firm and wide by the time I was fully literate. Though I met verse before meeting her words—in carols and hymns, hand games, nursery and jump rope rhymes, songs my parents sang and played—her words held a singular resonance for their cool fierce precision. That she was not only African American, but female in urban, north, twentieth century America was the richest of affirmation in the time when little black girls like us, were set upon by dog and bombed in the South or stoned and jeered at on the way to school in Queens, New York. My father had Countee Cullen and Langston Hughes; I had Gwendolyn Brooks. My favorite aunt's name is Gwendolyn. It was my special honor to escort her when she came to Williams College, where I was among the first class of women accepted to the previously all-male school where Sterling Brown now taught. Few women and even fewer black women studied or taught there, so having her radiant talent shine on the cold Berkshire hills was exalting. She took the slim folder of poems and commented on each one, affirming, critiquing, and spending time with me, discussing my work. I was giddy at the audience, at the time alone with her, who I had read most of my then young life. She was warm, welcoming, wonderful, accessible, and incisive. I remain grateful for Gwendolyn Brooks' being.

SANDRA JACKSON-OPOKU

Being Born into Brooks

Trying to remember when I first met Gwendolyn Brooks is like reaching through the mists of memory to recall my birth. I know for a fact that I was born, though I don't remember the actual event. Nor can I pinpoint the exact time and day of meeting Miss Brooks, the moment and manner of the encounter. Ah, this memory of mine, the edges of it curling like snapshots in a fading photo album. Such as it is.

This is what I do know for sure. It had to be in the early 1970s, when I was a college student, probably my first year majoring in journalism at Columbia College Chicago. I had been lurking on the margins of an organization I would one day join then eventually go on to head—OBAC Writers Workshop.

OBAC is pronounced *obasi*, a Yoruba word for leader. It was the fulcrum of the Black Arts Movement, a heady era of political awareness, cultural nationalism and Pan-Africanism. We wore the garb of the times, mile-high Afros and bellbottom blue jeans, dashikis of Dutch Javanese prints some of us thought were authentically African. Straightened hair was out, dark skinned sisters were finally in, and James Brown had cut his processed pompadour to sing, "Say it Loud (I'm Black and I'm Proud)."

Founded by Hoyt W. Fuller, Haki Madhubuti (Don L. Lee at the time), and Abdul Alkalimat (née Gerald McWhorter), OBAC began in 1967 as a multidisciplinary arts organization with theater, visual arts, and literature workshops.

The theater component under Val Gray Ward evolved into Kuumba Theater. The visuals arts workshop created the "Wall of Respect," a fluid expanse of iconic black images painted and repainted on the side of a building in the heart of a black Chicago community that would one day reclaim its old name, Bronzeville. The Wall of Respect ignited a rebirth of the mural movement across the nation and worldwide. Accompanied by African drumming, Gwendolyn Brooks (and others) read poetry in front of it, wrote poems about it. Some of the artists would go on to found AfriCOBRA, a visual arts collective still active today.

What endured for a time was the writer's workshop that would continue through the early years of twenty-first century, albeit on an on-again, off-again basis. Headed in the early days by *Black World Magazine* editor, Hoyt W. Fuller, OBAC introduced me to a world of ideas and literature I'd never known before. At Mr. Fuller's invitation, any black writer of note passing through Chicago would pass through OBAC's doors at a storefront on 35th Street. I sat at the feet of literary giants and learned from them—Haki Madhubuti, Sterling Plumpp, Alex Haley, Sonia Sanchez, Toni Morrison, Conrad Kent Rivers. It was at one of these gatherings, I can't remember which, that I first met a slight, dark skinned woman who wore an endless collection of head-ties and a downturned smile.

Some people remember Gwendolyn Brooks as gentle soul, but I didn't see her that way. Gracious, nurturing, and kind, yes. But gentleness is not synonymous with generosity. I remember Gwendolyn as a woman of quiet fierceness, scrupulous fairness, and a deep thoughtfulness that was as much her personal presence as it was infused into her writings. She was sweet but could be stern. If people didn't know better not to step out of line with her, they'd soon learn, and then some.

While not necessarily a gentle woman, Gwendolyn Brooks was a gentlewoman. Her exquisite courtesies and manners made her seem like someone from another era. She wrote so many notes and cards and letters to the many people she met, I'd worry when she would find the time to write poetry. She even sent thank you notes in response to other people's thank you notes!

Cash prizes for the annual poet laureate awards went to schoolchildren writing poetry as well as Significant Illinois Writers; I was honored to have received two of them. The fund came from Miss Brooks' very own pockets. We all know that poets, even successful ones like Miss Brooks, have never been Rockefeller-wealthy.

More valuable even than the handwritten notes and cash awards was the way Gwendolyn Brooks gave of herself. While devoting time to family, friends, a sometimes hectic travel schedule, and her own writing, Miss Brooks was known for reading and commenting on the writings of people she didn't know, that sometimes she'd never met. Now, she would never sugarcoat her critique to plump up anyone's ego. Yet she gave so freely of feedback and encouragement, urging us to become our best writer selves. To Gwendolyn Brooks, all writers had potential but they must be willing to polish it.

As a worker, a writer, and a teacher of literature and creative writing, I have taken these lessons into my own practice. While jealous of encroachments into my writing time, I've discovered what fueled Miss Brooks' legendary generosity. It feels good to give.

"We are each other's business," after all. "We *are* each other's magnitude and bond."*

Gwendolyn Elizabeth Brooks ain't never lied yet.

*Brooks, Gwendolyn. "Paul Robeson," *Family Pictures*. Detroit: Broadside Press. 1970

I remember the first time I read "We Real Cool." I immediately set to writing, attempting in my own way to reconstruct a rhythm so evident in the cadence of Gwendolyn Brooks' poem. Miss Brooks' simple yet powerful poem got me thinking about how to write about the black-American community without sounding overly dramatic or patronizing. The results of that are "Keloid Cells" and "Genetic Codes." I was born in Jamaica and raised in Brooklyn, New York. The result of which is a double consciousness of sorts—there is a part of me deeply linked to the black-American experience having spent most of my life in the United States, and there is another part very entrenched with a Caribbean identity and aesthetics. However, no matter what country you were born in, black people this side of the Atlantic have a very pervasive common history—"the bitter stench of slavery" as Dione Brand aptly refers to it in *No Language is Neutral*. So I set off to write a poem that could not only pay homage to the history of African American musical production that Miss Brooks' poetry is an extension of, but also to make the poem speak to my understanding of the black-American experience as someone who is almost but not quite linked to that identification.

The aftermath of slavery is something that I think of not solely on the larger scale of society but also within the microcosms of black family dynamics impacted by the lasting emotional and psychological scars that many have not yet dealt with. These themes are addressed in "Keloid Cells" and "Genetic Codes." Having grown up with an absent father, who was imprisoned for most of my adolescent years, the unprecedented numbers of black men who enter the prison industrial complex, and the subsequent negative effects on black families, is very personal to me. I try to trace this as a problem that predates incarceration, making a link between slavery and psychological imprisonment that plagues the black community. Out of that agony has come much cultural creativity, especially in the twentieth century.

The poem that has most profoundly affected me is "The Mother." The first two lines, "Abortions will not let you forget. You remember the children you got that you did not get," resonate with me as the daughter who is constantly reminded that I could have been aborted. I have never had an abortion much less been pregnant. But I know what it feels like to be constantly reminded of the choice of not having an abortion. I am the product of that choice and my deeply religious grandmother uses me as the poster child for her pro-life stance all the time. I wanted to write a poem from the point of view of the child. My poem isn't pro-life but it also isn't necessarily pro-choice either. It is just reflecting on the experience of being the child that wasn't really wanted; the child that represented the doubt that you felt about whether or not to get the abortion; the child that makes you question if you made the right decision after all. Or so it may feel, from the perspective of the child. I also see this as an extension of the conversation I am trying to have with Gwendolyn Brooks' poetry about the lasting effects of slavery on the back community because abuse, whether physical or emotional, is something taken as a matter of course and seldom interrogated as a pathology passed down from generations of dehumanizing torture. My own, perhaps misguided, solution to this is "Barbed Wire," which talks about ending the cycle of pain through the willful decision to not reproduce. The title comes from a line from Gayl Jones' *Corregidora* in my effort to create conversations between multiple black women speaking on similar issues—an attempt which I think Gwendolyn Brooks would have approved of.

JOAN WIESE JOHANNES

In 1993 I had the pleasure of hearing Gwendolyn Brooks read and discuss her poetry, an experience that impacted me as a novice poet. After the reading, Miss Brooks and I talked briefly while she autographed her book for me. When she asked my name, I said, "Joan Johannes," and she commented about the name's wonderful alliteration. I replied that I had married it! "Shame on you," she kindly chastised, then told me how important it is to acknowledge our families of origin. That conversation, along with the realization that I had already lost my mother, and my father would not be with me much longer, motivated me to use my maiden name. I published my first chapbook in 2000 under the name Joan Wiese Johannes and continue to use that form of my name.

More importantly, Miss Brooks improved my poetry by freeing me from the misconception that many people who grow up reading confessional poets have—to assume that first-person poems are always autobiographical. One of Miss Brooks most powerful poems is the first person, "The Mother," which she read that day. During the question and answer session that followed, a young woman asked if Miss Brooks felt guilty about the abortions. The poet laughed a loud and easy laugh, but it was clear she was not laughing at the questioner, but in response to the question. Then she said that the poem was not about her, and explained that it was true, having been based on the experiences of women living in her neighborhood, but it was not her truth. The realization that I could write truth without it always being autobiographical was pivotal in my development as a poet, as was Miss Brooks' relaxed reaction to the suggestion that she had behaved in a way considered immoral by some. This response by her gave me the courage to allow my narrators to sometimes be more heartless than I am and/or commit acts I wouldn't commit. Because of her example, I no longer need to separate myself from those narrators and temper their unflattering or socially controversial voices. Therefore, it is fair to say that Gwendolyn Brooks gave me my poetic license!

I had an opportunity to meet Gwendolyn Brooks at the 1996 Black Arts Festival in Atlanta, Georgia. It was the first time I ever heard her read. I remember being in awe of her unique cadence and rhythm. No one read poetry like she did, then or now. Gwendolyn Brooks was so at home in her own bones and soul. I also had the chance to talk with her during this same festival. I saw her in the lobby just sitting at table. She was simply dressed, sitting alone. I remember running up to her and hugging her and exclaiming out loud, "This is Gwendolyn Brooks," as folks came over to greet her. She was not a dressy poet, but the very last reading she did on the east coast was at the Dodge Poetry Festival. She was dressed to the nines in a gray satin coat jacket. I stood up for her entire reading, again in awe but deeply aware I might not see her again. Perhaps the most intimate reading was when Yari Yari hosted her at a fancy restaurant on 5th Avenue. She made us all laugh about being a poet and reading in humble places that were not so grand. I remain thankful for the few times I was in her presence and able to hear her voice. I am even more thankful for her poems, literary example, and pursuit of craft.

CAROLYN JOYNER

I met Gwendolyn Brooks up close and personal in the mid to late nineties at Chicago State University's annual Black Writers' Conference. I attended several years in a row, and remember her leaning forward in her seat, her rapt attention to every word during open mic session. It gave us the jitters, because we knew she'd hear the bad stuff along with the good, but we loved it.

Workshopping with her at these conferences gave me the understanding of how essential honest critical feedback is from experienced and legendary writers. I witnessed many "sow's ears turn into silk." We were warned to avoid cliched and hackneyed expressions by remembering that if we thought of something in ten minutes, everybody else could too.

I came to the poetry genre late, in comparison to most, but "Mama Gwen" impressed upon me how young I was, and I love her for this. She urged me to make my words my own, and to claim my own light.

EMILY HOOPER LANSANA

Fresh out of Yale undergrad, I moved to Chicago in 1988. I came to Chicago because I'd been told that it had a wonderful, supportive theater community that believed in diverse casting. Unfortunately, I found many closed doors in the world of traditional theater. Fortunately I started branching out into other areas of performance such as storytelling and spoken word.

I came across an opportunity to audition for a poetic tribute to Gwendolyn Brooks being designed by a small theater company. I was cast in the project. Each poet was given the opportunity to select one of Miss Brooks' poems to perform as a solo piece. I chose, "To the Diaspora."

For me poetry gives voice to the places we cannot speak. "To the Diaspora," so profoundly spoke to the truths of my journey as a young black woman struggling to be "conscious" and whole. I picked the poem apart and tried to make it live in my voice, my body, my breath. When we received confirmation that she would attend the performance, I was both excited and terrified. I will never forget performing the poem for her. She let out an audible breath and she smiled broadly. At the end of the evening, I was honored to meet her for the first time. We exchanged information. I couldn't believe this was actually happening.

That night was the beginning of a tender friendship. As time passed, my fiancée then husband and I often drove her to events. When one has the pleasure of driving Miss Brooks, there are certain things to keep in mind. Most importantly, be prepared to take your time. She was the most gracious person I have ever met. She shook hands with everyone who wanted to meet her. No matter how long the line, she always signed every autograph. She loved to take people to dinner. She would select wonderful restaurants, and in later years, she seemed to take much more joy in watching her guests eat than in doing so herself. Spending time with her was a lesson in generosity and humility.

She was among the first to be called after our sons were born. She gently held them in her arms and schooled my husband on how to hold his sons more like babies and less like footballs. Just before we moved to New York, she invited us over and insisted that we bring the boys. She welcomed our sons, both under three at the time, into her home. I scrambled to make sure that the toddlers did not destroy her lovely place. Chasing them and holding them tightly trying to avoid carefully organized stacks of paper and piles of books. We posed for a picture. We wanted to remember this summer afternoon colored with laughter. This was the last time we saw Miss Brooks alive. I still think of her almost every day.

I can't walk through Chicago's South Side and not remember how much she loved this place and it's people. She taught me to look closely, to listen carefully, and to love deeply.

Thank you, Miss Brooks.

ROY LEWIS

Description of Portrait of Gwendolyn Brooks

My portrait of Gwendolyn Brooks was commissioned by a Black women's group in Chicago in 1969, and was taken at Northeastern Illinois University in Chicago, where we worked as faculty and staff.

In January 1968, Miss Brooks came to my first traveling photography exhibition at the South Side Community Art Center in Chicago. The exhibit, "Black and Beautiful," opened at the New School of African American Thought in Washington, DC, in 1967, and traveled to Pittsburgh and New York and Chicago.

Miss Brooks commented about the exhibition that I, Roy Lewis, was a trailblazer in terms of creating a narrative about Black people. She offered her support, as her poetry is similar to mine, which includes narratives about people of color.

I began to cover Miss Brooks' poetry readings and appearances in Chicago, her collaboration with Oscar Brown Jr. on the play "Opportunity Please Knock" with the Blackstone Rangers.

Gwendolyn Brooks was the first African-American woman to win a Pulitzer Prize for Poetry, and was appointed Poet Laureate of Illinois in 1968, a position held until her death, and Poet Laureate Consultant in Poetry to the Library of Congress In 1985. I continued to document her career as a poet and teacher.

My relationship with Miss Brooks was that of friend, teacher, supporter, and mentor. I traveled with her to schools, prisons, and award ceremonies around the country. When Miss Brooks passed away in December 2000, I went out a day early and was able to circumvent one of the largest snowstorms in Chicago. Although many people were unable to make the funeral services due to the snowstorm, Miss Brooks still made it to the interment on time.

When I arrived at the funeral, I asked about the photographer protocol. Her daughter, Nora Blakely, said I had full access, as I was Miss Brooks' photographer for her Life and now for her funeral.

TONY LINDSAY

My Gwendolyn Brooks experience

When I was in the seventh grade at Nicolas Copernicus Elementary School, Nora Blakely was a teacher there, and there were times when her mother, Gwendolyn Brooks, would come and visit with the students. She would have lunch with us and "hang out." Her conversation was always encouraging of the arts; she would look at our drawings, poetry, and my stories. And to her, all the work that we did was great. I remember thinking what a cool job she had that allowed her to hang out with us, and that was when the initial writer's seed was planted in my mind. I wanted a "job" that allowed me the freedom to hang out. Years later while taking a summer class at Chicago State University, we passed each other on campus. She shocked me by remembering me, and she shocked me further by asking if I was still writing, and I was.

In 2000, I was a PhD student, all but dissertation, at the University of Texas-Dallas. I am a poet, and was so at that time, having recently had my poem "Here" selected for inscription on a memorial to honor former enslaved African Americans in Dallas. I did not begin work on my PhD until I was almost fifty, and with an urgency borne of the need to make up for lost time, I applied to many conferences—places I could recite my poetry, work with poets I admired, and present my scholarly work. On Friday, December 1, 2000, I attended a conference at Chicago State University. There I read poetry and took a photograph with Sonia Sanchez. I was excited about the possibility of sharing poetry with Miss Gwendolyn Brooks; however conference participants received word that Miss Brooks felt ill and would not come to campus that day. By the time I returned home to Dallas, Texas on Sunday, December 3, 2000, I learned that Miss Brooks had died. I felt a deep sadness for all that was lost with Miss Brooks' passing. It seems even the weather reacted to her death: on December 1, the day of the conference, the Chicago weather was gorgeous—lots of sunshine and no need for coats, gloves, or even thick sweaters. By December 3, snow covered the area and the cold breath of winter made me understand more fully Lou Rawls' song about "the hawk" in Chicago and the weather being so that one had to "get fully dressed before going to bed."

I was influenced by Miss Brooks as a young poet, and I am still influenced by her work today. I write about my neighborhood—in both a local and global sense. I attempt, at every opportunity, to "exhaust the little moment."

It was 1980, my first year as a poet under a California Arts Council Art-ist-in-Residency at the San Francisco African American Historical and Cul-tural Society. An opportunity came to have Gwendolyn Brooks speak at our institution. A hotel close to the center was booked, a caterer was hired, a small theater was secured that could welcome the few hundred estimated guests, flyers were produced and press releases submitted. I was so excited that I was going to meet Gwendolyn Brooks. Her work watered my spindly poetry roots and helped to make them stronger, reaching down, deeper and deeper. Much of the poet I had become was because of the body of work she had produced. I wanted her to see me as a poet, but didn't consider myself—or any of the poets who read in my series, came to the open readings, or attended the work-shops— as able readers with this queen of poetry. My director suggested I bring a manuscript with a SASE which he would give to her. Miss Brooks arrived and was taken first to the hotel and then to the event.

When she was brought to the venue, which had filled with a respectable audience, we were introduced. She was warm and gracious with my sincere gushing. Opening the clearest smile I had seen in a while, she asked who was going to read with her. I was so embarrassed. I stumbled over my words telling her we had only planned on her reading and doing a Q&A and being at the reception. We had not planned a longer program. She smiled and without scolding let me know I should always include young poets. She wanted to hear what they had to say. It should always be a conversation. I had forgotten the manila envelope with my underdeveloped manuscript in my sweaty hand. She saw it and asked what it was. I stumbled again, "My work . . . I wanted to but . . . " She smiled and took the manuscript. Her reading was, of course, incredible, and all attendees seemed pleased with the event.

Dewey Crumpler, an incredible painter and muralist was the Executive Director of the San Francisco African American Historical and Cultural So-ciety at that time. After the reading Miss Brooks was returned to her hotel which, unknown at the time of booking, was under renovations. She found a rat sharing her room. While she waited for Dewey to return and rebook her in another hotel, she sat in the hotel lobby and read my entire manuscript. Then she took the time to write me a brief letter supporting my work, encouraging me to stay on the road, applauding a courage that I didn't know I had. Dewey delivered the letter and manuscript to me the next day. I was humbled and elated. Through that encounter, Gwendolyn Brooks showed me that a poet should not only write with grace and integrity, but live that way, too.

ADRIAN MATEJKA

Remembrance

Gwendolyn Brooks was one of the first poets I felt was speaking to and for me, even before I recognized that I was supposed to be listening. The particular struggle of hunger and hope she gave voice to made sense to me. And while the poems were often situated in Chicago, the struggle was movable. Grumbling stomachs, absent fathers, and paycheck-to-paycheck living work the same way in Chicago as they do in Detroit, St. Louis, or Indianapolis, where I grew up. The poems included here are directly inspired by her intense collection, *The Bean Eaters*, where character and setting are as central to the poems as form and music.

Though I never met Miss Brooks, I got the opportunity to hear her read in September 2000. Shryock Auditorium on Southern Illinois University Carbondale's campus was packed with people of all ages—almost 1,400 in attendance—and I sat in the upper deck next to a group of middle school children. Miss Brooks read a handful of her own poems, then spent the rest of her time reading poems by some of the elementary children she worked with as part of her never ending community outreach. I have never been a part of an audience so grateful for a poet's work and presence.

It made sense, really, that she was reading as part of the "What I Have Learned and What I Would Like to Pass On" lecture series. The whole night was about giving. That the crowd laughed and exclaimed as she read poems by eight-year-olds was a testament to the power Miss Brooks uncovered and shared with us in poetry. That she signed books from the end of the reading at 8:30 p.m. to almost 1:00 a.m.—making sure that no one who waited left without a signature—is a testament to her power and grace. I didn't wait in that line, but I wish I had. She died a few months later, and I never had the opportunity to thank her for what she'd given me.

GWENDOLYN A. MITCHELL

Finding My Own Sunset and Thoughts on Reading Gwendolyn Brooks

I first met Gwendolyn Brooks in 1977, during my senior year at Penn State, when I traveled to Philadelphia for a Black Writer's conference hosted by Sonia Sanchez and Houston Baker. Gwendolyn Brooks was one of the featured participants. I remember walking with her and a group of young writers as she made her way across the campus to her reading and book signing. I met a number of writers that weekend, and I was introduced to a new world of Black poetry and a new understanding of being in this world—as a poet.

Maybe it was because we shared a name, or maybe because I found something comforting as well as intimidating and challenging about her disposition, that I kept writing and kept finding ways to push beyond my own self-limiting expectation. Over the years and whenever possible, I tried to be in her presence. I wanted to learn and understand the messages that she, with such apparent ease, was able to share through her writing and spoken words.

I moved to Chicago in the late 1990s to work for Third World Press. Gwendolyn Brooks was an integral part of this community of writers and an integral part of this publishing house.

Now that I am older, I have discovered that my interpretation of Gwendolyn Brooks's poetry has also grown with me. It has matured. As a younger poet, I may have overlooked the poignant dignity of the woman presented to us in "A Sunset in the City." In this poem, Miss Brooks avoids giving us a self-absorbed version of a woman's life or the perspective and exclusivity of the personal experiences of the poet. This poem was and remains the embodiment of the "woman" experience. Here Miss Brooks writes of a woman with full awareness of her power and place in this world. Miss Brooks tells us not to be afraid to confront the selves we become as we age. If we are honest, this confrontation—coupled with the choices that we make for ourselves—may change us for the better. I found Miss Brooks again as if for the first time through the reading of responding to "A Sunset." I am thankful for this exchange and for this renewed understanding of her voice and presence in this world.

LENARD D. MOORE

In the 1980s and 1990s, Gwendolyn Brooks and I exchanged letters. One of her letters was an invitation to participate in a Mini-Poetry Festival at the Library of Congress when she was the Poetry Consultant to the Library of Congress. It was an honor for me to talk to Gwendolyn Brooks and read my poetry at the Library of Congress. I remember meeting her husband Henry Blakely in June of 1983, at Alice Browning's International Black Writers Conference in Chicago. I think the conference was held at Hotel International. Thus, I also think Gwendolyn Brooks was at the conference, too. Also, in the 1980s, I was a student in Gerald W. Barrax's Beginning Poetry Writing Class and Advance Poetry Writing Class at North Carolina State University. We studied Gwendolyn Brooks' poetry. During one of those semesters, Gwendolyn Brooks taught at one-day poetry workshop at North Carolina State University. One of the students who was invited to participate in Miss Brooks' poetry workshop, I listened closely to her comments on my workshop poem. After her workshop, I asked her to sign one of her poetry pages in my textbook. She saw her picture in the textbook and said, "That's my favorite picture."

In 1997, I was one of the eighty poets who was invited to read an original poem as a tribute to Gwendolyn Brooks for her eightieth birthday in Chicago. For several years, I have taught Gwendolyn Brooks' poetry in my creative writing classes, poetry classes, and African American literature classes.

My poem "Fun In The Backyard" was inspired by Gwendolyn Brooks' poem "A Song In The Front Yard." I like the persona's message in her poem. I also like the movement of the poem. Yet, I marvel at all of the good details in the poem. Gwendolyn Brooks' poems are gems of brilliant light that shine on the people who are depicted so fully. I am grateful for her poems and how they teach us to live on this planet.

I met Gwendolyn Brooks when she spoke at Chicago State University (CSU) during the national Delta Sigma Theta (DST) conference in 2000 (she was an honorary member of the sorority). The activity I was part of was a tribute to Dr. Elnora Daniel, the president of CSU at that time. Some members of the Sapphire and Crystals collective exhibited their art. Besides me, founders Marva Pitchford Jolly, a CSU professor, and Felicia Grant-Preston, a CSU grad and member of DST were part of it.

The memory of her speech at this event has lasted these past sixteen years. The theme of her address was, "I may be old, I may be sick, but I am not dead, yet!" She gave many examples of what she was, and continued the idea that she was alive as long as she was alive! She spoke to the eternal optimist in me! At the time I did not know she had a terminal disease.

The painting expresses her directness (look at those eyes) and her creativity (note the humming bird representing so many people attracted to the sweet nectar of her intelligence). The gems around her are mined from her own source within; she was a gem who attracted other people, such as the poet Haki Madhubuti. The title "More Than Cool" means she is more than the one poem, "we real cool," and universally a superlative.

I first met Gwendolyn Brooks in 1989 when she was awarded the Frost Medal from the Poetry Society of America. At that time, I was the PSA's new Executive Director. Seated in the Grand Gallery of the National Arts Club at the dinner in her honor, I was awed by her presence, passion, and integrity. Soon afterward, we invited Gwendolyn to join the Board of Governors of the PSA, and I was thrilled to work with her during the years to come. She was overwhelmingly generous with her time and her commitment to poetry and, whenever asked to participate in events, she always said yes.

At the Harold Washington Library in 1996, Gwendolyn helped to celebrate the inauguration of *Poetry in Motion* in Chicago. Her poem, "Speech to the Young, Speech to the Progress-Toward (among them Nora and Henry III)" had been included in New York's *Poetry in Motion* program. We also featured "We Real Cool" in Chicago's *Poetry in Motion* program. At her last reading for the PSA, in 1999, she commanded the crowd in PSA's *Poetry in Public Places: Poetry and Drama event at Steppenwolf Theatre* where she shared the stage with Frank Bidart and John Mahoney.

Several weeks before our first child, Alexandra, was born, I received this note from Gwendolyn: "It's Almost time for the BABY! =Blessings on you ALL!!!! Love, Gwen Brooks." I can hear Gwendolyn's voice when I read this note. Her excitement about the arrival of the baby was palpable!

I have always been fascinated with the ferocity of her poem, "A Lovely Love"—how she harnesses wildness within the formal strictures of the sonnet. The poem begins: "Let it be alleys. Let it be a hall . . . " One day, in attempting to emulate Gwendolyn, I hope to capture that wild abandon. For now, I have taken the end words she used in her sonnet to create a love poem of my own.

MIKE PUICAN

My First Contact with Gwendolyn Brooks

In the early 1990s, I attended a Guild Complex event called the Gwendolyn Brooks Open Mic Awards—a poetry contest where some fifty poets read one of their poems onstage for the chance to win $500. The $500 was generously provided by Gwendolyn Brooks herself. Miss Brooks attended these events, and, without taking a single break, she would sit through over three hours of open mic poetry.

Even though I was not a very experienced writer, I had entered the contest. I was pretty nervous. I had never read in front of a crowd as large as this, let alone one that included a Pulitzer Prize winner. When my name was announced, my heart started pounding. I walked onto the stage, read my poem, and returned to my seat. As I was listening to the next reader still in a bit of a daze from having read my poem, someone tapped me on the shoulder, handed me a folded note and said, "This is from Miss Brooks." I opened the note. It read, "You are unique/—and splendid! —G."

I didn't win the $500, but I received a gift more valuable and more lasting. The encouragement I received from her that day has nurtured me for years. Her note is framed and hangs above my writing desk. Gwendolyn Brooks was so generous with her attention. There are many stories of how she gave encouragement to both new and established writers. As I look up from writing at my desk, she is still giving it.

EUGENE B. REDMOND

A Slice of Prose for Gwendolyn Brooks, Poet

Although like all poets of the pre-, during- and post-BAM generation/s, "I could write a book about" Gwen; just let me say this:

I was thirteen and she was thirty-three when I first encountered Gwendolyn Brooks at Hughes-Quinn Junior High School in East St. Louis, Illinois, a river/blues town with schools named after Paul Laurence Dunbar and James Weldon Johnson. It was 1950 and a couple of teachers echoed in classrooms what the "current events" board in the hallway yelled: Another "Negro first!" —Miss Brooks had won the Pulitzer Prize for poetry. (Years later, I'd meet and be hugely-hugely influenced by her; but I always felt that, even though I wasn't shown examples of her poetry at that Pulitzer moment, she'd had a photosynthetic impact on the boy-poet aborning.

BAM! Enter the Jump Bad BLACK '60s in Chicago & THE WHOLE BLACK WORLD in the '70s, '80s, '90s—

("If I had died before the age of 50, I'd have died a Negro fraction"—GB)—

with Report From Part One & Report From Part Two—bejeweled with Beckonings . . .

Hundreds of meetings, readings, workshops (including in East St. Louis), writers conferences (Fisk University-'67, Medgar Evers College-'88, Chicago/Chicago/Chicago, Sacramento, MLA, CLA, a 1990 homage to Hayden at U. of Michigan with Dove, Harper, Long Madgett, Lane [Pinkie], Chrisman, Darwin Turner & Williams [Shirley Anne]), festivals (NBAF-Atlanta, New York [where I introduced Gwen at Columbia University re: Troupe's "Black Roots '77"]), book signings, photographs, phone calls, written exchanges, accidental run-ins, and contributions to publications I edited: a special double issue of *Black American Literature Forum* on Henry Dumas [1988]; and several issues of *Drumvoices Revue* in the '90s) . . . not to mention her active participation on the Board of Trustees of the East St. Louis-based Eugene B. Redmond Writers Club (1986–), which celebrates its thirtieth birthday this year (2016).

Her Poet LaureateShip! (State of Illinois)

Her Poetry ConsultantShip! (US Library of Congress)

Her Poetry ScholarShip (National Endowment for Humanities' Lecturer)

In part, I owe my career to Gwen. So does Black Poetry. And Black Literature. And Black Studies (especially Black Literary Studies and Black Feminist/Womens Studies). I attempt to acknowledge these debts in my homage, "Journaling with Gwendolyn Brooks Kwansaba-Style 2016: A Pastiche of Poetic Reports on Her Life & Works."

CRYSTAL SIMONE SMITH

A decade ago, when I started writing poetry, I was acutely underread and newly grasping the fundamentals of imagery and metaphor when I purchased the monumental anthology, *Blacks*. At 500 plus pages and with Miss Brooks' incredible virtuosic style, it was daunting to say the least. I read, pondered, and took what I could from it, then moved on to poets I deemed more accessible like Lucille Clifton and Philip Levine. It was only when I realized I was writing race and class that I returned to Miss Brooks whose sonnets and ballads on the themes were absolutely masterful. Her poems are esoteric, yet sane, and proficient in musicality. And, no poet answers the question "why" as assuredly as Miss Brooks.

Nowadays, I'm constantly asked to teach poetry workshops in public schools and colleges, and I find, more than often, the general knowledge and praise of black poets rarely extends beyond the likes of Langston Hughes and Maya Angelou—that the works of Lucille Clifton, Audre Lorde, and Miss Brooks, who is arguably the most honored African-American poet, are not experienced or recognized. I consider this a crisis—black poetry without Gwendolyn Brooks!

To Make a Thing Sing and Mean: Reflections on Gwendolyn Brooks

All writers and readers understand this humble but beguiling truth: the experiences of reading a poem and of *hearing* it recited offer contrasting pleasures. Book in hand, one can dawdle through successive readings, dillydally among one's favorite image or phrase, even pour another cup in hopes of savoring the tastes of word and brew. Hearing a poem recited by its author, however, delivers the intimacy of human voice and the immediacy of art dropped in one's lap, as Walter Benjamin reminds us, art experienced *in situ*. We inhabit the church of art, and art's church resides in us. Yes, it's necessarily brief but also redemptive.

Although I'd lived with her poems for many years, the first time I heard Miss Brooks read from her work I was among a throng of some 300 Illinois writers of various stripes. We'd gathered for a celebration of Illinois authors in the State Library's beatific setting, a library crowned with names of our state's venerable authors and a venue now fittingly named in honor of Miss Brooks. Writers, notoriously the worst audience for other writers, are customarily slow to shutter their literary gossiping and late to find their chairs. Not this time. By the time Miss Brooks rose to the podium, the place fell quiet as midnight chapel. Then that voice, hers and only hers.

When I read Miss Brooks' poems, I always engage them first as sonic indulgences. I wrestle the surprisingly big-shouldered vowels, rise up with their musical chiming and sudden silences—so much so the poem itself seems a physical thing to me, another being in the room, a presence. And then, amid all that body given body, there comes the punch of idea and emotion: twin fists or feathered kisses. From Miss Brooks I learned to aspire to realms of the aesthetically improbable made possible—to sing a thing and to make it mean, to say a thing and make it croon.

That night's reading modeled another central human notion for me as well, something I mention whenever I speak to Illinoisans in my role as state poet laureate. It was Miss Brooks' grace and generosity with her audience, the honest elegance of the true artist. From a distant corner of the library atrium, I watched Miss Brooks greet each person wishing for a signed book or simple handshake. Her eyes never wavered from the person right in front of her, no matter the long line trailing behind like El cars at a busy stop. At that moment, all the world resolved itself within two beings brought together by poetry, the people and the poem, hand in open hand.

Conversations about race in America are not only essential but also existential matters. The work of nationhood remains unfinished. It's work that defines what we may become as much as what we have been. The many poems I've chanced about racial matters offer my contribution to this conversation, shout outs that trouble as well as settle the waters we sail together, you and me.

Gwendolyn Brooks blazed trails for me to look up to—following her path—I
was able to strategize—dream and pray—to find my own voice-freedom.
I am so grateful to her—for each living word—syllable and scribble.
Her voice echoes of times before, very present and beyond.

JEANNE TOWNS

Wordweaver

(for Gwendolyn Brooks)

She weaves words into
a web of intrigue and delight.
A song of pain so searing
until God bows his head and
weeps overwhelmed by the sweet melody
she plays with simple, unassuming words.

They are lovers, she and words
tried and true.
Theirs is a love
strengthened and heightened by time
stretching beyond barriers
to embrace all our selves.
Words move inside of her
like a tumultuous wind across a once quiet sky
like thunder folding into sunlight.

She is a wordsmith, a wordwonder, a wordwizard
Working words into marvel and awe.
Working words into woe and titillation.
Working words into hard and soft strokes,
into whispers and wailings
into love and pain.

She becomes her words.
Draping them around her like precious cloth.
Folding them into a magical healing balm.

Her words are a river
rich and wide, deep, and unyielding
flowing gracefully with the tide
enriched by all that flows in them

Her words are a generous lover.
They tremble and rise.
Make you weep an moan
Her words are love at its purest

And when she pours them into verse
They give birth to magic and marvel.

In 2015, I sat next to my aunt and across from my mentor, playwright Sandra Seaton, at the Society for the Study of Midwestern Literature's award luncheon. I may have eaten everyone's desert at the table as I waited to receive the Gwendolyn Brooks Poetry Prize for my poem "Social Regard," a piece primarily about life in the 1980s in Flint, Michigan. Unlike some prizes named for poets, the Brooks Prize was funded by Miss Brooks and she selected the winners prior to her passing.

Thinking back, I incessantly read *A Street in Bronzeville* (in my mind it is required reading for black poets) during the time I wrote my poem. Naturally, Miss Brooks' work influenced my writing. I think it was her ability to capture the lives of the people of Bronzeville and bring it to the page that created a mold for me. It piqued my interest in writing about the happenings of my hometown and I haven't stopped writing about Flint. Miss Brooks influenced me then and she continues to do so.

After the ceremony, one person in attendance, a man who'd known Miss Brooks when she was a member of SSML, came to me and said, "This is the poem *she* would have selected." Maybe he said more; I don't remember. I was consumed with the thought that Miss Brooks would have appreciated my work enough to select my poem for her prize named in her honor. The thought still blows me away...

Put simply, Gwendolyn Brooks is my favorite poet. I have written countless poems inspired by her poetry, and read her collection *Blacks*, and written in the margins, so much that the book is as much written by me as by Miss Brooks (though of course the portions worth reading are easily discernible as hers).

As a person/artist who insists my work examines the resilience and boldness of blkness, Mama Gwen's work offers a roadmap to how to maneuver through the cannon to get and stay within the pulse of my people.

REGGIE SCOTT YOUNG

A Bluesville Tribute for Gwendolyn Brooks

I was a student at Farragut High School on Chicago's West Side when I first met Gwendolyn Brooks, the famous poet from the South Side's historic Bronzeville community. It was the late 1960s and I was a member of a generation of inner city youths who were still trying to be cool in a manner similar to the *boyz* Miss Brooks wrote about in "We Real Cool." We were just beginning to get caught up in the cultural metamorphosis that had transformed most Negroes and colored folks into people who were Black and proud, and this made some of us a bit rebellious. My friends and I gladly embraced the concept of blackness, despite our lack of knowledge about Black life except for what we had observed with our own eyes. And we lacked tolerance for anything or anyone that reeked of Negro.

After having been force-fed the alien works of British poets in a previous English class, poetry was anything but cool to me. I had read an article about Miss Brooks that compared her poems to those of John Keats, so when I heard the announcement about her visit I never thought once about attending. I also remembered her being referred to in both the local papers and *Ebony* and *Jet* magazines as the first Negro to win the Pulitzer Prize in literature. Those issues in our school library were frayed and discolored by the time I got my hands on them, but it angered me to know that a *Negro* poet, one snobbish white people seemed to like quite well, would visit our Black school. To top it off, our Irish principal, a man who tried to look tough as Jimmy Cagney, came into my English class that Monday boasting about the respectable Chicago Negro poet who would visit our school that week. "She is the first really good Negro poet this country has seen and I want each of you to allow her dignified manner to rub off on you." After that, I hated the idea of a Gwendolyn Brooks because of how she was introduced to us by a principal who did his best to censor any notion of Black talk inside of what he claimed to be his building.

Gwendolyn Brooks' appearance was part of an effort by the Board of Education to sponsor visits by leading Blacks in ghetto schools that had never been offered those kinds of programs before—possibly to pacify students after we responded to the assassination of Martin Luther King by boycotting classes the next day—many of us joined the rebellions that were taking place in the streets. After the principal left our class that day, I started complaining: "Like Langston Hughes wasn't any good. Like Paul Laurence Dunbar wasn't any good. Like Claude McKay wasn't any good . . ." At the end of my litany, I mumbled, "I bet I can write better poems than she can."

Outbursts of that nature were forbidden in Mrs. Beverly's class, but instead of sending me to the office she offered me an opportunity that I found too difficult to pass up. "Mr. Young," she said—and she never called you by your last name unless something was up—"since you know so much about poetry, let me offer *you* the opportunity to represent us by reading a poem of your own as part of Thursday's program." My first inclination was to say "HELL NO!" but she then said if I wrote one it would excuse me from having to write an upcoming paper on Edgar Allen Poe. I knew it would be easy enough for me to come up with some rhymes since my friends and I used rhyming language all of the time when we signified on each other. I also remembered a scene from an old television show about a boy asking his "Pa" about what to say in a poem he had to write for his teacher. What his Pa said was this: "Write about something you know."

It didn't matter to me that my anti-Black principal would be in attendance or that our visitor was a well-known Negro because what I knew, or thought I knew really well, was about the realities of being poor and oppressed, which I assumed most Black people were, despite the fact that my own family had never been poor. My goal was to write a masterpiece that spoke about the true conditions of Black life. I can barely remember what I wrote in that poem, but I know it started something like this: "When you have no food or clothing and no money to pay the rent / The last thing you wanna hear is the white man tell you to be content." I had heard a couple of brothers read poems of that nature to the sounds of Congo drums in nearby Douglas Park and that was why I felt extremely proud of my series of rhyming couplets and clichés of ghetto life.

I thought I read some hot stuff that day, but Miss Brooks did not offer the praise I thought I deserved; instead, she asked me to repeat my name to make sure she had it right. Then she said, "Now, Reggie, I know you can do a better job than that." I thought she was trying to put me down because the contents of my poem had offended her Negro sensibilities, but a few minutes later she rebuked the principal after he called her a Negro for the second or third time. "Excuse me," she told him with a look that reminded me of a teacher informing a young student that something he said was inappropriate." "It would be good for you to know that that I no longer identify with that name. I am very proud to call myself *Black* and I insist that you do the same." She also told the now red-faced man that it would also be very nice if he would no longer use that word—*Negro*—in the presence of the Black students in the school. "After all, they look for you to set a positive example." What she said was delivered in a very polite and a matter-of-fact tone, but something I learned about Gwendolyn Brooks over the years was that she could use the most softly spoken words to convey very stringent commands.

What Miss Brooks said shocked me because it wasn't anything you would expect from a Negro poet at all, especially one who looked like some of the women who served with my mother on the usher board at Douglas Park Baptist Church—none of them would ever speak like that to a white man in authority. It would not be until I began to research her career years later while writing a paper on her for a conference that I would learn about the Black writers' conference she attended two or three years before her visit to my high school. While there, she found herself exposed to younger Black writers, including Amiri Baraka, who were advocating for a cultural nationalism that she also embraced. Miss Brooks' experience at that conference influenced her to no longer answer to the word Negro.

I must admit I was impressed by the way Gwendolyn Brooks humbled a white man who had shown a lack of respect for her at my school, but I couldn't get the words "Now Reggie" out of my head. As badly as she had slammed the principal, she had also slammed my poem, even if I did only write it in trigonometry class the period before.

Over the next thirty years I would hear Gwendolyn Brooks, the Poet Laureate of the State of Illinois and Poetry Consultant to the Library of Congress, say those words or similar words to me in different places around the country, especially when when I had the pleasure to introduce her before a reading at one of the colleges or universities where I worked. If I said something about her background or any of her poems that she felt the need to quibble with, she would interrupt me by saying, "Now Reggie," or something similar, before setting the record straight. I must admit that whenever I heard those words, no matter what she said after, it reminded me of the day when I read my first poem for her back in high school. I had already come to realize that she never spoke those words to serve as a rebuke and usually when she spoke to me like that it was meant serve as a preface to useful information or wise advice she had to offer. Eventually, I learned to embrace those words, no matter how she expressed them, even when they left me feeling a bit chastised.

I saw Miss Brooks a few more times in Chicago after her visit to my high school at readings she gave in the main library building downtown and at other civic festivities, but I never tried to approach her because I didn't want her to recognize me as the student who had read her such a terrible poem. However, I continued to write poetry on the sly because it was important for me to prove that I could write good poems if I put my mind to it. I wasn't a natural poet by any means and, frankly, I found a lot of the stuff I read to be a waste of time, but I was encouraged by the poetry being played on local Black radio stations by Nikki Giovanni, Gill Scott-Heron, and The Last Poets. I was also interested in exploring the New Black Poetry scene that was emerging on the South Side.

After high school I enrolled in the recently opened Chicago Circle Campus branch of the University of Illinois, but dropped out at the end of my first year. One of the reasons was a class I took with the poet Haki Madhubuti, although he was still known as Don L. Lee at the time. I had read his books and heard about the Black cultural nationalism movement he was helping to spearhead on the South Side and decided I could obtain a more practical education, one focused on blackness, by going out there to work as a volunteer for his Institute of Positive Education and its book publishing affiliate, Third World Press. The South Side was a more jazzy part of town than my native West Side, and jazz represented the most vibrant musical expression of the new blackness that had piqued my romantic inclinations. The West Side was known as the home of the blues in the city and Madhubuti along with several other New Black poets had riffed on the blues as being the most backward and least progressive aspect of Black culture. I remember hearing Madhubuti proclaim while reading one of his poems, "We not blue / we black." I figured spending time on the South Side would help cleanse me of any traces of the blues in me and help me to develop into one of the New Black Poets. It didn't work. Despite my attempt to become acculturated in the new blackness that so many young Black poets were writing about, I was still little more than a proverbial ghetto child and the lure of returning to ghetto life on the West Side was something I could not resist for very long. I ended up spending most of the seventies running the streets and after wasting the entire decade I realized I had become just another chump who was in line to die a meaningless death and that's why I decided to return to the university.

I read the introduction to Stephen E. Henderson's *Understanding the New Black Poetry* in a Black Studies class and his argument about the three characteristics that were ideally present in works of Black poetry: structure (racially distinctive or coded use of language), theme (content about distinctly Black experiences), and saturation (expressions that illustrate a poem's fidelity with the experiences of Black life). Henderson's book became my poetic Bible since it was a virtual instruction manual for writing Black poems and I began to draft scores of them. When I ran into Miss Brooks again it was a chance meeting downtown on an overcast and breezy Chicago day with her carrying a purse and shopping bags and me with a backpack on my shoulder and a used copy of Henry Dumas's *Play Ebony Play Ivory* in my hand. I might have shyly walked past her if she hadn't spoken and complemented me on my book selection. Not knowing if she was interested in me or simply the book, I tried to tell her about some of the times I had neem around her but she interrupted by saying, "I know who you are, Reggie" and proceeded to treat me like I was an old friend. I had no idea if she remembered me from my high school poem or some of the South Side literary events I had attended, or if it could have been because I had worked with her husband, Henry Blakely, as a member of the selection panel for *Dial-A-Poem, Chicago*. Her greeting encouraged me a great deal because I was anxious to discuss poetry with her and receive comments on my more recent poems. I was confident her response would be much better than the one she had from my high school effort. She proved to be more than generous with her time and invited me to accompany her to a deli down on

Wabash Avenue for a bowl of soup. It was during our discussion that I heard her utter that phrase containing my name for the second time.

Like any young poet anxious for an opportunity to show off her or his poems, I always had a stack of mine in my backpack, and I was sure they would impress her because they were not full of juvenile rhymes, and I'd learned to keep my distance from clichés. But once again the praise I expected was not forthcoming, although there were several poems she separated from the pile because she thought they were better than the others. She pointed out how many of them were merely pronouncements about Black life and how they tended to lump all Black people together instead of offering portraits about specific individuals. She then said, "*Now Reggie*, why don't you write about some of the people you see on a daily basis around where you live on the West Side?" She was convinced that if I wrote about life on the West Side from my male perspective in the early eighties I would produce very different poems than the ones she wrote as a young woman on the city's South Side in the forties.

Thinking about our conversation that day is what made me realize that if she was able to give her early poems a sense of place by using the name Bronzeville then the best name I could use for the community I wanted to write about was Bluesville. After all, as West Siders we were newcomers to the city and although we shared the same hue as our South Side racial brethren, many of us felt like distant cousins. They were well-established residents of the North, but we were people who had only recently moved up from places such as Louisiana, Mississippi, Alabama, and Arkansas. We might have become citizens of the Midwestern Metropolis, but we were still the same folks that Baraka once characterized as blues people. We lived in the same buildings, on the same blocks, and as members of the same neighborhoods, but we lacked the shared history and sense of community that many on the South Side grew up with as an inheritance. I began to write Bluesville poems, stories, and essays that day, and, in a sense, every time I used that name it represented a tribute to Gwendolyn Brooks.

Before my lunch meeting with Miss Brooks, I had already published a few poems in newspapers such as *The West Side Journal* and *Haymarket*, a small campus literary journal, *The Red Shoes Review*, and also *The Chicago Poetry Letter News*, but none that I would want anyone to read today. It was only after I started writing Bluesville poems that I began to receive more prestigious publications in magazines and journals such as *The Spoon River Quarterly*, *Contact II*, and *Black American Literature Forum*. That was when I started feeling confident enough to think of myself as a poet and it led me to get involved with members of the city's larger community of writers and poets, including Sandra Cisneros, David Hernandez, Julie Parsons, and Carlos Cumpián. I had dreams of transforming the West Side into an important literary place, to what Harlem was during the Harlem Renaissance. In an effort to bring about this change I created a community arts organization called Lawndale Renaissance/Bluesville and organized a series of neighborhood writing workshops. I wrote a successful grant proposal to help pay for weekly Saturday morning creative writing and literature classes for junior high school students in the community. A number of leading Chicago poets and writers agreed to attend as special guests, including Madhubuti, Carolyn Rodgers, Angela Jackson, Walter Bradford, and Gwendolyn Brooks. I am not sure the others would have been willing to spend precious time on a Saturday morning with young school kids all the way over on the city's West Side for the measly $25 honorarium I had to offer, but once Miss Brooks agreed to come everyone else soon followed.

I eventually defended a volume of Bluesville poems for my thesis and a multi-genre novel titled *Crimes in Bluesville* for my dissertation at UIC. It was about a young West Sider who used poetry to escape from the bondage of inner city streets. I also included a wise high school counselor who encouraged him to use poetry to make something positive out of his life. In the final version the counselor goes by the name of Azusa Beets, but the original name that I gave her was Henrietta Brooks.

Brooks
Biography

When you have forgotten Sunday halves in bed,
Or me sitting on the front-room radiator in the limping afternoon
Looking off down the long street
To nowhere…

When you have, I say, forgotten all that,
Then you may tell,
Then I may believe
You have forgotten me well.

—Gwendolyn Brooks, " when you have forgotten Sunday: the love story"

We Remember Sunday: Portrait of the Artist as an Ancestor

Kansas, Oklahoma, Nebraska, Colorado, Utah, New Mexico. Remember that these were once "Indian Territories" of the western frontier, resettled into statehood after the Civil War. They are the advance beginnings of Gwendolyn Brooks, she who would one day become our national poet laureate.

The World War I years in Topeka, Kansas saw firmly rooted black communities with their churches and schools and businesses. People called their parents Exodusters, those who'd fled the South in the violent aftermath of Reconstruction a full generation earlier. But Jim Crow segregation had followed them there. Lynchings too had tagged along.

A Great Migration had ebbed and flowed since World War I, that massive movement that led millions of souls from Down-South to "Up-South." The opportunity of a better life beckoned a bright young couple named David and Keziah Brooks.

Perhaps they sensed the trouble to come, the dustbowl dervish uprooting topsoil on great swathes of the prairie, the Great Depression, a massacre of black folks in Tulsa, just 200 miles due south of Topeka. The newlyweds arrived in Chicago during the wartime economic boom to work as janitor and schoolteacher respectively.

"I've always resented the fact that my parents were living in Chicago, but my mother wanted me to be born in her home town," Miss Brooks said in an interview. "I feel I'm really a native Chicagoan."

Gwendolyn Brooks arrived on the scene on June 7, 1917, soon to be Chicago bound. It was in her blood, her amniotic fluid. Topeka may have been her birthplace but Chicago was the site of her conception, the place she'd abide for a lifetime.

The South Side grew Gwendolyn into girlhood. Books were consumed like food in the Brooks family household. Beggars were fed at the family table. Perched on the back steps of their house on Champlain Avenue, Miss Brooks was writing and rhyming from the age of seven. "You're going to be the Lady Paul Laurence Dunbar one day," Keziah predicted.

Shy and dark skinned, Gwendolyn Brooks was sheltered within the bosom of family but often shunned outside of it. Poetry was a practice that nurtured her lonely spirit. In the place of fast friendships, writing kept her company. She also nurtured connections with several literary godfathers, writing fan letters to James Weldon Johnson, sharing sheaths of poems with Langston Hughes.

> Yet do I marvel at this curious thing:
> To make a poet black, and bid him sing!
> —Countee Cullen, "Yet do I Marvel"

Cullen was another of Miss Brooks' literary influences. In the New Negro Renaissance some thirty years before, he had penned a poem some read as an affirmation, some as a lament. "Curious" or not, young Miss Brooks was a poet black, already singing the song of her soul.

And there was plenty to sing about.

Her first poem was published when she was thirteen. By sixteen she was a weekly columnist at the *Daily Defender*. At the age of twenty her works had been in two anthologies.

Gwendolyn Brooks met Henry Lowington Blakely Jr. in 1938, married him the next year and gave birth to children, Henry III in 1940 and Nora Brooks in 1951. In the meantime she wrote poetry, won prizes, and spent time teaching, working, mothering, wife-ing, and eventually publishing books. *Annie Allen*, her second poetry volume, won the Pulitzer Prize in 1950, making her the first black person to be so honored. *The Bean Eaters* was dedicated to her father David, who had recently passed away.

In his study, "African-American Marriage in 1910: Beneath the Surface of Census Data," St. Clair Drake appears to blame women when men decide to abandon their marriages. In response, Miss Brooks penned the proto-feminist essay, "Why Negro Women Leave Home." She discusses how the presence of black women in the labor force, family finances, spousal abuse, infidelity, and other issues motivated black women to seek extramarital affairs or leave their husbands altogether. These were topics she would also explore in her creative works. Significantly, Gwendolyn and Henry had separated. In fact, they would live apart at two different points in their sixty-year marriage.

For an urban poet, Miss Brooks deployed a surprising number of nature images: birds, skies, yards, front and back. She was especially fluent in the language of flowers. Flowers to train, to throw away. She wrote of the coora, of furious flowerings. She praised the "demure prettiness" of dandelions and oh, the startling declamation of one trapped in the protection of her own front yard: "A girl gets sick of a rose!" (exclamation mine).

Already celebrated as a poet, Miss Brooks' skills as novelist, essayist, and memoirist were now emerging. *Maud Martha*, her first and only book length work of fiction was published in 1953. The discrete vignettes in this slim semi-autobiographical novella explore race, identity, gender, class, and colorism in the world of a black girl coming of age in South Side Chicago.

Then came the famous epiphany at Fisk University's Second Writers Conference. Gwendolyn Brooks was now fifty years old, an age when many become calcified in their beliefs. This was 1967, the height of the Black Power Movement and its sister in solidarity, the Black Arts Movement (BAM). The bright, the beautiful, the revolutionary young writers and thinkers converged upon Nashville and crashed into Miss Brooks' awareness.

In her own words, "[M]y blackness . . . confronted me with a shrill spelling of my name." Gwendolyn Brooks was entering "the kindergarten of consciousness," embracing the beauty of her dark brown skin, growing and grooming the natural hair she would keep for the rest of her life, and forever changing her writing direction.

Easing away from the strictness of structures like the sonnet, she began experimenting with looser forms. More significantly, her subject matter changed, its political message growing more overt.

Miss Brooks' newfound social consciousness also extended to her life off-page. She began hosting writing workshops with the Blackstone Rangers street gang and holding poetry salons in her home for BAM writers like Haki Madhubuti and Carolyn Rodgers. While not an official member of OBAC, she was closely aligned with the writers and artists, helping to dedicate the Wall of Respect in 1967. Leaving behind her mainstream publisher she began publishing her work with small black presses like Broadside Press and Third World Press.

Yet Gwendolyn Brooks' sense of compassion was expansive. Firmly rooted in the African American experience, her outreach also extended beyond the black community. During the decades that followed Miss Brooks toured widely, reading her work and conducting workshops across the nation and around the world. She started an annual magazine, visited Africa, and read at the White House with twenty other distinguished poets. A time of great progress became a time of great sadness when she lost her beloved mother, Keziah Wims Brooks.

Just as her parents once shared food with the neighborhood, Miss Brooks now brought poetry to the people with contests and competitions, awards, and in some cases, patronage. Gwendolyn Brooks once declared that, "People are my religion."

Miss Brooks created her work against the clamor of critics who warned that "if being a Negro is the only subject, the writing is not important." She knew that Negroes are important and demonstrated this through the ordinary heroism, the complex challenges and the sometimes terrible truths of living in the "hurt Black of our skin."

Gwendolyn Brooks burst the seams of straightjacketed stereotypes to give us a universe of full, flawed, and complicated characters. She made us see the drylongso, the everyday wonder of Old Marrieds and the Bean Eaters. She let us know the Bronzeville Boys and Girls, the Annie Allens, the Sadies and Maudes. She gave us Emmett Till, DeWitt Williams, and Satin Legs Smith.

As she approached elderhood Miss Brooks began to wrap her hair. In her study, "The African American Woman's Headwrap: Unwinding the Symbols," Helen Bradley Griebel noted that, "In the 1970s, the headwrap reemerged as an item of clothing worn publicly by some black women . . . Thus, over time, the headwrap displays a dynamic quality in gathering new meanings and shedding older nuances."

An African belief suggests that ancestors live on as long as they are remembered. A Chinese proverb also warns, "to forget one's ancestors is to be a brook without a source, a tree without a root."

Gwendolyn Brooks died at her home in Chicago, succumbing to cancer in the year 2000. Yet those who embrace her as a root of our cultural tree, a source of our literary brook, know that she lives on in ancestral memory. Whether or not we were in her presence, we remember still her sojourn amongst us, for by her fruits she is known.

And no, we have not forgotten Sundays, the "nothing-I-have-to-do and I'm-happy-why?/And if-Monday-never-had-to-come—"

Monday has come and we still remember. We have not forgotten Gwendolyn Brooks, nor shall we forget.

Brooks Bibliography

Look at what's happening in this world. Every day there's something exciting or disturbing to write about. With all that's going on, how could I stop?

—Gwendolyn Brooks

KATHLEEN E. BETHEL

AFRICAN AMERICAN STUDIES LIBRARIAN, NORTHWESTERN UNIVERSITY

Gwendolyn Brooks: A Selected Bibliography 1979-2015

"She was our irreplaceable visionary poet. And our charge is to make sure that her work, her legacy, and her ideas forever reign in the ears and minds of our children and our children's children. She was indeed a gift to us for eighty-three years."
—Haki R. Madhubuti, *Mosaic Literary Magazine*, Summer 2007

This list of references is an answer to poet and publisher Haki Madhubuti's charge to honor the legacy of Gwendolyn Brooks by sharing published responses to her life and work. The following bibliography covers material published after the book, *Langston Hughes and Gwendolyn Brooks: A Reference Guide*, by R. Baxter Miller (G. K. Hall, 1978). This is a marvelous compilation covering her early career before 1979.

As this Pulitzer Prize winner is featured in many publication types, the following pages include books, chapters, journals, and magazine articles. It does not include newspaper articles, academic theses and dissertations, audiovisual materials, sheet, book reviews, conference papers, government publications, obituaries, or blogs. Gwendolyn Brooks is a crucial presence in our literary canon, as she is a powerful, insightful, and brilliant voice of the twentieth century.

A Street in Bronzeville. New York: Harper & Brothers, 1945.

Annie Allen. New York: Harper & Brothers, 1949.

Maud Martha. New York: Harper & Brothers, 1953.

Bronzeville Boys and Girls. New York: Harper & Brothers, 1956.

The Bean Eaters. New York: Harper & Brothers, 1960.

Selected Poems. New York: Harper, 1963.

We Real Cool. Detroit: Broadside Press, 1966.

The Wall. Detroit: Broadside Press, 1967.

In the Mecca. New York: Harper, 1968.

Riot. Detroit: Broadside Press, 1969.

Family Pictures. Detroit: Broadside Press, 1970.

Aloneness. Detroit: Broadside Press, 1971.

Black Steel: Joe Frazier and Muhammad Ali. Detroit: Broadside Press, 1971.

Jump Bad: A New Chicago Anthology. Detroit: Broadside Press, 1971.

The World of Gwendolyn Brooks. New York: Harper, 1971.

Report from Part One. Detroit: Broadside Press, 1972.

The Tiger Who Wore White Gloves, Or What You Are You Are. Chicago: Third World Press, 1974.

Beckonings. Detroit: Broadside Press, 1975.

Primer for Blacks. Chicago: Black Position Press, 1980.

Young Poet's Primer. Chicago: Brooks Press, 1980.

To Disembark. Chicago: Third World Press, 1981.

Black Love. Chicago: Brooks Press, 1981.

The Progress. Chicago: Turtle Press, 1982.

Mayor Harold Washington; and, Chicago, the I Will City. Chicago: Brooks Press, 1983.

Very Young Poets. Chicago: Third World Press, 1983.

The Near-Johannesburg Boy, and Other Poems. Chicago: The David Company, 1986.

Blacks. Chicago: The David Company, 1987.

Gottschalk and the Grande Tarantelle. Chicago: The David Company, 1988.

The Second Sermon on the Warpland: For Walter Bradford. Tucson, AZ: Chax Press, 1988.

Winnie. Chicago: Third World Press, 1988.

Children Coming Home. Chicago: The David Company, 1991.

Maud Martha. Chicago: Third World Press, 1993; New York: Harper, 1953.

Brooks, Gwendolyn, and Seitu Jones. *Young Heroes II: To Don at Salaam*. Minneapolis: Minnesota Center for Book Arts and the Friends of the Public Library, 1995.

Report from Part Two. Chicago: Third World Press, 1996.

Selected Poems. New York: Harper Perennial, 1999, c1963.

In Montgomery, and Other Poems. Chicago: Third World Press, 2003.

Brooks, Gwendolyn, and Gloria J. W. Gayles. *Conversations with Gwendolyn Brooks*. Jackson: University Press of Mississippi, 2003.

Brooks, Gwendolyn, and Elizabeth Alexander. *The Essential Gwendolyn Brooks*. New York: Library of America, 2005.

Bronzeville Boys and Girls. Illustrated by Faith Ringgold. New York: Amistad/HarperCollins Publishers, 2007, c1956.

WRITINGS BY GWENDOLYN BROOKS

"'Aching' for Balance." *Education Week* 13.33 (1994): 33.

"An Arrival." *Ebony*. 51.1 (1995): 32.

"Art." *New American Writing* 5 (1989): 63.

"Astonishment of Heart." *U.S. Catholic* 75.5 (2010): 51.

"The Audre Lorde I Knew." *Eyeball* 2 (1993): 18.

"Ballad of Pearl May Lee." *Socialism and Democracy* 22.2 (2008): 45-48.

"Ballad of Pearl May Lee." *An Anthology of Interracial Literature: Black-White Contacts in the Old World and the New*. Edited by Werner Sollors. New York: New York University Press, 2004: 577-580.

"Beverly Hills, Chicago." *The 20th Century in Poetry*. Edited by Michael Hulse and Simon Rae. New York: Pegasus Books, 2013, 2011: 1.

"Big Persons And The Littles." *Farrakhan Factor: African-American Writers on Leadership, Nationhood, and Minister Louis Farrakhan*. New York: Grove Press, 1998: 270-274.

"Black Love." *Ebony* 36.10 (1981): 29.

"Black Love." (Poem) *Ebony* 41.1 (1985): 158.

"A Black Wedding Song." *Black Writer Magazine* 3.1 (1983): 20.

"A Black Wedding Song." *I Hear a Symphony: African Americans Celebrate Love*. Paula L. Woods and Felix H. Liddell, compilers. New York: Anchor Books, 1994: 151-152.

"A Black Wedding Song." *It's All Love: Black Writers on Soul Mates, Family, and Friends*. Edited by Marita Golden. New York: Broadway, 2009: 6.

"Black Woman in Russia." *Humanities* 15.3 (1994): 24-29.

"Boy Breaking Glass." *Poems to Read: A New Favorite Poem Project Anthology*. Edited by Robert Pinsky and Maggie Dietz. New York: W.W. Norton, 2002.

"Comment." *Poetry* 151.1/2 (1987): 202.

"Cynthia in the Snow." Illustrated by Julianna Brion. *Cricket* 42.4 (2015): 12.

"Excerpts from the poetry of Gwendolyn Brooks." [Includes: "The Life of Lincoln West," "A Song in the Front Yard," and "The Blackstone Rangers."] *Humanities* 15.3 (1994): 10-11.

"Foreword." Madhubuti, Haki R. *GroundWork: New and Selected Poems of Don L. Lee/Haki R. Madhubuti from 1966-1996*. Chicago: Third World, 1996: xiv-xvii.

"45 Years in Culture and Creative Writing." *Ebony* 46.1 (1990): 110, 112.

"From 'The Womanhood,' VI. The Rites for Cousin Vit." *American Poet* 35 (2008): 13.

"Gay Chaps at the Bar." Poetry 200.1 (2012): 44.

"Gwendolyn Brooks: Distinctive and Proud at 77." *Smokestacks & Skyscrap ers: An Anthology of Chicago Writing*. Edited by David Starkey and Richard Guzman. Chicago: Wild Onion, 1999: 392+.

"Gwendolyn Brooks." [Six poems] *The Garden Thrives: Twentieth-Century African-American Poetry*. Edited by Clarence Major. New York: Harper Perennial, 1996: 56-62.

"Gwendolyn Brooks (b.1917)." [10 poems] *Every Shut Eye Ain't Asleep: An Anthology of Poetry by African Americans Since 1945*. Boston: Little, Brown, 1994: 30-59.

"Gwendolyn Brooks (1917-2000)." [Three poems] *Angles of Ascent: A Norton Anthology of Contemporary African American Poetry*. Edited by Charles Henry Rowell. New York: W. W. Norton & Co., 2013: 4-11.

"Gwendolyn Brooks Summarizes Her Year As the 29th Consultant in Poetry." *Library of Congress Information Bulletin* 46.7 (1987): 69-70.

"Gwendolyn Brooks With Kamili Anderson: Belles Lettres Interviews." *Belles Lettres* 1.3 (1986): 9-10.

"Henry Dumas: Perceptiveness and Zeal." *Black American Literature Forum* 22.2 (1988): 177.

"I Am a Black." *Drumvoices Revue* 4.1 (1994): 126.

"I Am a Black." (Poem) *Essence* 34.12 (2004): 239.

"Interview (Autobiography)." *TriQuarterly* 60 (1984): 405-410.

"Jack Conroy, 'A Poem.'" *New Letters* 57.4 (1991): 3.

"Jane Addams." *Beloit Poetry Journal* 51.1-2 (2000): 237-238.

"Jane Addams." *Mosaic Literary Magazine* 19 (2007): 21.

"Keziah (Memoir)." *TriQuarterly* 75 (1989): 38-50.

"Last Inauguration of Mayor Harold Washington." *The Black Scholar* 19.4 (1988): 7.

"The Life of Lincoln West." *SOS/Calling All Black People: A Black Arts Movement Reader*. Edited by John H. Bracey Jr., Sonia Sanchez, and James Smethurst. Amherst: University of Massachusetts Press, 2014: 270-73.

"A light and diplomatic bird . . ." (untitled). *Field* 61 (1999): 6.

"Malcolm X." *SOS/Calling All Black People: A Black Arts Movement Reader*. Edited by John H. Bracey Jr., Sonia Sanchez, and James Smethurst. Amherst: University of Massachusetts Press, 2014: 312.

"Malcolm X: For Dudley Randall." Drumvoices Revue 2.1 (1992): 210.

"Marie Lucille." Storyworks 23.5 (2016): 29.

"Martin Luther King Jr." Storyworks 17.4 (2010): 3.

"Martin Luther King Jr." *In the Spirit of Martin: The Living Legacy of Dr. Martin Luther King, Jr.* By Gary Miles Chassman. Atlanta: Tinwood, 2002: 208.

"Martin Luther King Jr.: April 4, 1968. (Cover story)." *Scholastic Scope* 53.10 (2005): 19.

"Michael is Afraid of the Storm." *Storyworks* 14.6 (2007): 31.

"The Mother." *Literature and Medicine* 13.2 (1994): 201-02.

"The Mother." *Cries of the Spirit: A Celebration of Women's Spirituality.* Edited by Marilyn Sewell. Boston: Beacon, 1991: 101-103.

"My Dreams, My Works, Must Wait Till after Hell." *Ms.* 11.4 (2001): 83.

"The Near-Johannesburg Boy." *The Black Scholar* 19.4 (1988): 6-7.

"Negro Hero." *Field* 61 (1999): 24-25.

"'Parents' From Report From Part One." *Mosaic Literary Magazine* 19 (2007): 26-27.

"A Poet Honors Dr. King." *Scholastic Scope* 58.9 (2010): 13.

"Poets Who Are Negroes." *Afro-American Writers*, 1940-1955. Dictionary of Literary Biography Vol. 76. Edited by Trudier Harris-Lopez. Vol. 76. Detroit: Gale, 1988: 269.

"The Poetry of Gwendolyn Brooks." *Ebony* 39.6 (1984): 78-80+.

"The Poetry of Gwendolyn Brooks." *Ebony* 52.11 (1997): 50-52.

"The Progress." *Women on War: Essential Voices for the Nuclear Age.* Edited by Daniela Gioseffi. New York: Simon & Schuster, 1988: 33.

"Reader, Interrupted." *O, The Oprah Magazine* 7.7 (2006): 95.

"The Richness of Poetry." *New Letters* 59.1 (1992): 55.

"The Rites For Cousin Vit." *Field* 61 (1999): 29.

"Sadie and Maud." *Massachusetts Review* 34.2 (1993): 242-243.

"The Second Sermon On The Warpland." *Field* 61 (1999): 55-56.

"Sick Man Looks at Flowers." *Black Nature: Four Centuries of African American Nature Poetry.* Edited by Camille T. Dungy. Athens: University of Georgia Press, 2009: 172.

"{Sit down. Inhale. Exhale}." *Poetry* 177.4 (2001): 361.

"A Song In The Front Yard." *Field* 61 (1999): 11.

"A Song in the Front Yard." *Harper's* 269.1611 (1984): 47.

"Still Do I Keep My Look, My Identity..." *Poetry* 200.1 (2012): 45.

"Telephone Conversations." (Poem) *Black American Literature Forum* 17.4 (1983): 148.

"To an Old Black Woman, Homeless and Indistinct." *Drumvoices Revue* 2.1 (1992): 120-121.

"To Black Women." (Poem) *Ebony* 52.11 (1997): 51.

"To Gwen with Love." *Ebony* 56.4 (2001): 82-86.

"To Prisoners." *Illinois Issues* July (1981): 20.

"To Those of My Sisters Who Kept Their Naturals." *Essence* 19.10 (1989): 129.

"Tommy." *Ideals* 60.2 (2003) 79+.

"Twenty Four Poems From Four Decades." *Time Capsule* Summer/Fall (1983).

"Uncle Seagram." *Drumvoices Revue* 4.1 (1994): 127.

"We Real Cool." *Field* 61 (1999): 45.

"We Real Cool." *Mosaic Literary Magazine* Summer 19 (2007): 63.

"We Real Cool." *Hip-hop Poetry and the Classics: Connecting Our Classic Curriculum to Hip-hop Poetry through Standards-based, Language Arts Instruction.* By Alan Sitomer and Michael Cirelli. Beverly Hills: Milk Mug Pub., 2004: 47-49.

"Weaponed Woman." *Essence* 14 (1983): 147.

"When You Have Forgotten Sunday: The Love Story." *Mosaic Literary Magazine* 19 (2007): 20.

"When You Have Forgotten Sunday: The Love Story." *Ebony* 52.11 (1997): 52

"Winnie." *Poetry* 151.1/2 (1987): 20.

PUBLICATIONS ABOUT GWENDOLYN BROOKS

Ahern, Megan K. "Creative Multivalence: Social Engagement Beyond Naturalism in Gwendolyn Brooks's *Maud Martha*." *African American Review* 47.2/3 (2014): 313-326.

Alexander, Elizabeth. "Meditations on 'Mecca:' Gwendolyn Brooks and the Responsibilities of the Black Poet." *The Black Interior: Essays.* Saint Paul, MN: Graywolf Press, 2004: 45-58.

"Meditations on 'Mecca:' Gwendolyn Brooks and the Responsibilities of the Black Poet." *By Herself: Women Reclaim Poetry.* Edited by Molly McQuade. Saint Paul, MN: Graywolf Press, 2000: 368-379.

"Ode to Miss Gwendolyn Brooks (Ten Small Serenades)." *Power and Possibility: Essays, Reviews, and Interviews.* Ann Arbor: University of Michigan Press, 2007: 28-32.

—."Our Miss Brooks." *Black Issues Book Review* 2.6 (2000): 54.

"Posthumous Jewels: Gwendolyn Brooks left us many rich words." *Black Issues Book Review* 6.1 (2004): 54.

The Essential Gwendolyn Brooks. New York: Library of America, 2005.

Alexandra, Elizabeth. "New Ideas About Black Experimental Poetry." *Michigan Quarterly Review* 50.4 (2011): 598-621.

Anaporte-Easton, Jean. "Etheridge Knight: Poet and Prisoner an Introduction." *Callaloo* 19.4 (1996): 941-46.

Andrews, Larry R. "Ambivalent Clothes Imagery in Gwendolyn Brooks's 'The Sundays Of Satin-Legs Smith.'" *CLA Journal* 24 (1980): 150-163.

Avilez, GerShun. "Housing the Black Body: Value, Domestic Space, and Segregation Narratives." *African American Review* 42.1 (2008): 135-147.

Axelrod, Steven Gould. "Gwendolyn Brooks and the Middle Generation." *Jarrell, Bishop, Lowell & Co.: Middle Generation poets in context.* Edited by Suzanne Ferguson. Knoxville: University of Tennessee Press, 2003: 26-40.

"The Middle Generation and WWII: Jarrell, Shapiro, Brooks, Bishop, Lowell." *War, Literature, and the Arts* 11.1 (1999): 1-41.

Banks, Margot Harper. *Religious Allusion in the Poetry of Gwendolyn Brooks.* Jefferson, NC: London: McFarland, 2012.

Barnes, S. Brandi. "The Poet in the House of Evans Ave." *Mosaic Literary Magazine* 19 (2007): 34-36, 59-60.

Bass, Patrik Henry. "Gwendolyn's Words: A Gift to Us." *Essence* 31.11 (2001): 16

Beckwith, Naomi. "The Necessary Fluster." *Poetry* 200.3 (2012): 266-67.

Betts, Tara. "Gwendolyn's Gatekeeper, Interview with Nichole Shields." *Mosaic Literary Magazine* 19 (2007): 28-31, 60.

Bloom, Harold. *Gwendolyn Brooks.* Philadelphia: Chelsea House, 2000.

Gwendolyn Brooks: Comprehensive Research and Study Guide. Philadelphia: Chelsea House Publishers, 2003.

Bolden, Barbara Jean. *Urban Rage in Bronzeville: Social Commentary in the Poetry of Gwendolyn Brooks, 1945-1960.* Chicago: Third World Press, 1998.

Boyd, Melba Joyce. "'Prophets for a New Day': The Cultural Activism of Margaret Danner, Margaret Burroughs, Gwendolyn Brooks and Margaret Walker During the Black Arts Movement." Revista Canaria de Estudios Engleses 37 (1998): 55-67.

Bresnahan, Roger J. Jiang. "The Cultural Predicaments of Ethnic Writers: Three Chicago Poets." *Midwestern Miscellany* 27.2 (1999): 36-46.

Bridgforth, Sharon. "From Dyke/Warrior-Prayers: Redux." *Cream City Review* 39.1 (2015): 165-66.

Brown, Martha H. and Marilyn Zorn. "GLR Interview: Gwendolyn \ Brooks." *Great Lakes Review* 6.1 (1979): 48-55.

Bryant, Jacqueline. *Gwendolyn Brooks'* Maud Martha: *A Critical Collection*. Chicago: Third World Press, 2002.

Gwendolyn Brooks and Working Writers. Chicago: Third World Press, 2007.

Bryant, Marsha. "Gwendolyn Brooks, 'Ebony,' and Postwar Race Relations," *American Literature* 79.1 (2007): 113-141.

Bubíková, Šárka. "Maud Martha and the Tradition of the Ethnic Female Bildungsroman." *Litteraria Pragensia* 21 (2011): 7-21.

Burr, Zofia. *Of Women, Poetry, and Power: Strategies of Address in Dickinson, Miles, Brooks, Lorde and Angelou*. Urbana: University of Illinois Press, 2002.

Callahan, John F. "Essentially an Essential African: Gwendolyn Brooks and the Awakening to Audience." *North Dakota Quarterly* 55.4 (1987): 59-73.

Campbell, Alex. "Gwendolyn Brooks Meets the Conquering Lion of Judah." *Drumvoices Revue* 12.1/2 (2004): 125-26.

Campbell, Christian. "Three Kinds of Edges for P.S." (Poem) *Mosaic Literary Magazine* 19 (Summer 2007): 44.

Chapman, Danielle. "Sweet Bombs." *Poetry* 189.1 (2006): 54.

Cherry, James E. "On Hearing of the Death of Gwendolyn Brooks." (Poem) *Role Call: A Generational Anthology of Social and Political Black Art & Literature*. Edited by Tony Medina, Samiya A. Bashir, and Quraysh Ali Lansana. Chicago: Third World, 2002: 208.

Clarke, Cheryl. "The Loss of Lyric Space and the Critique of Traditions in Gwendolyn Brooks's *In the Mecca*." *Kenyon Review* 17.1 (1995): 136-147.

Conrad, Rachel. "'And Stay, a Minute More, Alone': Time and Subjectivities in Gwendolyn Brooks's Bronzeville Boys and Girls." *Children's Literature Association Quarterly* 38.4 (2013): 379-398.

"Children Coming Home: The Anticipatory Present in Gwendolyn Brooks's Poems of Childhood." *Callaloo* 37.2 (2014): 369-388.

Cordell, Sigrid Anderson. "'The Case Was Very Black Against' Her: Pauline Hopkins and the Politics of Racial Ambiguity at the Colored American Magazine." *American Periodicals: A Journal of History & Criticism* 16.1 (2006): 52-73.

Cummings, Allison. "Public Subjects: Race and the Critical Reception of Gwendolyn Brooks, Erica Hunt, and Harryette Mullen." *Frontiers: A Journal of Women Studies* 26.2 (2005): 33-36.

Dawkins, Laura. "It Could Have Been My Son: Maternal Empathy in Gwendolyn Brooks's and Audre Lorde's Till Poems." *Emmett Till in Literary Memory and Imagination*. Edited by Harriet Pollack and Christopher Metress. Baton Rouge: Louisiana State University Press, 2008: 112-127.

Dawson, Emma Waters. "The Vanishing Point: The Rejected Black Woman in the Poetry of Gwendolyn Brooks." *Obsidian II: Black Literature in Review* 4.1 (1989): 1-11.

Debo, Annette. "Reflecting Violence in the Warpland: Gwendolyn Brooks's Riot." *African American Review* 39.1/2 (2005): 143-152.

"Signifying Afrika: Gwendolyn Brooks' Later Poetry." *Callaloo* 29.1 (2006): 168-181.

Doreski, Carole K. "Brooks, Gwendolyn 1917–." *American Writers: A Collection of Literary Biographies, Supplement 3*. Edited by Lea Baechler and A. Walton Litz. New York: Charles Scribner's Sons, 1991: 69-90.

Dove, Rita. "Bearing Witness Tribute to Gwendolyn Brooks." *Humanities* 15.3 (1994): 8-9.

"Testifying: A Tribute from Poet Laureate of the United States Rita Dove." *Black Issues in Higher Education* 11.18 (1994): 14.

Duncan, Bryan. "'And I Doubt All': Allegiance and Ambivalence in Gwendolyn Brooks's 'Gay Chaps at the Bar'." *Journal of Modern Literature* 34.1 (2010): 36-57.

Dworkin, Ira. "'The Evading Eye': The Transgeneric Prose of Gwendolyn Brooks." *CLA Journal* 47.1 (2003): 32-54.

Edford, Rachel. "Forms of Identity in Gwendolyn Brooks's World War II Poems." *College Literature* 41.4 (2014): 71-93.

Engleman, Paul. "Written on the Wind." *Chicago* 44.6 (1995): 82.

Evans, Robert C. "'Abortions Will Not Let You Forget': A Close Reading of Gwendolyn Brooks's 'The Mother.'" *CLA Journal* 54.3 (2011): 223-238.

Faulkner, Howard. "A Note on Sonnet 2 of Brooks's *The Children of the Poor*." *Explicator* 67.1 (2008): 51-53.

Fleissner, Robert F. "'Real Cool' Fire and Ice: Brooks and Frost." *Robert Frost Review* 4 (1994): 58-62.

Floreani, Tracy. "Maud Martha Versus I Love Lucy: Taking on the Postwar Consumer Fantasy." *Complicating Constructions: Race, Ethnicity, and Hybridity in American Texts*. Edited by David S. Goldstein and Audrey B. Thacker. Seattle: University of Washington Press, 2007: 180-203.

Flynn, Richard. "'The Kindergarten of New Consciousness': Gwendolyn Brooks and the Social Construction of Childhood." *African American Review* 34.3 (2000): 483-499.

Ford, Karen Jackson. "These Old Writing Paper Blues: The Blues Stanza and Literary Poetry." *College Literature* 24.3 (1997): 84-103.

"The Last Quatrain: Gwendolyn Brooks and the Ends of Ballads." *Twentieth Century Literature* 56.3 (2010): 371-395.

"The Sonnets of Satin-Legs Brooks." *Contemporary Literature* 48.3 (2007): 345-373.

Francini, Antonella. "Sonnet vs Sonnet: The Fourteen Lines in African American Poetry." *RSA Journal* 14 (2003): 37-66.

Franklin, V. P. "Chapter 9: Gwendolyn Brooks and Amiri Baraka: The Creation of a Black Literary Aesthetic." *Living Our Stories, Telling Our Truths: Autobiography and the Making of the African-American Intellectual Tradition*. New York: Scribner, 1995.

Frazier, Valerie. "Domestic Epic Warfare in *Maud Martha*." *African American Review* 39.1/2 (2005): 133-141.

Full of Pepper and Light: Welcoming the Gwendolyn Brooks Papers to the University of Illinois: An Evening of Poetry, Song, and Appreciation: 24 April 2014, Lincoln Hall Theatre, Urbana, Illinois. Urbana, IL: Rare Book & Manuscript Library, 2014.

Gayle, Addison, Jr. "Gwendolyn Brooks: Poet of the Whirlwind." *Black Women Writers (1950-1980): A Critical Evaluation*. Edited by Mari Evans. New York: Anchor Press/Doubleday, 1984: 79-87.

Georgoudaki, Ekaterini. *Race, Gender, and Class Perspectives in the Works of Maya Angelou, Gwendolyn Brooks, Rita Dove, Nikki Giovanni, and Audre Lorde*. Thessaloniki, Greece: Aristotle University of the Thessaloniki, 1991.

Gery, John. "Subversive Parody in the Early Poems of Gwendolyn Brooks." *South Central Review* 16.1 (1999): 44-56.

Gibbons, Reginald. "Gwendolyn Brooks at 70." *Book World* (1987).

Giles, Ron. "Brooks's 'A Song in the Front Yard.'" *Explicator* 57.3 (1999): 169-171.

Gilfoyle, Timothy J. "A Chicago School of Literature—Gwendolyn Brooks and Studs Terkel." *Chicago History* 26.1 (1997): 62-72.

Gilmore, Susan. "'It Had the Beat Inevitable': Gwendolyn Brooks's Report from the Fifties." *Sagetrieb: A Journal Devoted to Poets in the Imagist/ Objectivist Tradition* 19.3 (2006): 105-140.

Giovanni, Nikki. "No Complaints for Gwendolyn Brooks... (1917-2001)." *Black Collegian* 31.3 (2001): 99.

Gonsalves, Joy. "20/20, For Ms. Gwendolyn Brooks." *Mosaic Literary Magazine* 19 (2007): 37.

Goodman, Jenny. "Revisionary Postwar Heroism in Gwendolyn Brooks's *Annie Allen*." *Approaches to the Anglo and American Female Epic, 1621-1982*. Edited by Bernard Schweizer. Aldershot; Burlington, VT: Ashgate (2006): 159-180.

Greasley, Philip A. "Africa and Gwendolyn Brooks's America." *Midwestern Miscellany* 37 (2009): 17-32.

"Gwendolyn Brooks at Eighty: A Retrospective." *MidAmerica: The Yearbook of the Society for the Study of Midwestern Literature* 23 (1996): 124-135.

"Gwendolyn Brooks: The Emerging Poetic Voice." *The Great Lakes Review* 10.2 (1984): 14-23.

"Gwendolyn Brooks's Afrika." *MidAmerica: The Yearbook of the Society for the Study of Midwestern Literature* 8 (1986): 9-18.

Griffin, Farah Jasmine. "Gwendolyn Brooks (7 June 1917-)." *American Poets Since World War II: Fourth Series. Dictionary of Literary Biography Vol. 165*. Edited by Joseph Mark Conte. Detroit: Gale, 1996: 81-91.

Gruesser, John C. "Afro-American Travel Literature And Africanist Discourse." *Black American Literature Forum* 24.1 (1990): 5-21.

Guinn, Michael. "A tribute to Ms. Gwendolyn Brooks." (Poem) *Role Call: A Generational Anthology of Social and Political Black Art & Literature.* Edited by Tony Medina, Samiya A. Bashir, and Quraysh Ali Lansana. Chicago: Third World, 2002: 442.

Hacker, Marilyn. "The Sonnet as a Wild Woman's Blues." *Field: Contemporary Poetry and Poetics* 61 (1999): 29-35.

"Brooks, H. D., and Rukeyser: Three American Women Poets in the First Century of World Wars." *American Poet* 35 (2008): 8-12.

Hackney, Sheldon. "Conversation with Gwendolyn Brooks." *Humanities* 15.3 (1994): 4-6, 36-38.

Hall, James C. "A Way with Words." *Footsteps* 7.2 (2005): 32-35.

Hansell, William H. "The Uncommon Commonplace in the Early Poems of Gwendolyn Brooks." *CLA Journal* 30.3 (1987): 261-277.

Harrington, Su. "Gwendolyn Brooks." *Ms.* 14.1 (2004): 84.

Harris, Victoria F. "The Voice of Gwendolyn Brooks." *Interpretations* (1979): 56-66.

Hawkins, B. Denise. "Conversation." *The Furious Flowering of African American Poetry.* Charlottesville: University Press of Virginia, 1999: 274-280.

"An Evening with Gwendolyn Brooks." *Black Issues in Higher Education* 11.18 (1994): 16-17, 20-21.

"A Furious Flowering of Poetry: Conference to Document, Analyze Black Arts Movement of the '60s." *Black Issues in Higher Education* 11.13 (1994): 40.

Hedley, Jane. "Race and rhetoric in the poetry of Gwendolyn Brooks." *I Made You to Find Me: The Coming of Age of the Woman Poet and the Politics of Poetic Address.* Columbus: Ohio State University Press, 2009.

Heller, Janet Ruth. "Gwendolyn Brooks's Dramatic Monologues in A Street In Bronzeville." *MidAmerica* 29 (2002): 54-60.

Henderson, Aneeka A. "Red, Black, and Left: Communist Counterdiscourses." *WSQ: Women's Studies Quarterly* 43.3/4 (2015): 72-75.

Hill, Christine M. *Gwendolyn Brooks: "Poetry Is Life Distilled."* Berkeley Heights, NJ: Enslow Publishers, 2005.

Hirshfield, Jane. "Poetry, Transformation, and the Column of Tears." *American Poetry Review* 42.6 (2013): 37-41.

Hobby, Blake G. "Gwendolyn Brooks's Bronzeville and Tate Taylor's Jackson: 'Art Hurts.'" *Movies in the Age of Obama: The Era of Post Racial and Neo-racist Cinema.* Edited by David Garrett Izzo. Lanham: Rowman & Littlefield, 2014: 15-30.

Horvath, Brooke Kenton. "The Satisfactions of What's Difficult in Gwendolyn Brooks's Poetry." *American Literature* 62.4 (1990): 606-616.

Howe, Susan Elizabeth and Jay Fox. "A Conversation with Gwendolyn Brooks." *Literature and Belief* 12 (1992): 1-12.

Hubbard, Stacy Carson. "'A Splintery Box': Race and Gender in the Sonnets of Gwendolyn Brooks." *Genre* 25.1 (1992): 47-64.

Hughes, Gertrude Reif. "Making It Really New: Hilda Doolittle, Gwendolyn Brooks, and the Feminist Potential of Modern Poetry." *American Quarterly* 42.3 (1990): 375-401.

Hughes, Sheila Hassell. "A Prophet Overheard: A Juxtapositional Reading of Gwendolyn Brooks's 'In the Mecca.'" *African American Review* 38.2 (2004): 257-280.

Israel, Charles. "Gwendolyn Brooks." *American Poets Since World War II: Part 1. Dictionary of Literary Biography Vol. 5.* Edited by Donald J. Greiner. Detroit: Gale, 1980: 100-106.

Jack, Z. M. "'That No Performance May Be Plain or Vain': Self as Art in Gwendolyn Brooks' Bronzeville." *Wasafiri: The Transnational Journal of International Writing* 45 (2005) 5-10.

Jackson, Angela. "In Memoriam Gwendolyn Brooks (1917-2000)." *Callaloo* 23.4 (2000): 1163-1169.

Janssen, Ronald R. "Brooks' 'A Song in the Front Yard.'" *Explicator* 43.3 (1985): 42-43.

Jefferson, Margo. "A Journal for Adrienne Kennedy (after People Who Led to My Plays)." *Modern Drama* 55.1 (2012): 55-69.

Jimoh, A. Yemisi. "Double Consciousness, Modernism and Womanist Themes in Gwendolyn Brooks's 'The Anniad.'" *MELUS: Multi-Ethnic Literature of the U.S.* 23.3 (1998): 167-186.

Johnson, Mark. "Brooks's Gang Girls." *Explicator* 61.4 (2003): 229-231.

Joyce, Joyce Ann. "The Poetry of Gwendolyn Brooks: an African-Centered Exploration." *Warriors, Conjurers and Priests: Defining African-Centered Literary Criticism.* Chicago: Third World Press, 1994.

Kavanaugh, Ron. "Editorial." *Mosaic Literary Magazine* 19 (Summer 2007): 13.

Kearful, Frank J. "Poetry: The 1940s to the Present." *American Literary Scholarship* 2007.1 (2007): 409-436.

Kent, George E. "Aesthetic Values in the Poetry of Gwendolyn Brooks." *Black American Literature and Humanism.* Edited by R. Baxter Miller. Lexington: University Press of Kentucky, 1981: 75-94.

"Gwendolyn Brooks (7 June 1917-)." *Afro-American Writers, 1940-1955. Dictionary of Literary Biography* Vol. 76. Edited by Trudier Harris-Lopez. Vol. 76. Detroit: Gale, 1988: 11-24.

"Gwendolyn Brooks' Poetic Realism: A Developmental Survey." Evans, Mari. *Black Women Writers (1950-1980): A Critical Evaluation.* New York: Anchor Press/Doubleday, 1984: 88-105.

"Gwendolyn Brooks Portrait, in Part, of the Artist as Young Girl and Apprentice Writer." *Callaloo* 7 (1979): 74-83.

A Life of Gwendolyn Brooks. Lexington: University Press of Kentucky, 1990.

Kiell, Matthew. "Taking Gwendolyn Brooks Back to Her Neighborhood." *Humanities* 15.3 (1994): 12-13, 42-43.

Kitta, Gergely. *Gwendolyn Brooks's Poetry: Some Special Characterisics of African-American Art through the Verse of a Poet Laureate.* Saarbrücken: VDM Verlag Dr. Müller, 2008.

Koch, Matthew. "Rhythm in Gwendolyn Brooks's We Real Cool." *Explicator* 69.1 (2011): 27-29.

Kufrin, Joan. "The Poet." *Uncommon Women: Gwendolyn Brooks, Sarah Caldwell, Julie Harris, Mary Mccarthy, Alice Neel, Roberta Peters, Maria Tallchief, Mary Lou Williams, Eugenia Zukerman.* Piscataway, NJ: New Century Publishers, 1981: 35-53.

Kukrechtová, Daniela. "The Death and Life of a Chicago Edifice: Gwendolyn Brooks's 'In the Mecca.'" *African American Review* 43.2/3 (2009): 457-472.

Lansana, Quraysh, Ali. "Giant Steps: First-person Observation of Ms. Brooks' Guiding Hand." *Mosaic Literary Magazine* 19 (2007): 41-43, 60.

Latimore, Jewel C. "For Gwendolyn Brooks—a Whole & Beautiful Spirit." *SOS/Calling All Black People: A Black Arts Movement Reader*. Edited by John H. Bracey Jr., Sonia Sanchez, and James Smethurst. Amherst: University of Massachusetts Press, 2014: 385.

Lattin, Patricia H. and Vernon E. "Dual Vision in Gwendolyn Brooks's *Maud Martha*." *Critique: Studies in Contemporary Fiction* 25.4 (1984): 180-188.

Lempke, Susan Dove. "Bronzeville Boys and Girls." *Horn Book Magazine* 83.1 (2007): 79.

Leyda, Julia. "Space, Class, City: Gwendolyn Brooks's *Maud Martha*." *Japanese Journal of American Studies* 19 (2008): 123-137.

Lieberman, Laurence. "On the Brink of Secession." *American Poetry Review* 43.6 (2014): 29-30.

Lindberg, Kathryne V. "Whose Canon? Gwendolyn Brooks: Founder at the Center of the 'Margins.'" *Gendered Modernisms: American Women Poets and Their Readers*. Edited by Margaret Dickie and Thomas J. Travisano. Philadelphia: Pennsylvania University Press, 1996: 283-311.

Lowney, John. "'A Material Collapse That Is Construction': History and Counter-Memory in Gwendolyn Brooks's 'In the Mecca.'" *MELUS: Multi-Ethnic Literature of the U.S.* 23.3 (1998): 3-20.

Lupack, Alan C. "Brooks' 'Piano after War.'" *Explicator* 36.4 (1978): 2-3.

McBride, Mekeel. "The Second Sermon on the Warpland: Two Streaks of Sun." *Field: Contemporary Poetry and Poetics* 61 (1999): 55-61.

McKay, Nellie. "The Autobiographies of Zora Neale Hurston and Gwendolyn Brooks: Alternate Versions of the Black Female Self." *Wild Women in the Whirlwind: Afra-American Culture and the Contemporary Literary Renaissance*. Edited by Joanne M. Braxton and Andrée Nicola McLaughlin. New Brunswick, NJ: Rutgers University Press, 1990: 264-281.

Gwendolyn Brooks (1917-)." *Modern American Women Writers*. Edited by Elaine Showalter, Lea Baechler, and A. Walton Litz. New York: Scribner, 1991:37-48.

McKibbin, Molly Littlewood. "Southern Patriarchy and the Figure of the White Woman in Gwendolyn Brooks's 'A Bronzeville Mother Loiters in Mississippi. Meanwhile, a Mississippi Mother Burns Bacon.'" *African American Review* 44.4 (2011): 667-685.

Madhubuti, Haki R. "Eighty-three is a Wise Number." *Mosaic Literary Magazine* 19 (2007): 32.

—."Gwendolyn Brooks (1917-2000)." *Black Issues in Higher Education* 17.22 (2000): 15.

Honoring Genius: Gwendolyn Brooks: The Narrative of Craft, Art, Kindness and Justice: Poems. Chicago: Third World, 2011.

Say That the River Turns: The Impact of Gwendolyn Brooks. Chicago: Third World Press, 1981.

"'The Roads Taken.' ("Poets We've Known")." *Poetry* 192.4 (2008): 380-81.

Malewitz, Raymond. "'My Newish Voice': Rethinking Black Power in Gwendolyn Brooks's 'Whirlwind.'" *Callaloo* 29 (2006): 531-544.

Mangharam, Mukti Lakhi. "'The Universal Is the Entire Collection of Particulars': Grounding Identity in a Shared Horizon of Humanity." *College Literature* 40.3 (2013): 81-98.

Massa, Suzanne Hotte. "Gwendolyn Brooks (1917-)." *Contemporary African American Novelists: A Bio-Bibliographical Critical Sourcebook.* Edited by Emmanuel S. Nelson. Westport: Greenwood Publishing Group, Inc., 1999: 47-52.

May, Vivian M. "Maids Mild and Dark Villains, Sweet Magnolias and Seeping Blood: Gwendolyn Brooks's Poetic Response to the Lynching of Emmett Till." *Emmett Till in Literary Memory and Imagination.* Edited by Harriet Pollack and Christopher Metress. Christopher. Baton Rouge: Louisiana State University Press, 2008: 98-111.

Meadows, Doris M. "African-American Poetry And History: Making Connections." *OAH Magazine Of History* 13.2 (1999): 36-41.

Melhem, D. H. "Cultural Challenge, Heroic Response: Gwendolyn Brooks and the New Black Poetry." *Perspectives in Black Popular Culture.* Edited by Harry B. Shaw. Bowling Green, OH: Bowling Green University Press, 1990: 71-84.

"Gwendolyn Brooks and Emily Dickinson." *Emily Dickinson International Society Bulletin* 7.1 (1995): 14-15, 17.

"Gwendolyn Brooks, Black Poetry, and Me." *Callaloo* 32.4 (2009): 1208-1212.

"Gwendolyn Brooks: An Appreciation." (Cover story) *Humanities* 15.3 (1994): 7.

"Gwendolyn Brooks: Humanism and Heroism." *Heroism in the New Black Poetry: Introductions & Interviews.* Lexington: University Press of Kentucky, 1990: 11-39.

Gwendolyn Brooks: Poetry & the Heroic Voice. Lexington: University Press of Kentucky, 1987.

Metress, Christopher. "'No Justice, No Peace': The Figure of Emmett Till in African American Literature." *MELUS: Multi-Ethnic Literature of the U.S.* 28.1 (2003): 87-103, 188.

Mihaila, Rodica. "Metamorphoses of Blackness in the Poetry of Gwendolyn Brooks." *British and American Studies* (1998): 61-66.

Miller, E. Ethelbert. "Gwendolyn Brooks on Langston Hughes." *Langston Hughes Review* 15.2 (1997): 92-109.

Miller, R. Baxter. "Define ... The Whirlwind: 'In the Mecca'—Urban Setting, Shifting Narrator and Redemptive Vision." *Obsidian* 4.1 (1978): 19-31.

"'Does Man Love Art?': The Humanistic Aesthetic of Gwendolyn Brooks." *Black American Literature and Humanism.* Lexington: University Press of Kentucky, (1981): 95-112.

Langston Hughes and Gwendolyn Brooks: A Reference Guide. Boston: G. K. Hall, 1978.

"On the Ruins of Leftist Modernity: Gwendolyn Brooks." *On the Ruins of Modernity: New Chicago Renaissance from Wright to Fair.* Champaign, IL: Common Ground Pub., (2012): 55-74.

Mootry, Maria K. "Brooks's 'A Bronzeville Mother Loiters in Mississippi. Meanwhile, a Mississippi Mother Burns Bacon.'" *Explicator* 42.4 (1984): 51-52.

"'Chocolate Mabbie' And 'Pearl May Lee': Gwendolyn Brooks and the Ballad Tradition." *CLA Journal* 30.3 (1987): 278-293.

"Growing Up Black and Female, Black and Male in Chicago in Gwendolyn Brooks' *Maud Martha* and Ron Fair's *Hog Butcher.*" ["Curriculum Materials" by Edna Capehart.] *Illinois History Teacher* 3.2 (1996): 45-51.

"'The Step of Iron Feet': Creative Practice in the War Sonnets of Melvin B. Tolson and Gwendolyn Brooks." *Obsidian II: Black Literature in Review* 2 (1987): 69-87.

Mootry, Maria K. and Gary Smith. *A Life Distilled: Gwendolyn Brooks, Her Poetry and Fiction*. Urbana: University of Illinois Press, 1987.

Moss, Thylia. "A Song in the Front Yard: A Meditation on the Fortunate Illness That Occurs When 'a Girl Gets Sick of a Rose'." *Field: Contemporary Poetry And Poetics* 61 (1999): 11-17.

Mullen, Bill. "Engendering the Cultural Front: Gwendolyn Brooks, Black Women, and Class Struggle in Poetry." *Popular Fronts: Chicago and African-American Cultural Politics, 1935-46*. Urbana: University of Illinois Press, 1999: 148-180.

Müller, Timo. "The Vernacular Sonnet and the Resurgence of Afro-Modernism in the 1940s." *American Literature* 87.2 (2015): 253-73.

Muse, Daphne. "Our Literary Mecca: A Tribute to Gwendolyn Brooks." *Black Masks* 14.5 (2001): 10.

Myers, Ardie S. "Former LC Consultant in Poetry Delivers Jefferson Lecture." *Library of Congress Information Bulletin* 53 (1994): 261-62.

Najar, Lubna. "The Chicago Poetry Group: African American Art and High Modernism at Midcentury." *Women's Studies Quarterly* 33.3/4 (2005): 314-23.

Nelson, Emanuel S. "Gwendolyn Brooks (1917-2000)" *African American Autobiographers: A Sourcebook*. Edited by Emanuel S. Nelson. Westport: Greenwood, 2002: 47-50.

Nelson, Marilyn. "Negro Hero." *Field: Contemporary Poetry And Poetics* 61 (1999): 24-28.

"1988 Essence Awards: Gwendolyn Brooks." *Essence* 19.6 (1988): 68.

Ortega, Kirsten Bartholomew. "The Black "Flâneuse": Gwendolyn Brooks's 'In the Mecca.'" *Journal of Modern Literature* 30.4 (2007): 139-55.

Owens, Clarke W. "Brooks's 'First Fight, Then Fiddle.'" *Explicator* 52.4 (1994): 240-242.

Parascandola, L. J. "Religious Allusion in the Poetry of Gwendolyn Brooks." *Choice: Current Reviews for Academic Libraries* 50.6 (2013): 1046-46.

Park, You-Me. "Native Daughters in the Promised Land: Gender, Race, and the Question of Separate Spheres." *American Literature* 70.3 (1998): 607-633.

Parrott, Jill M. "How Shall We Greet the Sun? Form and Truth in Gwendolyn Brooks's 'Annie Allen.'" *Style* 46.1 (2012): 27-41.

Pettis, Joyce. "Gwendolyn Brooks (1917-2000)." *African American Poets: Lives, Works, and Sources.* Westport, CT: Greenwood Press, 2002: 32-40.

Phillips, Carl. "A Light and Diplomatic Bird: Twist, Tact, and Metaphysics." *Field Contemporary Poetry and Poetics* 61 (1999): 36-44.

Phillips, Michelle H. "Moving in and Stepping Out: Gwendolyn Brooks's Children at Midcentury." *African American Review* 47.1 (2014): 145-160.

Presson, Rebekah. "The Richness of Poetry: An Interview with Gwendolyn Brooks." *New Letters* 59.1 (1992): 53-68.

Prestianni, Vincent. "Bibliographical Scholarship on Three Black Writers." *Obsidian II: Black Literature in Review* 5.1 (1990): 75-85.

Preston, Rohan B. "The Furious Flower." *Emerge* 9.9 (1998): 50.

Quashie, Kevin Everod. "'Maud Martha' and the Practice of Paying Attention." *The Sovereignty of Quiet: Beyond Resistance in Black Culture.* New Brunswick, N.: Rutgers University Press, 2012: 47-72.

Rabinowitz, Paula. "Domestic Labor: Film Noir, Proletarian Literature, and Black Women's Fiction." *Modern Fiction Studies* 47.1 (2001): 229-254.

Randall, Dudley. "Gwendolyn Brooks." *Black Writer Magazine* 3.1 (1983): 20.

Randall, Dudley, and Lena Ampadu. "The Message Is in the Melody: An Interview with Dudley Randall." *Callaloo* 22.2 (1999): 438-45.

Reardon, Patrick T. "Live It Up!" *U.S. Catholic* 66.12 (2001): 22.

Reed, Kathleen Rand. "The Poet's Voice." About ...Time 33.3/4 (2005): 20-21.

Rinner, Jeni. "From Bronzeville to the Mecca and After: Gwendolyn Brooks and the Location of Black Identity." *MELUS: Multi-Ethnic Literature of the U.S.* 40.4 (2015): 150-72.

Rochman, Hazel. "The Booklist Interview: Gwendolyn Brooks." *Booklist* 90 (1993): 426-27.

Rozga, Margaret. "The Grammar of Segregation in the Sonnets of Gwendolyn Brooks." *MidAmerica* 37 (2010): 63-73.

Rubin, Anne Sarah. "Reflections on the Death of Emmett Till." *Southern Cultures* 2.1 (1995): 45-66.

Rushin, Kate. "When You Have Forgotten Sunday: The Love Story: Not Just Another Poem." *Field: Contemporary Poetry And Poetics* 61 (1999): 18-23.

Ryan, William F. "Blackening the Language." *American Visions* 3.6 (1988): 32-37.

Saber, Yomna Mohamed. *Brave to Be Involved: Shifting Positions in the Poetry of Gwendolyn Brooks*. New York: Peter Lang, 2010.

Sakthi, P., and Stella Thangaraj. "Segregation: An Abomination." *IUP Journal of English Studies* 7.1 (2012): 32-38.

Salaam, Kalamu, ya. "How I Fell So Deeply in Love with Us." *Mosaic Literary Magazine* 19 (2007): 22-24.

"No Ordinary Waterfall (for Gwen Brooks)." *Mosaic Literary Magazine* 19 (2007): 24.

Sanchez, Sonia. "Eulogy." *Time* 156.25 (2000): 25.

Satz, Martha. "Honest Reporting: An Interview with Gwendolyn Brooks." *Southwest Review* 71.4 (1989): 25-35.

Saunders, Judith P. "The Love Song of Satin-Legs Smith: Gwendolyn Brooks Revisits Prufrock's Hell." *Papers on Language and Literature* 36.1 (2000): 3-18.

Schmidt, Tyler T. "War City: Gwendolyn Brooks, Edwin Denby, and the Private Poetics of Public Space." *Desegregating Desire: Race and Sexuality in Cold War American Literature*. Jackson: University Press of Mississippi, 2013: 87-135.

Schwartz, Lloyd. "We Real Cool: Cool Brooks: Gwendolyn Brooks's Tragic Jazz." *Field Contemporary Poetry and Poetics* 61 (1999): 45-47.

Schweik, Susan M. "(Not) Playing with Mimesis: Gwendolyn Brooks and the Stuff of Letters." *A Gulf so Deeply Cut: American Women Poets and the Second World War*. Madison: University of Wisconsin Press, 1991: 109-139.

Scott, Heidi. "'Gay Chaps at the Bar': A Close Look at Brooks's Sonnets." *Explicator* 66.1 (2007): 37-42.

Seals, Marc. "Cross-Examining the Myth of Southern Chivalry: Gwendolyn Brooks's Emmett Till Poems." *MidAmerica* 37 (2010): 74-80.

Seligman, Dee. "The Mother of Them All: Gwendolyn Brooks's 'Annie Allen.'" *The Anna Book: Searching for Anna in Literary History*. Edited by Mickay Perlman. Westport, CT: Greenwood Press, 1992: 131-138.

Shaw, Harry B. *Gwendolyn Brooks*. Boston: Twayne Publishers, 1980.

"Perceptions of Men in the Early Works of Gwendolyn Brooks." *Black American Poets Between Worlds, 1040-1960*. Edited by R. Baxter Miller. Knoxville: University of Tennessee Press, 1986: 136-159.

Smethurst, James Edward. "Hysterical Ties: Gwendolyn Brooks and the Rise of a 'High' Neomodernism." *The New Red Negro: The Literary Left and African American Poetry*, 1930-1946. New York: Oxford University Press, 1999: 164-179.

Smith, Derik. "Quarreling in the Movement: Robert Hayden's Black Arts Era." *Callaloo* 33.2 (2010): 449-66.

Smith, Gary. "Brooks's 'We Real Cool.'" *Explicator* 43.2 (1985): 49-50.

"Gwendolyn Brooks's A Street in Bronzeville, the Harlem Renaissance and the Mythologies of Black Women." *MELUS: Multi-Ethnic Literature of the U.S.* 10.3 (1983): 33-46.

Smith, Patricia. "For Gwendolyn." *Ms.* 11.3 (2001): 94.

"Gwendolyn Brooks." *Poetry* 200.1 (2012): 58-61.

"To Keep From Saying Dead." *Black Renaissance* 11.2/3(2012): 97.

Smith, Tabathia. "Gwendolyn Brooks." *Umoja Sasa* 5.7 (1979): 1, 5.

Solomon, Asali. "Indispensable Maud Martha." *Mosaic Literary Magazine* 19 (2007): 38-39.

Spillers, Hortense J. "Gwendolyn the Terrible: Propositions on Eleven Poems." *Shakespeare's Sisters: Feminist Essays on Women Poets*. Edited by Sandra M. Gilbert and Susan Gubar. Bloomington: University of Indiana Press, 1979: 233-234.

"'An Order of Constancy': Notes on Brooks and the Feminine." *Centennial Review* 29.2 (1985): 223-248.

Stanford, Ann Folwell. "An Epic with a Difference: Sexual Politics in Gwendolyn Brooks's 'The Anniad.'" *American Literature* 67.2 (1995): 283-301.

"Dialectics of Desire: War and the Resistive Voice in Gwendolyn Brooks's 'Negro Hero' and 'Gay Chaps at the Bar.'" *African American Review* 26.2 (1992): 197-211.

"'Like Narrow Banners for Some Gathering War': Readers, Aesthetics, and Gwendolyn Brooks's the Sundays of Satin-Legs Smith." *College Literature* 17.2/3 (1990): 162-182.

Stern, Frederick C. "The 'Populist' Politics of Gwendolyn Brooks's Poetry." *MidAmerica: The Yearbook of the Society for the Study of Midwestern Literature* 12 (1985): 111-119.

Stetson, Erlene. "'Songs after Sunrise' (1935-1936): The Unpublished Poetry of Gwendolyn Elizabeth Brooks." *CLA Journal* 24 (1980): 87-96.

Strange, Sharan. "In Praise of the Young and Black: After Gwendolyn Brooks." *Callaloo* 26.2 (2003): 279-80.

Struthers, Ann. "Gwendolyn Brooks' Children." *Iowa English Bulletin* 29 (1979): 15-16.

Sullivan, James D. "Killing John Cabot and Publishing Black: Gwendolyn Brook's 'Riot.'" *African American Review* 36.4 (2002): 557-569.

"Writing About Gwendolyn Brooks Anyway." *White Scholars/African American Texts*. Edited by Lisa Long. New Brunswick, NJ: Rutgers University Press, 2005: 198-208.

Taylor, Henry. "Gwendolyn Brooks: An Essential Sanity." *Kenyon Review* 13.4 (1991): 115-131.

Thomas, Lorenzo. "A Timely Godmother: The Fiftieth Anniversary of Gwendolyn Brooks's Lyrical Narrative 'Annie Allen.'" *Biblio* 4.4 (1999): 16.

Thorsson, Courtney. "Gwendolyn Brooks's Black Aesthetic of the Domestic." *MELUS: Multi-Ethnic Literature of the U.S.* 40.1 (2015): 149-76.

Upton, Lee. "Bronzeville Woman in a Red Hat: Language in a Red Hat." *Field Contemporary Poetry and Poetics* 61 (1999): 48-54.

Vijayalakshmi, S. "Bard of the Black: A Study of Select Poems of Gwendolyn Brooks." *Labyrinth: An International Refereed Journal of Postmodern Studies* 4.3 (2013): 151-155.

Tracey L. "Gwendolyn Brooks' 'The Anniad' and the Interdeterminacy of Genre." *CLA Journal* 44.3 (2001): 350-366.

Walther, Malin Lavon. "Re-Wrighting Native Son: Gwendolyn Brooks's Domestic Aesthetic in 'Maud Martha.'" *Tulsa Studies in Women's Literature* 13.1 (1994): 143-145.

Walton, Anthony. "Gwendolyn Brooks 1917-2000." (Poem) *Role Call: A Generational Anthology of Social and Political Black Art & Literature*. Edited by Tony Medina, Samiya A. Bashir, and Quraysh Ali Lansana. Chicago: Third World, 2002: 441.

Warren, Nagueyalti. "She Real Cool." *Mosaic Literary Magazine* 19 (2007): 45.

Washington, Mary Helen. "Plain, Black, and Decently Wild: The Heroic Possibilities of Maud Martha." *The Voyage in: Fictions of Female Development*. Edited by Elizabeth, Abel, Marianne Hirsch, and Elizabeth Langland. Hanover, NH: Published for Dartmouth College by University Press of New England, 1983: 254-270.

"'Taming All That Anger Down': Rage and Silence in Gwendolyn Brooks' 'Maud Martha.'" *Massachusetts Review* 24.2 (1983): 453-466.

Watkins, Mel. "In Memoriam: Gwendolyn Brooks (1917-2000)." *Black Scholar* 31.1 (2001): 51-54.

Weaver, Afaa Michael. "The Way of All Bridges... In Memory of Gwendolyn Brooks." *Mosaic Literary Magazine* 19 (2007): 14-18.

Werner, Craig. "On the Ends of Afro-American "Modernist" Autobiography." *Black American Literature Forum* 24.2 (1990): 203-20.

Wheeler, Lesley. "Heralding the Clear Obscure: Gwendolyn Brooks and Apostrophe." *Callaloo* 24.1 (2001): 227-235.

Whitaker, Charles. "A Poet for All Ages." *Ebony* 42.8 (1987): 154-162.

Williams, Gladys Margaret. "Gwendolyn Brooks's Way with the Sonnet." *CLA Journal* 26.2 (1982): 215-240.

Wolosky, Shira. "The Ethics of Foucauldian Poetics: Women's Selves." *New Literary History* 35.3 (2004): 491-505.

Wright, Stephen A. "Beneath the Rhetoric... Answering the Higher Call: The Prophetic Voices of Johnson, Hansberry, Baldwin, and Brooks." *Zora Neale Hurston Forum* (2003): 55.

Wright, Stephen Caldwell. "Gwendolyn Brooks (June 7, 1917-December 3, 2000." *Writers of the Black Chicago Renaissance*. Edited by Steven C. Tracy. Urbana: University of Illinois Press, 2011: 96-120.

On Gwendolyn Brooks: Reliant Contemplation. Ann Arbor: University of Michigan Press, 1996.

Zodrow-MacDonald, Esme. "The Last Word." *New Moon Girls* 21.2 (2013): 33.

GWENDOLYN BROOKS ONLINE: SELECTED WEBSITES

Finding Aid to the Gwendolyn Brooks Papers, 1917-2000, (bulk: 1950-1989) at
The Bancroft Library, University of California, Berkeley, Online Archive of
California:
   http://www.oac.cdlib.org/findaid/ark:/13030/kt1580234v/
Gwendolyn Brooks. Academy of American Poets. Poets.org:
   https://www.poets.org/poetsorg/poet/gwendolyn-brooks
Gwendolyn Brooks. Famous Black Writers, AfroPoets.net:
   http://www.afropoets.net/gwendolynbrooks.html
Gwendolyn Brooks: Online Resources. Compiled by Peter Armenti. Library of
Congress:
   https://www.loc.gov/rr/program/bib/brooks/
Gwendolyn Brooks, 1917-2000. The Poetry Foundation:
   https://www.poetryfoundation.org/poems-and-poets/poets/detail/
   gwendolyn-brooks
Gwendolyn Brooks, 1917-2000. Modern American Poetry.
   http://www.english.illinois.edu/maps/poets/a_f/brooks/brooks.htm

CONTRIBUTORS

Opal Palmer Adisa
Opal Palmer Adisa travels in the skirt of the ocean. A daughter of the Caribbean, she gained her voice through reading the works of African American writers. The author of sixteen books of stories, novels, poems, and children's books, and the founder and editor of the journal, *Interviewing the Caribbean*, Adisa is Distinguished Professor of the MFA program at California College of the Arts. She spends the rest of her time in St. Croix, the US Virgin Islands, where she directs community theatre and curates art shows.

Lana Hechtman Ayers
Lana Hechtman Ayers is a poetry publisher, movie addict, and time travel enthusiast. She facilitates Write Away™ generative writing workshops, leads private salons for book groups, and teaches at writers' conferences. She is obsessed with exotic flavors of ice cream, Little Red Riding Hood, and monochromatic cats and dogs. She's authored seven collections of poetry thus far. In addition to thriving in the book-loving culture, she enjoys the Pacific Northwest's bountiful rain and copious coffee shops. Her favorite color is the swirl of Van Gogh's *Starry Night*.

Khari B.
Discopoet Khari B. is a spoken word musician and educator working internationally in the literary arts. With a reputation for delivering intense performances with live instrumental accompaniment, Khari B.'s energetic nature is inextricably tied to growing up in Chicago's House music scene and being the son of two educators, one being the renown woodwindist, Mwata Bowden.

Personally recognized for his talents by the late Gwendolyn Brooks and having performed around the globe, Khari B.'s start began with a simple class project in 1992 where he discovered an appetite for using his talent for poetry to reach, teach, and entertain willing ears.

A recent chair of the Association for the Advancement of the Creative Musicians (AACM), Khari guided the organization into their fiftieth anniversary. He creates programming for "Parent University," an integrated learning venture between parents and students in elementary schools on the West Side of Chicago. He is also Artist-In-Residence at Purdue University.

L.D. Barnes

L.D. Barnes has been published in the *BAC Street Journal*, literary magazine of the Beverly Arts Center, *The Villager*, newspaper of the Beverly Area Planning Association, and at ChicagoSmooth.typepad.com, the Smooth Jazz blog of Rick O'Dell. Her short story about detectives won second place in the 2015 Printer's Row Literary Festival's Sara Paretsky Flash Fiction contest.

Tina Jenkins Bell

Tina Jenkins Bell is a freelance writer, fiction writer, and playwright who lives in Chicago with her husband, two sons, and neighborhood dog, Bella. Her short stories and a novel excerpt were published in *Hair Trigger, BAC Street, Expressions* and *Guildworks Journals*. She has also written for the *Chicago Tribune, Crain's Chicago Business*, and *Upscale Magazine*, among others. She is a member of FLOW (For Love of Writing) and recently completed two short story fellowships with Colgate University and the Midwest Writer's Conference.

Wayne-Daniel Berard

Wayne-Daniel Berard, PhD is Professor of English at Nichols College in Dudley, Massachusetts. He is a Peace Chaplain, an interfaith clergyperson commissioned by the Peace Abbey in Sherborn, Massachusetts. Raised in Taunton, Massachusetts, Wayne-Daniel spent five years in Franciscan seminary. An adopted child, his discovery of his Jewish birth-parentage led to years of on-going Torah study with Rabbi Alan Ullman's School for Judaic Studies in Newton, Massachusetts. He is a published poet and essayist, and his chapbook *The Man Who Remembered Heaven* received the 2003 chapbook award from the journal *Ruah*. His first full-length book *When Christians Were Jews (That Is, Now): Recovering the Lost Jewishness of Christianity with St. Mark's Gospel*, was published in 2006 by Cowley Publishing. He is a member of B'nai Or, a Jewish Renewal Community in Newton, Massachusetts, and of the Emmaus Community in Bridgewater, Massachusetts. Wayne-Daniel resides in Mansfield, Massachusetts with his wife Christine; their shared families include six children, numerous cats, a rescued black shepherd, and very spoiled dachshund.

Kathleen Bethel

Kathleen E. Bethel is the African American Studies Librarian at Northwestern University in Evanston, Illinois, with responsibilities for Gender and Sexuality Studies and Caribbean Studies. A member of the American Library Association and the Black Caucus of ALA, Kathleen is committed to library leadership, recruitment, and research.

Early in her career, Bethel worked at the Johnson Publishing Company Library, the Newberry Library, Maywood Public Library, and Wilmette Public Library, all in Illinois. She serves on the boards of the Center for Black Genealogy, the Project on the History of Black Writing, and the SonEdna Foundation. A Life Member of the Association for the Study of African American Life and History, Inc., Kathleen belongs to the Chicago Branch and has served on the Executive Council. She served fourteen years on the Board of Chicago's DuSable Museum of African American History. A Life Member of the Toni Morrison Society, she chaired the Bibliography Committee. Kathleen received the 1999 DEMCO/ALA Black Caucus Award for Excellence in Librarianship and the 1999 Irma Kingsley Johnson Distinguished Service Award from the Chicago Friends of the Amistad Research Center.

Tara Betts

Tara Betts is the author of *Break the Habit* and *Arc & Hue*, as well as the chapbooks *7 x 7: kwansabas* and *THE GREATEST!: An Homage to Muhammad Ali*. Tara holds a PhD from Binghamton University and an MFA from New England College. She currently teaches at University of Illinois-Chicago. Tara Betts heard Miss Brooks read several times in the late 1990s as a young college graduate and finally greeted her once in 2003 when Miss Brooks signed Tara's hardcover copy of *Blacks*. Tara was also the winner of the 1999 Gwendolyn Brooks Open Mic Award, one of the many prizes funded for years by Miss Brooks herself.

Roger Bonair-Agard

Roger Bonair-Agard is a native of Trinidad and Tobago and Brooklyn and author of four collections of poems including *Bury My Clothes* (Haymarket Books, 2013), which was long listed for the National Book Award and won the Society of Midland Authors Award for Poetry, and the forthcoming *Where Brooklyn At?!* (Willow Books, 2016). The founder of NYC's louderARTS Project and writer in residence at NYC's National Sawdust, Roger is the founder/facilitator of the Baldwin Protocols, a reading series and program towards arts-based interventions. He is the Director of Creative Writing at Free Write Arts and Literacy at Cook County Juvenile Temporary Detention Center. He lives in Chicago. He is Nina's father.

Jericho Brown

Jericho Brown is the recipient of a Whiting Writers' Award and fellowships from the John Simon Guggenheim Foundation, the Radcliffe Institute for Advanced Study at Harvard University, and the National Endowment for the Arts. His poems have appeared in *New York Times*, *New Yorker*, *The New Republic*, *Buzzfeed*, and *The Best American Poetry*. His first book, *Please* (New Issues, 2008), won the American Book Award, and his second book, *The New Testament* (Copper Canyon, 2014), won the Anisfield-Wolf Book Award and was named one of the best of the year by *Library Journal*, *Coldfront*, and the Academy of American Poets. His is an associate professor of English and creative writing at Emory University in Atlanta.

Rose Blouin

Rose Blouin has worked in the medium of photography since 1980. Her areas of particular interest include documentary and fine art photography. Her work has been exhibited in a number of museums and galleries and was selected for inclusion in an artists' billboard project (juried) coordinated by The Randolph Street Gallery in Chicago.

Blouin's photographs have been published on the covers of *South Side Stories*, *Columbia Poetry Review*, *Killing Memory*, *Seeking Ancestors* by Haki Madhubuti, *The Chicago Musicale*, and *Menagerie*. A photo of Gwendolyn Brooks was included in *Say That the River Turns: The Impact of Gwendolyn Brooks*.

David R. Bublitz

David R. Bublitz is the son of a veteran. He completed an MFA at the Oklahoma City University Red Earth program. He is a 2015 Pangaea Prize finalist and a founding editor of the *Red Earth Review*. He has published poetry in *CON-SEQUENCE Magazine*, *Zero-Dark-Thirty*, and *Proud to Be: Writing by American Warriors*. He teaches journalism courses at Cameron University in Lawton, Oklahoma, while advising for the student-run newspaper, the *CU Collegian*.

Kalisha Buckhanon

Kalisha Buckhanon's novels are *Solemn*, *Conception*, and *Upstate*. Her short stories are widely published in many online and university print literary journals. Her articles and essays appear on several popular women's blogs and cultural websites. Her writing awards include an American Library Association ALEX Award, Friends of American Writers Award, Illinois Arts Council Fellowship, and Terry McMillan Young Author Award. Kalisha's work has received attention in major media outlets such as *Essence*, *The Guardian*, BBC-London, TV-One, *People*, *Elle*, *Entertainment Weekly*, and *Marie Claire*. She has an MFA from The New School in New York City, and her BA and MA in English from University of Chicago. She writes at her blog Negression.com and her website is www.Kalisha.com.

CM Burroughs

CM Burroughs' debut collection of poetry *The Vital System* was published by Tupelo Press in 2012. She is an assistant professor of poetry at Columbia College Chicago, and serves as senior editor for *Tupelo Quarterly* and coeditor for *Court Green*. Burroughs has been awarded fellowships and grants from Yaddo, the MacDowell Colony, Virginia Center for the Creative Arts, Cave Canem Foundation, Callaloo Writers Workshop, and the University of Pittsburgh. She has received commissions from the Studio Museum of Harlem and the Warhol Museum to create poetry in response to art installations. A Pushcart Prize nominee and a finalist for the 2009 Gift of Freedom Award, her poetry has appeared in journals including *Callaloo*, *jubilat*, *Ploughshares*, *VOLT*, *Bat City Review*, and *Volta*. Burroughs is a graduate of Sweet Briar College, and she earned her MFA from the University of Pittsburgh.

Adjoa Burrowes

Adjoa Burrowes is a visual artist, author, and illustrator of over a dozen books for children, including the award winning, *Grandma's Purple Flowers*, which she both wrote and illustrated. Burrowes designs and presents art and creative writing workshops locally and in museums, schools, and cultural centers across the country and world, including the National Museum of Women in the Arts and the National Civil Rights Museum. Several large-scale public art works based on her children's books were commissioned in Washington, DC including *The Gift of Words*, a painted mural at the Martin Luther King Jr. Memorial Library. Burrowes recently received an MA in Art Education at the Corcoran School of the Arts and Design at George Washington University and lives in Washington, DC.

Chirskira Caillouet

Chirskira Caillouet is a poet and spoken word artist who writes about love, life, and current events. In 2009, she published a chapbook entitled *Honey Licorice*, and in 2014 was a Gwendolyn Brooks Open Mic Awards semifinalist. She was recruited as a reader to participate in the Third Annual Gwendolyn Brooks birthday celebration and received top honors for "Rock the Ballot" at Saint Sabina's Rock the Mic Award for a piece. She is a lifetime Chicagoan and South Sider and a volunteer-activist, having participated in movements to help the less fortunate, like those affected by gun violence and building homes in El Paso, Texas and New Orleans, Louisiana with Habitat for Humanity.

Cortney Lamar Charleston

Cortney Lamar Charleston is a Cave Canem fellow, finalist for the 2015 Auburn Witness Poetry Prize, and semi-finalist for the 2016 Discovery/Boston Review Poetry Prize. His poems have appeared or are forthcoming in *Beloit Poetry Journal*, *Gulf Coast*, *Fugue*, *Hayden's Ferry Review*, *The Iowa Review*, *The Journal*, *New England Review*, *Pleiades*, *River Styx*, *Spillway*, and elsewhere.

Adrienne Christian

Adrienne Christian is the author of the poetry collection, *12023 Woodmont Avenue* (Willow Books, 2013). She is a Cave Canem fellow whose poems have been published or are forthcoming in *The LA Review, frogpond, Obsidian, Alimentum, Falling Star, Silk Road*, and other literary journals. Her nonfiction has appeared in *Heart & Soul, Today's Black Woman*, and *African Vibes*. Adrienne earned a BA in English from the University of Michigan and an MFA from Pacific University.

Sandra Cisneros
Sandra Cisneros is the founder of the Alfredo Cisneros del Moral Foundation, the Elvira Cisneros Award, and the Macondo Foundation, all of which have worked on behalf of creative writers. She is the recipient of numerous awards including a MacArthur. Her writings include the novels *The House on Mango Street* and *Caramelo*, the short story collection *Woman Hollering Creek*, the poetry collections *My Wicked Ways* and *Loose Woman*, and the children's books, *Hairs* and *Bravo, Bruno* with Leslie Greene, published in Italy. She is currently at work on several writing projects including a second volume of non-fiction "stories" about her romantic life, *How to be a Chignon*—life tips, *Infinto*—short stories, and *Cantos Y Llantos*—poems. Her most recent books are *Have You Seen Marie?* an illustrated book for adults with artist Ester Hernández and *A House of My Own: Stories from My Life*, non-fiction with photographs.

Kimberly A. Collins
Kimberly A. Collins' wish has always been for her writing to touch, heal, and inspire another soul and to be a tool for transformation. If any of one of those desires is realized, then her writing will not have been in vain. She works at this task as a mother, English instructor, blogger, and as the founder of SOAR (So Others Ascend Righteously) where she facilitates Writing For Healing Workshops. Ms. Collins published her first collection of *Poetry Slightly Off Center* in 1992. Her most recent poetry appears in *Syracuse Cultural Workers' 2017 Women Artist Datebook, Truth Feasting, Berkeley Review*, and *Black Magnolia Literary Magazine*. Her later work is also found in *Black Poets of the Deep South, In The Tradition: An Anthology of Young African American Writers, The Nubian Gallery, NOBO Journal of African American Dialogue, Theorizing Black Feminism*, and *Fingernails Across the Blackboard*. Her essays are found in several scholarly publications and magazines.

Esteban Colon

Esteban Colon is a poet and experiential educator who practices around the city of Chicago. He is a founding member of the Waiting 4 the Bus Poetry Collective and author of the full length book *Things I Learned the Hard Way*. His writings have appeared in a wide variety of journals, anthologies, and chapbooks. He's a short man, who is very big fan of anyone enjoying the work of the poets included in this collection.

Kevin Coval

Kevin Coval is the author of *Schtick, L-vis Lives: Racemusic Poems, Everyday People*, and the American Library Association "Book of the Year" Finalist *Slingshots: A Hip-Hop Poetica*. He is the founder of Louder Than a Bomb: The Chicago Youth Poetry Festival, Artistic Director at Young Chicago Authors, and teaches at the University of Illinois-Chicago.

Arlene Turner-Crawford

Arlene Turner-Crawford works in the media of drawing, painting, printmaking, and graphic illustration. She holds a BS in Education and an MS of Education in Art. As a student, Arlene met with many influential writers, artists, and activists, including Dr. Jeff Donaldson, founder of OBAC (Organization of Black American Culture) and AfriCOBRA (African Commune of Bad Relevant Artists), Nelson Stevens, Larry Neal, LeRoi Jones (Amira Baraka), Don L. Lee (Haki Madhubuti), Sonia Sanchez, Max Roach, Archie Shepp, Barbara Ann Tiers, Maya Angelou, Abena Joan Brown, Gwendolyn Brooks, and many others. Arlene believes that "Art is ritual, an attempt to interpret higher expressions of life. As an image-maker, my work is expressed through both realistic and symbolic forms."

Kimberly D. Dixon-Mays

Kimberly D. Dixon-Mays is a Cave Canem and Ragdale fellow whose work has appeared in *Reverie, Anthology of Chicago, Uproot, Consequence, Rhino*, the upcoming anthology *Trigger Warning*, and her collections *SenseMemory* and *More Than a Notion: Reflections on (Black) Marriage*. She is also a playwright and performer, and has been a recurring member of the Poetry Performance Incubator project of the Guild Literary Complex. She served as the Guild's Executive Director from 2010 to 2012.

Rita Dove

Rita Dove is a former US Poet Laureate (1993-1995) and recipient of the 1987 Pulitzer Prize in poetry for *Thomas and Beulah*. The author of numerous books, among them the 2009 tour de force *Sonata Mulattica*, a poetic treatise on the life of nineteenth century violinist George Bridgetower, and, most recently, *Collected Poems 1974-2004*, she also edited *The Penguin Anthology of Twentieth-Century American Poetry* (2011). Her drama *The Darker Face of the Earth* premiered in 1996 at the Oregon Shakespeare Festival and was produced at the Kennedy Center in Washington, DC, as well as the Royal National Theatre in London, among other venues. In 1998, the Boston Symphony debuted her song cycle "Seven for Luck," with music by John Williams, under the composer's baton. Among Rita Dove's many honors are the 2011 National Medal of Arts from President Obama, the 1996 National Humanities Medal from President Clinton, and twenty-five honorary doctorates. She is Commonwealth Professor of English at the University of Virginia.

Judy Dozier

Judy Dozier has published poetry and short stories in *US Catholic* Magazine and others. Two of her plays were produced at the ETA Creative Arts Foundation Readers Theatre. She is a past recipient of the Hoyt W. Fuller Play Festival Award sponsored by The African American Arts Alliance of Chicago, and the second place winner of the African American Women in the Arts Play Festival sponsored by the ETA Creative Arts Foundation.

Natasha Ria El-Scari

Natasha Ria El-Scari is a writer, Cave Canem fellow, 2016 Ragdale Residency recipient, and educator for over a decade. Her poetry, academic papers, and personal essays have been published in anthologies and literary and online journals. She has opened for and introduced many great writers, singers and activists, and has been featured at universities and venues nationwide. Born and raised in Kansas City, Missouri, Natasha has a BA from Jackson State University and an MA from the University of Missouri-Kansas City. Natasha's Black Feminist approach is reflected in her writing, poetry, and performance pieces. In 2015, Natasha released her first book, *Screaming Times* (Spartan Press, 2015). Of her work, critic and poet Denise Low writes, "Poems lift off the page, almost reading themselves. Unlike some performance poetry, her words translate well to the printed page." Her albums, "DragonButterFirefly" (2006), "This is Love..." (2010) and DVD *Live at the Blue Room* (2015) display how Natasha connects with any crowd with maternal warmth and unrelenting honesty. Her second book, *The Only Other* (Main Street Rag) was released in 2016. Find her at www.natasharia.com.

Malaika Favorite
Malaika Favorite received her BFA and MFA in art from LSU Baton Rouge. Her artwork is featured in: *Art: African American* by Samella Lewis and *The St. James Guide to Black Artists* by Thomas Riggs. Malaika won the 2016 Broadside Lotus Press Naomi Long Madgett Poetry Award for her collection of poems, *Ascension*, published in 2016 by Broadside Lotus Press. Her publications include *Dreaming at the Manor* (Finishing Line Press, 2014) and *Illuminated Manuscript* (New Orleans Poetry Journal Press, 1991).

kwabena foli
kwabena foli is a writer and teaching artist born in Belgium and raised on the South Side of Chicago. His poetry and writings has been featured on Russell Simmon's All Def Poetry and he performs spoken word throughout the country. kwabena is a Chicago Poetry Slam champion and was a finalist at the National Poetry Slam Group finals.

Calvin Forbes
Calvin Forbes currently teaches at the School of the Art Institute of Chicago and is the author of *Blue Monday* (Wesleyan University Press, 1974) and *The Shine Poems* (LSU Press, 2001). He has won grants or fellowships from the Fulbright Foundation, The National Endowment for the Arts and Illinois Art Council, and the District of Columbia Arts Council.

Diane Glancy

Diane Glancy is professor emeritus at Macalester College. She was a visiting professor at Azusa Pacific University from 2012-2014. She is the author of *Fort Marion Prisoners and the Trauma of Native Education* (University of Nebraska Press, 2014) and the poetry collection *Report to the Department of the Interior* (University of New Mexico Press, 2015). Wipf & Stock will publish three of her novels, *Uprising of Goats*, which features the voices of ten Biblical women, *One of Us*, about the BTK murders in Wichita, and *Ironic Witness*.

Mel Goldberg

After growing up on the Near North Side of Chicago, Mel Goldberg taught high school and college literature and writing in California, Illinois, and Arizona, and as a Fulbright Exchange Teacher at Stanground College in Cambridgeshire, England. His poetry has appeared online and in print in the United States, the United Kingdom, Australia, New Zealand, and Mexico. He has self-published five books of poetry: *The Cyclic Path* (1990), *Sedona Poems* (2003), *If We Survive* (2011), *A Few Berries Shaken From the Tree* (haiku in English and Spanish 2010), and *Seasons of Life* (haiku, 2013). He now lives in the village of Ajijic in Jalisco, Mexico.

Marita Golden

Marita Golden is a veteran teacher of writing and an acclaimed award-winning author of over a dozen works of fiction and nonfiction, many of which are taught in college and universities around the country. As a teacher of writing she has served as a member of the faculties of the MFA Graduate Creative Writing Programs at George Mason University, Virginia Commonwealth University, the Fairfield University low-residency MFA program, and as Distinguished Writer in Residence in the MA Creative Writing Program at Johns Hopkins University. She cofounded and serves as President Emeritus of the Hurston/Wright Foundation.

Among her books are the novels *After* and *The Edge of Heaven* and the memoirs *Migrations of the Heart*, *Saving Our Sons*, and *Don't Play in the Sun: One Woman's Journey Through the Color Complex*. She compiled the collection of interviews *THE WORD Black Writers Talk About the Transformative Power of Read-*

ing and Writing. Her most recent book is *Living Out Loud: A Writer's Journey.* She is the recipient of many awards, including the Barnes & Noble Writers for Writers award presented by Poets & Writers and the Black Caucus of the American Library Association's Fiction Award for her novel *After.*

Jaki Shelton Green
Jaki Shelton Green is a poet, cultural activist, creativity coach, and teacher. Her publications include *Dead on Arrival, Masks, Dead on Arrival and New Poems, Conjure Blues, singing a tree into dance, breath of the song,* and *Feeding the Light.* She was the 2016 Lenoir-Rhyne University Writer in Residence and teacher at the Duke University Center for Documentary Studies. She has been a Pushcart Prize nominee, a North Carolina Literary Hall of Fame inductee, a North Carolina Piedmont Laureate, and a recipient of the Sam Ragan Award in Fine Arts and a North Caorlina Award in Literature. She is the founder and owner of SistaWRITE, an organization that brings women and spaces together for writing retreats, sisterhood, and shared experiences.

Dirk Hagner
Dirk Hagner was born and educated in Germany where he received his MFA and has been living in California since the 1980s. He is an artist-printmaker working primarily on paper using woodcut, intaglio, and letterpress.

He has been included in over 100 juried group exhibitions, over twenty invitational and eighteen solo exhibitions in galleries and institutions, including Loyola University New Orleans, Biola University, Riverside Art Museum, Bakersfield Museum of Art, Pacific Asia Museum in Pasadena, Laguna Art Museum, Mt. San Antonio College, University of Wisconsin, and California State University Los Angeles.

Dirk is in the printmaking faculty at Mt. San Antonio College and a board member of the Los Angeles Printmaking Society. He is a member of The Boston Printmakers, the Society of Graphic Artists in New York, and the Southern Graphics Conference International.

Sam Hamill

Sam Hamill is the author of more than a dozen collections of poetry, including *Destination Zero: Poems 1970–1995* (1995), *Almost Paradise: New and Selected Poems and Translations* (2005), and *Measured by Stone* (2007). Hamill has also published several collections of essays and numerous translations, including *Crossing the Yellow River: 300 Poems from the Chinese* (2000). Hamill's own poetry has been translated into more than a dozen languages.

Monica A. Hand

Monica A. Hand is the author of *Me and Nina* (Alice James Books, 2012). Her poems have been published in *Cortland Review*, *Pleiades*, *Oxford American*, *Spoon River Poetry Review*, *Black Renaissance Noire*, *The Sow's Ear*, and *Drunken Boat*. She has an MFA in Poetry and Poetry in Translation from Drew University, and is currently a PhD candidate in Creative Writing-Poetry at the University of Missouri-Columbia.

Monique Hayes

Monique Hayes received an MFA from the University of Maryland College Park. Her work has appeared in *Prick of the Spindle*, *Midway Journal*, *Heart: Human Equity through Art*, and *Mused*, among others. She received a residency at Wildacres and currently works as a Manuscript Screener for *Callaloo*.

DaMaris B. Hill

DaMaris B. Hill writes poetry, fiction, and criticism. Her work critically examines the individual and collective realities of the human experience. She is inspired by the anxieties of our contemporary existence that are further complicated by fears that some popular narratives fail to be inclusive, stating "I belong to a generation of people who do not fear death, but are afraid that we may be forgotten." Currently, Dr. DaMaris B. Hill serves as an Assistant Professor of Creative Writing and African American and Africana Studies at the University of Kentucky.

Aries Hines

Aries Hines is a writer, fierce femme, queer, and giver of great hugs. She holds an MFA in Poetry from Mills College. Her film work has been featured at film festivals including The Austin International Gay and Lesbian Film Festival. Her poetry and performances have been published widely, and she was part of the San Francisco Queer Arts Festival for her one-woman show "My Dyscalculia Voice" about disability and race. Her work has also been produced or published by *The Queer Girl Theater Project*, *Colorlines Magazine*, *The Journal of Lesbian Studies*, *Black Girl Dangerous*, and more. Her work explores race, identity, queerness, and family. She is currently at work on her memoir and a collection of new poems. She resides in San Diego and sometimes performs for So Say We All.

Akua Lezli Hope

Akua Lezli Hope is a creator who uses sound, words, fiber, glass, and metal to create poems, patterns, stories, music, ornaments, wearables, jewelry, adornments, and peace whenever possible. A third generation Caribbean American, New Yorker, and firstborn, she has won fellowships from the New York Foundation for the Arts, Ragdale, Hurston/Wright writers, the National Endowment for The Arts, and is a Cave Canem fellow. Her manuscript, *Them Gone*, won Red Paint Hill Publishing's Editor's Prize and will be published in 2016. She won the Science Fiction Poetry Association's 2015 award for short poetry. Her first collection, *EMBOUCHURE, Poems on Jazz and Other Musics*, won a Writer's Digest Book Award. She is included in *The 100 Best African American Poems*, *Dark Matter*, the first anthology of African American Science Fiction, and *Erotique Noire*, the first anthology of black erotica, as well as many other anthologies and journals. A paraplegic, she has founded a paratransit nonprofit so that she and others may get around in her small town.

Randall Horton

Randall Horton is the author of three collections of poetry and most recently, *Hook: A Memoir* (Augury Books, 2015). He is a member of the experimental performance group: Heroes Are Gang Leaders and Associate Professor of English at the University of New Haven.

Angela Jackson

Angela Jackson—poet, novelist, playwright—is the recipient of the Shelley Memorial Award from the Poetry Society of America. Her latest volume of poetry, *It Seems Like a Mighty Long Time*, was nominated for the Pulitzer Prize. Forthcoming in 2017 are a novel, *Roads, Where There Are No Roads* (Northwestern University Press), and a biography of *Gwendolyn Brooks* (Beacon Press).

Sandra Jackson-Opoku

Sandra Jackson-Opoku is the author of the American Library Association Black Caucus Fiction award-winning novel, *The River Where Blood is Born*, and *Hot Johnny (and the Women Who Loved Him)*, an *Essence* Magazine Hardcover Fiction Bestseller in 2001. Her fiction, poetry, essays, articles, and reviews appear in *Ms.* Magazine, *The Literary Traveler*, *Transitions Abroad*, *Say That the River Turns: The Impact of Gwendolyn Brooks, Kweli, Nommo: A Literary Legacy of Black Chicago, Writing from Black Chicago: In the World, Not of it?*, and others. Her work has earned the National Endowment for the Arts Fiction Fellowship, a CCLM Fiction Award for Younger Writers, the Black Excellence Award in Literature, several grants from the Illinois Arts Council and Chicago Office of Cultural Affairs, and more.

Jodi Joanclair

Jodi Joanclair is an ex-essayist and an aspiring poet. For most of her life, she has struggled between not having the prudence to be silent in moments that required further deliberation and of being much too quiet when she should have exerted her freedom of speech. She hopes in her poetry to better direct the many thoughts in her head, much influenced by her travels, spirituality, and identity as a transnational queer of color. After her most recent retreat to India, she has been dwelling on her ancestral birthrights, capitalist exploitation, and what it means to be a woman of color living in a developing nation under neo-colonialist policies. She is a full time teacher and a part time healer. She hopes someday to reverse the order of those roles, or bring more healing into her teaching.

Joan Wiese Johannes

Joan Wiese Johannes has published four chapbooks, including *Sensible Shoes*, the 2009 winner of the John and Miriam Morris Chapbook Competition sponsored by the AL Poetry Society and *He Thought the Periodic Table Was a Portrait of God* from Parallel Press. Winner of the Mississippi Valley Poetry Contest, and the Trophy and Triad contests sponsored by Wisconsin Fellowship of Poets, her poetry has appeared in numerous literary journals and anthologies. She also has published creative nonfiction, articles, and compositions for the Native American-style flute, an instrument she often uses in her readings. Joan agrees with the stage manager in *Our Town*, who mused that only poets and saints truly appreciate life while living it. Although not a candidate for sainthood, she lives a good life in Port Edwards, Wisconsin with her poet/artist husband Jeffrey.

Jacqueline Johnson
Jacqueline Johnson is a multi-disciplined artist creating in both writing and fiber arts. She is the author of *A Woman's Season* and *A Gathering of Mother Tongues*, the winner of the Third Annual White Pine Press Poetry Award. Ms. Johnson has received awards from the New York Foundation of the Arts, the Middle Atlantic Writers Association's Creative Writing Award in poetry, and MacDowell Colony for the Arts. She is a Cave Canem fellow.

Carolyn Joyner
Carolyn Joyner is a Washington, DC poet who has been featured in several anthologies and poetry magazines, among them are *Gathering Ground, Beyond the Frontier, 360, A Revolution of Black Poets*, the 2004-2005 Cave Canem annual collections, and *Obsidian, Amistad*, and *Beltway Quarterly* magazines. During 2010, she co-hosted "Poet's Corner," a program on local FM radio station, WPFW, and in 2003 and 2013, she received an Artist Fellowship grant from the DC Commission on the Arts and Humanities. She has an MA in Creative Writing from Johns Hopkins University.

Dasha Kelly
Dasha Kelly is a nationally-respected writer, artist, and creative consultant. She travels extensively as an artist-in-residence, feature performer, speaker, and group facilitator. Dasha was thrice selected as a US Embassy Arts Envoy to teach and perform in Botswana, Africa, and was the first US Artist in

Residence through a partnership with Lebanon's Rafiki Hariri University and the American University of Beirut. Dasha has written for national, regional, and local magazines; published two collections of poems, essays, and short stories; four full-length spoken word recordings; a poetry chapbook; and two novels. Her latest novel, *Almost Crimson* (Curbside Splendor, 2015), was named by *BuzzFeed* one of the "16 Most Exciting Books of 2015 by Independent Publishers." She is an alum performer of HBO's Russell Simmons presents Def Poetry Jam and a featured artist of the National Performance Network. In 2015, Dasha was a finalist as Poet Laureate for the State of Wisconsin and, in 2016, named Artist of the Year by the City of Milwaukee. Dasha is founder of Still Waters Collective, an arts education and community-building initiative in Milwaukee, where she lives with her husband, family, and one imperious cat.

Emily Hooper Lansana

Emily Hooper Lansana is an arts administrator, educator, and performing artist. She serves as Associate Director of Community Arts Engagement for the Reva and David Logan Center for the Arts at the University of Chicago. She was a Curriculum Supervisor with Chicago Public Schools Office of Arts Education and Director of Education at the Lincoln Center Theater. She is recognized for her work with Performance Duo: In the Spirit. For more than twenty years, she has performed as a storyteller, sharing her work with audiences throughout Chicago and across the country. She has been featured at the National Storytelling Festival, the National Association of Black Storytellers Festival, and at a variety of museums, colleges, and performance venues. She also enjoys passing on traditions to young people as a coach and mentor with nationally recognized Ase Youth Group and Rebirth Poetry Ensemble. Her work seeks to give voice to those whose stories are often untold, especially those of the African diaspora.

Nile Lansana

Nile Lansana is a poet, writer, and student at Jones College Preparatory High School in Chicago. He is a member of the Rebirth Poetry Ensemble, winners of the 2016 Louder Than a Bomb Youth Poetry Festival. Rebirth will represent Chicago at the 2016 Brave New Voices International Festival, where they placed among the top sixteen youth poetry teams in the country in 2014. Nile is an alumnus of the Brother Authors summer writing institute at the University of Illinois-Chicago. An avid sports enthusiast, Nile's goal is to pursue a career in sports journalism.

Quraysh Ali Lansana

Quraysh Ali Lansana is the author of eight poetry books, three textbooks, three children's books, editor of eight anthologies, and co-author of a book of pedagogy. He is a faculty member of the Writing Program of the School of the Art Institute of Chicago and a former faculty member of the Drama Division of the Juilliard School. Lansana served as Director of the Gwendolyn Brooks Center for Black Literature and Creative Writing at Chicago State University from 2002-2011, where he was also Associate Professor of English/ Creative Writing until 2014. *Our Difficult Sunlight: A Guide to Poetry, Literacy & Social Justice in Classroom & Community* (with Georgia A. Popoff) was published in March 2011 by Teachers & Writers Collaborative and was a 2012 NAACP Image Award nominee. His most recent books include *The BreakBeat Poets: New American Poetry in the Age of Hip Hop* with Kevin Coval and Nate Marshall (Haymarket Books, 2015) and *The Walmart Republic* with Christopher Stewart (Mongrel Empire Press, 2014). Forthcoming titles include: *A Gift from Greensboro* (Penny Candy Books, 2016), *Clara Luper: The Woman Who Rallied the Children* with Julie Dill (Oklahoma Hall of Fame Press, 2017), and *The Whiskey of Our Discontent: Gwendolyn Brooks as Conscience and Change Agent* with Georgia A. Popoff (Haymarket Books, 2017).

Tony Lindsay

Tony Lindsay is the author of seven novels: *One Dead Preacher, Street Possession, Chasin' It, Urban Affair, One Dead Lawyer, More Boy than Girl, One Dead Doctor*, and five short story collections: *Pieces of the Hole, Fat from Papa's Head—Emotional Drippings, Stories of Love, Lust, and Addiction, Almost Grown*, and *Acorns in a Skillet, Stories of Racecraft in America*. He has published book critiques and reviews for *Black Issue's Book Review*. He was a contributor to the anthologies *Don't Hate the Game, Luscious*, and *Fire and Desire*. He has been published by the African American literary website *Timbooktu*, as well as the young adult magazine *Cicada*. He writes bimonthly articles for *Conversations* magazine and nonfiction book reviews for Hartman Publishing's *N'DIGO* Magapaper. He teaches at Calumet College of St. Joseph, Harold Washington College, and Ivy Tech Community College.

Roy Lewis

Renowned photographer and activist Roy Lewis grew up on a cotton plantation in Mississippi. His career as a photographer began in 1964 when *Jet* magazine published his photograph of musician Thelonius Monk. In 1970, Lewis videotaped an exclusive Interview with the Honorable Elijah Muhammad, which was featured in the film *A Nation of Common Sense*. In 1974, he traveled to Zaire to film the Ali-Foreman fight. This historic video would later be featured in the Hollywood film, "When We Were Kings." In 1975, Lewis began work on a pictorial book focusing on the African American people, life, and culture along the Mississippi River. In 1995, Lewis published "The Million Man March," a highlight of that historic day. Lewis also contributed work to the widely acclaimed photo book project, *Songs of My People*. His major assignments include coverage of Congressional Black Caucus conferences and events and the signing of the Affordable Health Care Act by President Barack Obama in 2012. His photojournalism awards include The Maurice Sorrell Lifetime Achievement Award, Lifetime Achievement Award from the National Press Club, and the National Press Photographers Association (NPPA) Award for Community Service.

Mary Catherine Loving

Mary Catherine Loving, PhD is a reader who writes. In her various incarnations from kindergarten teacher to college professor, she has taught reading, creative writing, world literature, and literary criticism, among other subjects. She publishes critical essays, poetry, and book reviews. Her poem, "Here," was inscribed on a memorial to honor former slaves. Her book reviews have appeared recently in *CALYX: A Journal of Art and Literature for Women*. Her recent critical work on Phillis Wheatley is available in the *Journal of African American Studies*, and her critical work on Lucille Clifton is forthcoming in an edited collection from Palgrave.

devorah major

A California born, San Francisco raised granddaughter of immigrants, documented and undocumented, devorah major served as San Francisco's Poet Laureate from 2002-2006. Her novels are *Brown Glass Windows* and *An Open Weave*. In addition to her four poetry books and four poetry chapbooks, she has two biographies for young adults and a host of short stories, essays, and individual poems published in anthologies and periodicals. Among her awards are a American Library Association Black Caucus First Novelist Award for An Open Weave and a PEN Oakland Josephine Miles Literary Award for her poetry book *street smarts*. In June 2015 she premiered her poetry play "Classic Black: Voices of 19th Century African-Americans in San Francisco" at the San Francisco International Arts Festival. In the Fall of 2016, City Lights Publishing released her fifth book of poetry, *and then we became*.

John C. Mannone

John C. Mannone has published work in *Windhover, Artemis, 2016 Texas Poetry Calendar, Southern Poetry Anthology (NC), Still: The Journal, Town Creek Poetry, Tupelo Press, Baltimore Review, Pedestal, Raven Chronicles*, and others. He is the author of two literary poetry collections: *Apocalypse* (Alban Lake Publishing) and *Disabled Monsters* (The Linnet's Wings Press), and is the poetry editor for *Silver Blade* and *Abyss & Apex*. He won the 2015 Joy Margrave award for creative nonfiction and has been nominated three times for a Pushcart Prize. He is a professor of physics in East Tennessee. "The Samaritan Women" received Honorable Mention in the Inspirational category of the 2016 Tennessee Mountain Writers contest. Visit *The Art of Poetry*: http://jcmannone.wordpress.com.

Adrian Matejka

Adrian Matejka is the author of *Map to the Stars, The Devil's Garden* (winner of the New York / New England Award) and *Mixology* (a winner of the 2008 National Poetry Series). His third collection of poems, *The Big Smoke*, was awarded the 2014 Anisfield-Wolf Book Award and was a finalist for the National Book Award and Pulitzer Prize. He is the Ruth Lilly Professor/Poet in Residence at Indiana University in Bloomington.

Tony Medina

Tony Medina is Professor of Creative Writing at Howard University. He is a two-time winner of the Paterson Prize for Books for Young People for *DeShawn Days* and *I and I, Bob Marley*. He is the author of a number of books for adults and young people, including *An Onion of Wars* and *Broke Baroque* and a finalist for the Julie Suk Book Award. He recently received the Langston Hughes Society Award from the College Language Association and the first African Voices Literary Award. Medina's most recent book is the anthology *Resisting Arrest: Poems to Stretch the Sky* (Jacar Press, 2016). Look for his work at tonymedina.org.

Gwendolyn A. Mitchell

Gwendolyn A. Mitchell, poet and editorial consultant, is co-editor of two anthologies, and author of three volumes of poetry including her forthcoming collection, *Among the Missing*.

jessica Care moore

jessica Care moore is the CEO of Moore Black Press, Executive Producer of Black WOMEN Rock!, and founder of the literacy-driven, Jess Care Moore Foundation. An internationally renowned poet, playwright, performance artist, and producer, she is the 2013 Alain Locke Award Recipient from the Detroit Institute of Arts. moore is the author of *The Words Don't Fit in My Mouth, The Alphabet Verses The Ghetto, God is Not an American, Sunlight Through Bullet Holes*, and a memoir, *Love is Not The Enemy*. Her poetry has been heard on stages like Carnegie Hall, Lincoln Center, and the London Institute of Contemporary Arts. She has performed on every continent. jessica Care moore believes poems belong everywhere and to everyone.

Lenard D. Moore

Lenard D. Moore, a North Carolina native and US Army Veteran, is the Founder and Executive Director of the Carolina African American Writers' Collective and co-founder of the Washington Street Writers Group. Moore's poems, short stories, essays, and reviews have appeared in over 400 publications. His poetry has been translated into several languages. He is the author of *The Open Eye* (NC

Haiku Society Press, 1985), *Forever Home* (St. Andrews College Press, 1992), *Desert Storm: A Brief History* (Los Hombres Press, 1993), *A Temple Looming* (WordTech Editions, 2008) and *The Open Eye, Limited 30th Anniversary Edition* (Mountains & Rivers Press, 2015). Moore has taught workshops, served on literary panels, and given readings at schools, festivals, colleges, and universities. Currently, Mr. Moore, Associate Professor of English, teaches Advanced Poetry Writing and African American Literature at the University of Mount Olive, where he directs the literary festival. He is working on two poetry collections, a novel, short stories, a play, and literary criticism.

Shahari Moore
Shahari Moore was born in South Central California and raised in Bronzeville on the South Side of Chicago. She holds an MFA with a focus in African American Literature from Chicago State University, and a Masters in Educational Psychology from Eastern Illinois University. Her career in academia has spanned over nineteen years and includes service as a Counselor, Lecturer, Assistant Professor, and a Department Chair. Her research led to landmark status being granted by the City of Chicago to the homes of Richard Wright, Lorraine Hansberry, and Gwendolyn Brooks. She is the inaugural coordinator for Brooksday, a day to honor the life and works of Gwendolyn Brooks, sponsored by Third World Press, The Guild Complex, The American Writers Museum, and Brooks Permissions. She has received fellowships from the National Endowment for the Humanities and the Hurston/Wright Foundation. She is the Historian Emeritus for the Guy Hanks and Marvin Miller Screenwriting Program at the University of Southern California's School of Cinematic Arts. She has published essays and short stories with Third World Press. In 2011 her short story, "Swimmin' Lesson," was adapted as a short film and screened at the Cannes Film Festival in France. It later won the Black Harvest Film Festival at the Gene Siskel Center in Chicago. In 2015, she wrote and co-directed *B Love*, which also screened in Cannes and premiered at Black Harvest. She is a Diverse Voices in DOCS fellow with Kartemquin Films. Shahari currently resides in Chicago and is completing her first documentary which will explore the life, legacy and impact of Gwendolyn Brooks.

Manuel Muñoz

Manuel Muñoz is the author of two collections of short stories: *The Faith Healer of Olive Avenue* (2007) and *Zigzagger* (2003). His first novel, *What You See in the Dark*, was published in 2011. A recipient of a Whiting Writers' Award and two O. Henry Prizes, Muñoz was a finalist for the 2007 Frank O'Connor International Short Story Prize. A native of Dinuba, California, he lives in Tucson, where he is Associate Professor in the English Department at the University of Arizona.

Satoki Nagata

Satoki Nagata is a Chicago-based visual artist. Born and raised in Japan, he first came to the United States as a scientist. After ten years in the field of neuroscience, Satoki recognized the connective limitations of science. He soon reallocated his professional focus on visual creatives. He has learned from Zen Buddhism that our existence is composed of various relationships—this notion has inspired him to use photography to create relationships with the world to find himself. He makes photographic images of ordinary people and their lives in the city of Chicago. He is working on various art forms including a movie and multimedia works with other creatives in addition to still photography. His work has been recognized internationally and introduced by various media, and are exhibited in various countries from Asia, North America, and Europe. Learn more at www.satoki.com.

Marilyn Nelson

Marilyn Nelson is the author or translator of over twenty-four books. Her awards include the 2013 Milton Kessler Poetry Award, the 1998 Poets' Prize, the PEN Winship Award, and the Lenore Marshall Prize. Her young adult books include *Carver: A Life in Poems* (2001), which received the Flora Stieglitz Straus Award and the Boston Globe/Horn Book Award, was a National Book Award finalist and was designated both a Newbery Honor Book and a Coretta Scott King Honor Book. *A Wreath for Emmett Till* won the 2005 Boston Globe/Horn Book Award and was designated a 2006 Coretta Scott King Honor Book, a 2006 Michael L. Printz Honor Book, and a 2006 Lee Bennett Hopkins Poetry Award Honor Book. Other honors include two NEA creative writing fellowships, the 1990 Connecticut Arts Award, an ACLS Contemplative Practices Fellowship, the Department of the Army's Commander's Award for Public Service, a Fulbright Teaching Fellowship, and a fellowship from the JS Guggenheim Memorial Foundation. In January 2013, she was elected a Chancellor of the Academy of American Poets. Her latest collection for young adults is *How I Discovered Poetry* (Dial, 2014), a memoir in verse with illustrations by Hadley Hooper.

Zoe Lynn Nyman

Zoe Lynn Nyman is a Baltimore raised artist and writer, currently residing in Chicago. She studied at the School of the Art Institute of Chicago for her BFA, and her work has appeared in the schools yearly BFAW magazine, *MOUTH*, two years in a row. Her writing deals with relationship dynamics, family matters, faith, fate, and introspective considerations.

Sharon Olds

The twelve collections published by poet Sharon Olds include *Satan Says* (1980), *The Dead and The Living* (1984), *The Wellspring* (1996), *Stag's Leap* (2013), which won both the Pulitzer and T.S. Eliot Prizes, and *Odes* (2016). Olds was New York State Poet Laureate 1998-2000 and currently teaches at New York University's Graduate Program in Creative Writing.

Joyce Owens

Artist Joyce Owens earned an MFA from Yale University, a BFA from Howard University, and has served as associate professor, curator, juror, panelist, consultant, or lecturer at the Art Institute of Chicago, Bradley University, the Illinois Arts Council, Arts Alliance Illinois at Art Expo, the College Art Association, Chicago Artists Coalition, the Chicago Department of Cultural Affairs, Columbia College Chicago, the Hyde Park Art Center, Wells Street Art Fair, Old Town Art Fair, Purdue University, the DuSable Museum, the Museum of Science and Industry, Chicago State University, the Museum of Greater Lafayette, Indiana, and other institutions. Owens' artwork has been exhibited in solo and group exhibitions on four continents. Her honors and awards include a 3Arts Award and Ragdale Fellowship, cash prizes or solo exhibitions from sculptor Martin Puryear, visual artists Faith Ringgold, Jon Pounds, Tony Tasset, and Margaret Hawkins, a correspondent for Artnews and former *Chicago Sun Times* art critic.

Elise Paschen

Poet and editor Elise Paschen was born and raised in Chicago. She earned a BA at Harvard University, where she won the Lloyd McKim Garrison Medal and the Joan Grey Untermeyer Poetry Prize. She has published several collections of poetry, including *Bestiary* (2009) and *Infidelities* (1996), which was the winner of the Nicholas Roerich Poetry Prize. She is the editor of *Poetry Speaks Who I Am* (2010), *Poetry Speaks to Children* (2005), and the co-editor of *Poetry Speaks* (2001) and *Poetry in Motion* (1996). Her own work has been included in the anthologies *Poetry 180: A Turning Back to Poetry* (2003), *The Poetry Anthology: 1912-2002* (2002), *Reinventing the Enemy's Language: Contemporary Native Women's Writings of North America* (1998), and *A Formal Feeling Comes: Poems in Form by Contemporary Women* (1994). Paschen has served as the executive director of the Poetry Society of America. She cofounded the Poetry In Motion program, which posts poems in subways and buses. She was the Frances Allen Fellow of the Newberry Library as well as poet laureate of Three Oaks, Michigan. Paschen teaches in the MFA Writing Program at the School of the Art Institute of Chicago.

Georgia A. Popoff

Georgia A. Popoff of Syracuse, New York, is an educator, arts-in-education specialist, *Comstock Review* senior editor, Downtown Writers Center Workshops Coordinator, and coauthor of a teachers' text on poetry in K-12 classrooms. She has three poetry collections, most recently, *Psalter: The Agnostic's Book of Common Curiosities* (Tiger Bark Press, June 2015).

Rohan Preston

Emmy Award-winning writer, critic, and photographer Rohan Preston authored the poetry book *Dreams in Soy Sauce* (Tia Chucha/Northwestern, 1992) and coedited the multi-genre anthology *Soulfires: Young Black Men on Love and Violence* (Penguin, 1996). His chapbooks include *Sweetie mango suite: poems &*

reveries of rural Jamaica, Jazz people: lyrics, toasts & chants, and *Falling into her eyes: fatherhood poems*. He was part of a team of *Star Tribune* journalists who won an Emmy for a documentary on the meaning of Barack Obama's election to the presidency. Other awards include the 1997 Henry Blakely Poetry Prize, the inaugural prize given by Gwendolyn Brooks. A member of the 2007 and 2012 Pulitzer Prize juries for drama, he placed silver in the 2007 Lowell Thomas travel writing competition for "Senegal: The Return." Born in Jamaica, raised in New York, and educated at Yale, he has written for the *Chicago Tribune*, the *Washington Post* and the *New York Times*. He lives with his family in the Twin Cities, where he is lead theater critic at the *Star Tribune*.

Mike Puican

Mike Puican was a member of the 1996 Chicago Slam Team and is currently Board President of the Guild Literary Complex.

Eugene B. Redmond

Eugene B. Redmond, emeritus professor of English at Southern Illinois University Edwardsville, was named Poet Laureate of East St. Louis (Illinois) in 1976, the year Doubleday released his critical history, *Drumvoices: The Mission of Afro-American Poetry*. Earlier, as a teacher-counselor and poet-in-residence at SIU's Experiment in Higher Education (1967-1969), he taught with Katherine Dunham and Henry Dumas (1934-1968). He has won a National Endowment for the Arts Creative Writing Fellowship, a Pushcart Prize, an Outstanding Faculty Research and Teaching Award, and lectured at universities in the US, Africa, and Europe. East St. Louisans created the Eugene B. Redmond Writers Club in his honor; the Club turns thirty this year. Winner of two American Book Awards, Redmond's most recent release, among more than twenty-five collections of diverse writings, is *Arkansippi Memwars: Poetry, Prose & Folklore 1962-2012* (Third World Press).

Felicia Grant Preston

Felicia Grant Preston received a BA in art from Southern Illinois University, an MS in Education from Northern Illinois University, and an MA from Chicago State University. In addition, she has studied at the University of Illinois,

The School of the Art Institute of Chicago, Governor State University, and The Savannah College of Art and Design. Her work has been exhibited at the Museum of Science and Industry's Black Creativity exhibition, ARC Gallery, Woman Made Gallery, Artemisia Gallery, Hyde Park Art Center, South Side Community Art Center, Susan Woodson Gallery, Nicole Gallery, the South Shore Cultural Center, Neleh Artistic Expressions, and Gallery Guichard, to name a few. She has also exhibited at Fort Wayne Museum of Art Alliance in Fort Wayne, Indiana, Vaughn Cultural Center in St. Louis, Missouri, the Art Exchange Gallery in Detroit, Michigan, the Savannah College of Art and Design in Savannah, Georgia, Florida Community College in Jacksonville, Florida, Art Jazz Gallery in Philadelphia, Pennsylvania, and in numerous private collections.

Patricia Smith

Patricia Smith is the author of seven books of poetry, including *Shoulda Been Jimi Savannah*, winner of the Lenore Marshall Prize from the Academy of American Poets and finalist for the William Carlos Williams Award from the Poetry Society of America; *Blood Dazzler*, a finalist for the National Book Award, and *Gotta Go Gotta Flow*, a collaboration with award-winning Chicago photographer Michael Abramson. Her most recent book, *Incendiary Art*, was published by Northwestern University Press in February 2017. Her other books include the poetry volumes *Teahouse of the Almighty*, *Close to Death*, *Big Towns Big Talk*, *Life According to Motown*; the children's book *Janna and the Kings*, and the history *Africans in America*, a companion book to the award-winning PBS series. Her work has appeared in *Poetry*, *The Paris Review*, *The Baffler*, *The Washington Post*, *The New York Times*, *Tin House*, and in *Best American Poetry*, and *Best American Essays*. Her contribution to the crime fiction anthology *Staten Island Noir* won the Robert L. Fish Award from the Mystery Writers of America for the best debut story of the year and was featured in the anthology *Best American Mystery Stories*. She is a Guggenheim fellow, a two-time winner of the Pushcart Prize, a former fellow at both Yaddo and the MacDowell Colony, and a four-time individual champion of the National Poetry Slam, the most successful poet in the competition's history. Patricia is a professor at the College of Staten Island and in the MFA program at Sierra Nevada College, as well as an instructor at the annual VONA residency and in the Vermont College of Fine Arts Post-Graduate Residency Program.

Crystal Simone Smith

Crystal Simone Smith is the author of two poetry chapbooks, *Routes Home* (Finishing Line Press, 2013) and *Running Music* (Longleaf Press, 2014). Her work has appeared in *Callaloo, Nimrod, Barrow Street, Frogpond, African American Review*, and elsewhere. She is an alumna of the Callaloo Creative Writing Workshop and the Yale Summer Writers Conference and lives in Durham, North Carolina. She teaches English Composition and Creative Writing and is the Founder and Managing Editor of Backbone Press.

Kevin Stein

Poet and critic Kevin Stein was named Illinois Poet Laureate in 2003. A professor of English and Director of Creative Writing at Bradley University, Stein is known for the humor and insight of his poems, and the lucidity of his prose. Stein's books of poetry include *A Circus of Want* (1992), which won the Devins Award, *Bruised Paradise* (1996) *Chance Ransom* (2000), *American Ghost Roses* (2005), which won the Society of Midland Authors Poetry Award, and *Sufficiency of the Actual* (2009). Stein's criticism includes a monograph on the poet James Wright—*James Wright: The Poetry of a Grown Man* (1988), the essay collection *Private Poets, Public Acts* (1996), and *Poetry's Afterlife: Verse in the Digital Age* (2010), a book that examines poetry's flourishing "underground" in the digital landscape.

Sharan Strange

As a founding member of the Dark Room Collective and cocurator of its Dark Room Reading Series, Sharan Strange helped to present over 100 established and emerging writers, musicians, and visual artists of color to audiences in the Boston area from 1988-1994. For many years she was also a contributing editor of *Callaloo*, the journal of African diaspora arts and letters.

Her honors include the Rona Jaffe Foundation Writer's Award, the Barnard New Poets Prize, a grant from the DC Commission on the Arts and Humanities, and residencies at the Gell Writers' Center, the MacDowell Colony, and Yaddo. Currently, she teaches creative writing at Spelman College and serves as a community board member of Poetry Atlanta.

Her poems and essays have appeared in journals and anthologies in the US and abroad, including *Angles of Ascent: A Norton Anthology of Contemporary African American Poetry*, *Best American Poetry*, *Black President: The Art and Legacy of Fela Anikulapo-Kuti*, *Callaloo*, among others. Her writings have also been featured in exhibitions at the Whitney Museum, the New Museum of Contemporary Art, and the Skylight Gallery in New York, and the Institute of Contemporary Art in Boston, as well as in concert performances with the American Modern Ensemble and *#SingHerName*, a commissioned collaboration with composer Courtney Bryan for The Dream Unfinished project.

Regina Taylor

With a body of work encompassing film, television, theater, and writing, Regina Taylor's playwriting credits include "Crowns" (winner of four Helen Hayes Awards), "Trinity River Plays" (Edgerton Foundation New American Play Award), "Oo-Bla-Dee" (Steinberg-ATCA New Play Award), "Drowning Crow" (produced with Broadway, Manhattan Theater Club), "The Dreams of Sarah Breedlove," "Escape from Paradise," "Ties that Bind," and "stop. reset.," which Taylor directed at NYC's Signature Theatre Company and Goodman Theatre. As an Artistic Associate of Goodman Theatre, Regina Taylor is one of its most produced playwrights. She is a resident playwright at NYC's Signature Theatre. She has received a Golden Globe Award, two Emmy nominations, two NAACP Image Awards, and an Oscar Micheaux Award from the Chicago Film Critics Association. Taylor's film credits include "The Negotiator," "Courage Under Fire," and "A Family Thing." Television audiences know Taylor for her roles in "I'll Fly Away," "The Unit," "Dig," and Masterpiece Theater's "Cora Unashamed." Learn more at www.reginataylor.com and www.stopreset.org.

Sheree Renée Thomas

Sheree Renée Thomas is the author of *Sleeping Under the Tree of Life* (Aqueduct Press, 2016) and *Shotgun Lullabies: Stories & Poems* (Aqueduct Press, 2011). She is also the editor of two World Fantasy Award-winning anthologies, *Dark Matter:*

A *Century of Speculative Fiction from the African Diaspora* and *Dark Matter: Reading the Bones*. Her work has been anthologized in *Stories for Chip: Tribute to Samuel R. Delany*, *Memphis Noir*, *A Moment of Change: Feminist Speculative Poetry*, *The Ringing Ear: Black Poets Lean South*, *So Long Been Dreaming: Postcolonial Science Fiction & Fantasy*, *Mojo: Conjure Stories*, *Bum Rush the Page: A Def Poetry Jam*, and other books. Her work also appears in *Callaloo*, *Transition*, *Drumvoices Revue*, *Obsidian*, *Renaissance Noire*, and other literary journals. In 2015 she served as the Lucille Geier Lakes writer-in-residence at Smith College, and received the Wallace Foundation Fellowship at the Millay Colony of the Arts, as well as fellowships at the Blue Mountain Center and VCCA. In 2016 she was named a Tennessee Arts Fellow in Creative Writing by the Tennessee Arts Commission. She has also received fellowships from Cave Canem, Writers Omi/Ledig House, and the New York Foundation for the Arts. A native of Memphis, Thomas first heard Gwendolyn Brooks read selections from her poetry during the poet's visit to the city in 1994. Thomas writes between a river and a pyramid and strives to celebrate the spirit and language of her people in every story and poem.

Clifford Thompson

Clifford Thompson received a Whiting Writers' Award for nonfiction in 2013 for *Love for Sale and Other Essays*. He is also the author of the memoir, *Twin of Blackness* (2015), both of which were published by Autumn House Press. His essays on books, film, jazz, and American identity have appeared in publications including *The Village Voice*, *The Threepenny Review*, *The Iowa Review*, *Commonweal*, *Film Quarterly*, *Cineaste*, *Oxford American*, the *Los Angeles Review of Books*, and *Black Issues Book Review*. He is the author of a novel, *Signifying Nothing*. For over a dozen years he served as the editor of *Current Biography*, and he has held adjunct professorships at Columbia University, New York University, and Queens College. He lives in Brooklyn.

Anastacia Renee Tolbert

Anastacia Renee Tolbert is a queer super-shero of color moonlighting as a writer, performance artist, and creative writing workshop facilitator. She has received awards and fellowships from Cave Canem, Hedgebrook, VONA, Jacks Straw, Ragdale, and Artist Trust. She was recently selected as the 2015-2016 poet-in-residence at Hugo House, a place for writers in Seattle. *Chapbook 26*, recently published by Dancing Girl Press, is an abbreviated alphabet expression of the lower and uppercase lives of women and girls. A Pushcart nominee (2015), her poetry, fiction, and nonfiction have been published widely. Recently Tolbert has been expanding her creative repertoire into the field of visual art, and has exhibited her painting and photography surrounding the body as a polarized place of both the private and political. This year she has begun a year-long theatrical mixed-media project in collaboration with the Project Room, *9 Ounces: A One Woman Show*. Lately, she's been obsessed with the body and the stories (true and not true) it holds.

Jeanne Towns
Jeanne Towns is a freelance writer and poet and a former member of the Organization of Black American Culture (OBAC). She has received the Essay of the Year Award, grants from the Illinois Arts Council, the City of Chicago Department of Cultural Affairs, Poets and Writers, and the Chicago Public Library. Her work has been published in the *Chicago Tribune, Essence, NOMMO, Black American Literature Forum*, the *Minnesota Review, Catalyst, N'digo, Grey City Journal, Rolling Out, Colorlines* and *Afrique*, to name a few. Her poetry has been performed at ETA Theater, on television, and choreographed as a dance number for Deeply Rooted (a dance troupe steeped in traditions of African-American dance, storytelling, and universal themes). Jeanne taught poetry in Chicago Public Schools with Urban Gateways to residents of the Chicago Housing Authority (CHA), Chicago Public Libraries, River North High School, Dwight Correctional facility, and the University of Illinois. Jeanne's book of poetry is *Lovin' Me As I Am*. She is developing a play set against the backdrop of the civil rights movement, on growing up in Chicago's often maligned West Side.

Qiana Towns
Qiana Towns's poem, "Social Regard," was selected for the Gwendolyn Brooks Poetry Prize by the Society for the Study of Midwestern Literature. She is a Cave Canem fellowship graduate and editor for *Reverie: Midwest African American Literature*. Most recently, her work appears in *The Crab Orchard Review*.

Bettina Marie Walker

Bettina Marie Walker is a pre-med graduate with a minor in Writing and Communications, Media Arts, and Theatre from Chicago State University. She is currently completing two Masters' programs, one for Executive Leadership and the other in Molecular Biology. Bettina has studied abroad in France and Ghana, and performed at the Panafest in Accra, Ghana. She is interested in translating contemporary poetry from Africa and France and will be attending a low-residency MFA creative writing program for poetry and screenwriting in the near future.

DeShaunte Walker

DeShaunte Walker was born and raised in Chicago. He joined the United States Marine Corps in 1999, completed a tour of duty in Iraq, and was honorably discharged in 2007. In 2013, Walker received his BA in Graphic Design from Jackson State University in Jackson, Mississippi. Earlier that year he participated in the Mississippi Collegiate Art Competition (MCAC), a unique juried exhibition, where he won the Award of Excellence in clay arts for a self-portrait entitled "Headstrong." In 2016, he presented his thesis research at the Gene Siskel Film Center on Black MEN.T.O.R. (Black Men Truly Owning Responsibility). Walker is a natural draftsman who is able to create using several forms of media and is currently pursuing his Masters Degree in Art Education at the School of the Art Institute of Chicago.

John Wilkinson

John Wilkinson is a British poet working in Chicago. His recent books include *Reckitt's Blue* (Seagull Books, 2012) and selected poems, *Schedule of Unrest* (Salt, 2014). A new collection, *Ghost Nets*, is appearing from Omnidawn in fall 2016.

Keith S. Wilson

Keith S. Wilson is an Affrilachian Poet, Cave Canem fellow, and graduate of the Callaloo Creative Writing Workshop, as well as a Virginia Center for the Creative Arts fellow and recipient of three Bread Loaf scholarships. His work has appeared or is appearing in the following journals: *American Letters & Commentary*, *32 Poems*, *Cider Press Review*, *Anti-*, *Muzzle*, *Mobius*, and *The Dead Mule*

School of Southern Literature. Additionally, he has had poems nominated for a Pushcart Prize and Best of the Net award.

avery r. young

Multidisciplinary artist avery r. young is a Cave Canem alum and 3Arts Awardee whose work has appeared in *The BreakBeat Poets* and other anthologies. His performance work, visual text, and sound design examines Black American culture. His first full-length album "booker t. soltreyne: a race rekkid" is a collection of sound design featuring narratives about race, gender, and sexuality.

Reggie Scott Young

Reggie Scott Young, a native of Chicago's West Side, is a scholar and writer who most recently served as Professor of Creative Writing and American Literatures at the University of Louisiana at Lafayette. His poems, stories, and works of nonfiction have appeared in *Fifth Wednesday Journal*, *Louisiana Literature*, *Oxford American*, and *African American Review*. He served as guest-editor of *Obsidian Literary Journal*'s special issue on Jeffery Renard Allen, and he also coedited *Mozart and Leadbelly: Stories and Essays by Ernest J. Gaines* and *This Louisiana Thing That Drives Me: The Legacy of Ernest J. Gaines*. His poems in this volume are excerpts from his recent book of poetry, *Yardbirds Squawking at the Moon*.

ACKNOWLEDGEMENTS

A work of this breadth and magnitude would not have been possible without the assistance of so many magnificent and munificent souls. We extend our sincerest gratitude for all such support, and sincerely apologize to any we may have missed:

- The poet Alison Joseph, who publicized the call for submissions on her Yahoo CWROPPS mailing list
- Karyn Calabrese, owner/proprietor of Karyn's Fresh Corner, who provided the respite of a workspace and delicious vegan ice cream
- School of the Art Institute of Chicago student interns: Jada-Amina Harvey, LaAndrea Mitchell, Zoe Lynn Nyman, Roderick Chancellor Sawyer, and Darius T. Thomas
- Kimberly Chapman, intern from the Red Earth MFA Program at Oklahoma City University
- Our wonderfully generous artists and writers who, in love and respect for Miss Brooks, contributed their work for little or no financial remuneration
- Librarian Kathleen Bethel, who researched and compiled the Brooks Bibliography at the zero hour
- Those respected members of the literary community who provided valuable book jacket endorsements: Ana Castillo, Cheryl Clarke, Edwidge Danticat, Joanne Gabin, Marita Golden, Reginald Gibbons, Angela Jackson, Major Jackson, and Michael Warr
- Our families, who suffered long weeks of absence and distraction as we read, re-read, edited, wrote, and assembled
- Our respective writing communities, particularly FLOW II (For Love of Writing)
- Lastly, but by no means least, Curbside Splendor Publishing, who invested in our dream and vision for this project